Bahamas

Fodor's 90

Bahamas

FODOR'S TRAVEL PUBLICATIONS, INC.
New York & London

ISBN 0–679–01741–0

Fodor's Bahamas

Editor: Andrew E. Beresky
Area Editors: Christopher Evans, Dorothy M. Zinzow
Cartographer: David Lindroth
Drawings: Michael Kaplan
Cover Photograph: Robert Holland/The Waterhouse

Cover Design: Vignelli Associates

SPECIAL SALES

MANUFACTURED IN THE UNITED STATES OF AMERICA
10 9 8 7 6 5 4 3 2 1

CONTENTS

FOREWORD vii
Map of the Bahamas viii

INTRODUCTION ix

FACTS AT YOUR FINGERTIPS 1
Facts and Figures 1; Planning Your Trip 2; Travel Agents and Tour Operators 2; Tips for British Visitors 4; Tourist Information Services 5; When to Go 6; Seasonal Events 7; How to Get There by Air 10; How to Get There by Sea 11; Getting Around the Bahamas 12; Packing 14; Passports and Visas 15; Customs 15; Airport Taxes and Other Charges 16; Money 17; What It Will Cost 17; Hotels and Other Accommodations 18; Dining Out 19; Tipping 20; Casinos 20; Telephones, Telegrams, and Telex 20; Postage 21; Language 21; Time Zone 21; Electric Current 21; Traveling with Pets 21; Traveling with Children 21; Student and Youth Travel 22; Hints to the Disabled 22; Health 22; Security 23

THE BAHAMAS: First Stop in the New World 27

NEW PROVIDENCE ISLAND: Nassau, Cable Beach, and 40
Paradise Island
Exploring Nassau 41
Map of Nassau and Paradise Island 42
Exploring New Providence 51
Map of New Providence 52
Practical Information for New Providence Island 58

GRAND BAHAMA ISLAND: Freeport, Lucaya, and West End 89
Map of Freeport/Lucaya 90
Exploring Freeport/Lucaya 91
Exploring Grand Bahama Island 94
Map of Grand Bahama Island 95
Practical Information for Grand Bahama Island 98

THE FAMILY ISLANDS 114
Map of the Abacos 115
The Abacos 116
Practical Information for the Abacos 121
Map of Andros 128
Andros 129
Practical Information for Andros 130
Bimini 133
Map of Bimini 134
Practical Information for Bimini 135
Cat Island 138
Practical Information for Cat Island 140
Chub Cay 140
Practical Information for Chub Cay 141
Crooked Island 141
Practical Information for Crooked Island 142

Eleuthera 142
  Map of Eleuthera 145
  Practical Information for Eleuthera 147
The Exumas 152
  Map of the Exumas 155
  Practical Information for the Exumas 156
Great Inagua 160
  Practical Information for Great Inagua 161
Long Island 161
  Practical Information for Long Island 162
Rum Cay 164
  Practical Information for Rum Cay 164
San Salvador 165
  Practical Information for San Salvador 166

INDEX   169

FOREWORD

The islands of the Bahamas offer three distinct vacation worlds to explore, each different and appealing. The best known and most popular is Nassau and Paradise Island; the second is Grand Bahama Island, with the resorts of Freeport, Lucaya, and West End; and the third, officially called the Family Islands, encompasses all the other islands in the Bahamas chain.

In the following chapters we present an island-by-island guide to the Bahamas, with practical information about each resort destination throughout the island chain. We begin with New Providence Island and the major resort centers of Nassau, Cable Beach, and Paradise Island. Our second Bahamas vacation destination is Grand Bahama Island, including Freeport, Lucaya, and West End. In the final section, we offer a guide to more than a dozen of the Family Islands, including the Abacos, Andros, Bimini, Cat Island, Chub Cay, Crooked Island, Eleuthera, the Exumas, Great Inagua, Long Island, Rum Cay, and San Salvador, and several of the resort centers of offshore cays that can be reached by ferry or water taxi from the main islands, such as Eleuthera's Harbour Island and Spanish Wells, and Abaco's Elbow Cay, Great Guana Cay, and Green Turtle Cay.

While every care has been taken to assure the accuracy of the information in this guide, the passage of time will always bring change, and consequently the publisher cannot accept responsibility for errors that may occur.

All prices and opening times quoted here are based on information available to us at press time. Hours and admission fees may change, however, and the prudent traveler will avoid inconvenience by calling ahead.

Fodor's wants to hear about your travel experiences, both pleasant and unpleasant. When a hotel or restaurant fails to live up to its billing, let us know and we will investigate the complaint and revise our entries where the facts warrant it.

Send your letters to the editors of Fodor's Travel Publications, 201 E. 50th Street, New York, NY 10022.

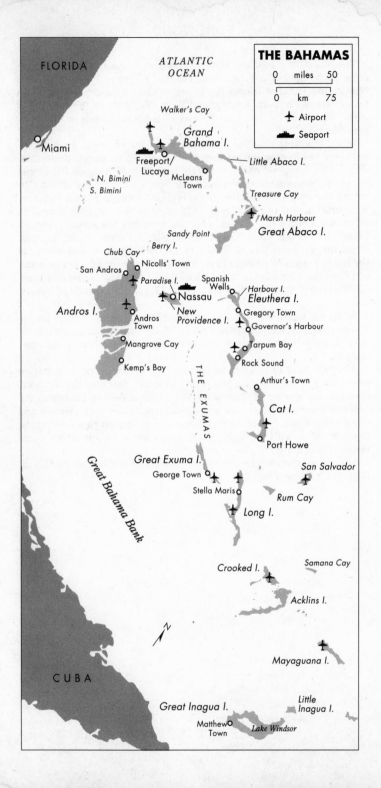

INTRODUCTION

The Commonwealth of the Bahama Islands is an archipelago that lies in the warm western waters of the Atlantic, beginning just 60 miles off the coast of Florida's Palm Beach and stretching in a great southeasterly arc for more than 750 miles to the Windward Passage, entrance to the Caribbean Sea. The more than 700 emerald islands in the Bahamas chain are scattered over 100,000 square miles of ocean waters.

They are the South Sea Islands of the North Atlantic, a Polynesia that lies just over the horizon, not half a world away. As a tropical island destination, the Bahamas are the nearest and most accessible to all of North America—Los Angeles is closer to Nassau than it is to Honolulu. Resort capitals in the Bahamas are only half an hour from Florida's Gold Coast, 2½ hours from New York, three hours from Toronto, and little more than a breakfast-to-dinner flight from Great Britain and the Continent.

Each island is bordered by powder-soft white-sand beaches lined with whispering casuarinas and swaying palms. Offshore, the islands are fringed by living coral reefs and surrounded by a palette of blue and green waters of unbelievable clarity and indescribable beauty. An astronaut, soaring more than a hundred miles above, once said they were "like nothing else on earth . . . a ribbon of turquoise lost in the midnight blue of the world's oceans."

Half of the islands in the Bahamas chain are subtropical, the other half tropical, with the Tropic of Cancer bisecting the archipelago. The warm waters of the Gulf Stream, which sweeps along the Bahamas' western shores, and the gentle trade winds that blow constantly from the southeast ensure a nearly perfect year-round climate that has attracted visitors to the Bahamas for two centuries. Early travelers called the Bahamas "the isles of perpetual June."

The northernmost island is Walkers Cay in the Abacos, which lies some 100 miles due east of Stuart, Florida; the southernmost is Inagua, less than 50 miles from Cuba. The nearest islands to the U.S. mainland are Bimini, 50 miles across the Gulf Stream from Miami, and Grand Bahama, 60 miles off Palm Beach. Nassau, capital city of the Bahamas, on the island of New Providence, is just 150 miles from the Florida coast, less than 35 minutes by jet from Miami or Fort Lauderdale.

Fewer than 250,000 people live in all of the Bahama Islands, most of them in the two major urban resort centers of Nassau and Freeport. The population is approximately 85% black and 15% white, and both races can trace their Bahamian ancestry back more than 200 years. For the most part, black and white Bahamians work with each other and socialize together in harmony.

Tourism, the most important industry in the Bahamas, accounts for some two-thirds of the national income and employs almost three-fourths of the population in related services. International banking, the second largest industry, has grown steadily in importance in the Bahamas during the past 20 years because of the political and economic stability of the country; the excellent communications network that links Nassau to the rest of the world; a favorable investment climate with no income, sales, or inheritance taxes; and strict bank secrecy laws that rival those of Switzerland. The Bahamas boast more than 350 banks and trust companies, representing many of the world's largest financial institutions. Nassau has become a leading international Eurodollar trading center, on a level with London, Paris, and Geneva.

The Bahamas are among the most politically and economically stable nations in the hemisphere, with one of the highest per capita incomes of any Third World nation. The election of a black majority government in 1967 ended 300 years of rule by the white minority. Under the leadership of Prime Minister Sir Lynden O. Pindling, the Bahamas became independent of Great Britain on July 10, 1973. The island nation has chosen to remain in the Commonwealth, however, and Queen Elizabeth II is recognized as monarch. English is the universal language here, and the Bahamas retain a European-style government of parliamentary democracy with free elections and a court system based on English law. The islands still offer much of the colorful pomp and pageantry derived from more than 300 years of British colonial rule and heritage.

Each year the Bahamas attract more than 3 million visitors. The lower-priced summer and autumn months, known as "low season," rival in popularity the higher-priced winter months, or "high season," making the islands a busy year-round vacation destination. Even though more than 20 of the islands in the entire archipelago have been developed as resort centers, and in spite of the fact that the Bahamas are not in the Caribbean, the islands present the broadest variety of vacation styles in the entire region, from Bermuda in the north to Barbados in the south.

The principal stop in a Bahamas itinerary is often New Providence Island, which combines British colonial charm and the historic landmarks of the centuries-old capital city of Nassau with the delights of international shopping and the sophistication of world-famous resorts and casinos on Paradise Island, just across the harbor, and along beautiful Cable Beach.

Grand Bahama Island offers the resort centers of Freeport and oceanside Lucaya, carved from the casuarina forests less than a generation ago. Here visitors find the features of a modern country club: half a dozen 18-hole championship golf courses, the internationally famous UNEXSO scuba-diving school, elegant hotels and casinos that rival the best of Nassau and Paradise Island, miles of beautiful beaches and challenging reefs, and shopping bargains from around the world at the colorful International Bazaar and the new festival marketplace at Port Lucaya.

The Family Islands, known to generations of natives and visitors as the Out Islands—"out" from the glamour of Nassau and Freeport yet very much "in" with sophisticated travelers—boast a casual, laid-back style and a rustic charm that make them favorite havens for the wealthy, the titled, and the famous, and a mecca for serious yachtsmen, fishermen, and diving enthusiasts. There are more than a dozen Family Islands to choose from, some large and some small, some just 50 miles off Florida's shores, others more than 350 miles from the capital city of Nassau. Whichever island you choose, you'll find the Family Island trademarks: seemingly endless, nearly empty beaches to roam; crystal-clear waters for swimming and snorkeling; colorful coral reefs for diving; fine fishing, good sailing, and a barefoot ambience ideal for getting away from it all.

INTRODUCTION   xi

The Bahamas in 1990

With the final rooms due to open early in 1990, **Carnival's Crystal Palace Hotel and Casino** becomes the biggest resort in the Bahamas, with over 1,550 rooms. At the end of 1988 Carnival bought the neighboring Cable Beach Hotel for $82.5 million and merged the two properties. Tourism director Baltron Bethel says: "The property will undoubtedly be the premier resort in all the Bahamas and the Caribbean." Carnival spent over $140 million building the hotel and is presently spending over $5 million on a face-lift of the former Cable Beach Hotel. The combined hotels boast a 2,000-foot-long private beach; an 18-hole, par-72 golf course; a health club; and a sports center with ten tennis, three indoor squash, and three racquetball courts. The casino—the Bahamas' biggest—has 750 slot machines and 51 blackjack, seven craps, and nine roulette tables as well as one mini baccarat and one big six table.

The **Royal Bahamas Police Force Band** celebrates its 150th birthday in 1990. In addition to the Changing of the Guard Ceremony—which takes place at Government House every other Saturday—some special concerts will be organized. Collectors note: A British toy company has produced a limited edition set of the bandsmen in miniature.

The Grand Bahama resort area of **Lucaya** has added three new developments: the **Port Lucaya complex,** with 85 shops, boutiques, and restaurants; the **Dolphin Experience,** where dolphins have been trained to swim out into the nearby canals with trainers and tourists (you can be an assistant trainer for a day); and improved facilities by the Bahamas National Trust at the **Lucayan National Park and Caverns.**

The Meridien hotel group, a subsidiary of Air France, has taken over the management of the **Royal Bahamian Hotel,** formerly the Balmoral Beach Hotel. The hotel is expected to attract upscale clients from Europe as well as the U.S. with its new five-star rating. A hotel spokesman said: "We will strive to achieve the right mix of the Bahamian culture with the French touch."

Work is underway on an office complex in downtown Nassau which is to be called the **Bahamas Financial Center.** This is the first major office development in the Bahamas' capital for over a decade. The site of the $25-million project is the former Charlotte Street parking lot at the intersection of Shirley and Charlotte streets. The architects say the four-story structure will combine contemporary design with a Bahamian flair.

Princess Hotels International has spent several million dollars refurbishing the **Princess Tower** on Grand Bahama. In 1988, 80 suites and rooms on the third and fourth floors were upgraded, and the remaining rooms on the first and second floors were given new furnishings and fixtures. The finishing touch for the 1990 season was to be a face-lift for the exterior of the building.

Carnival Cruise Lines is building a $150 million superliner. The ship, unnamed at press time, will carry 2,200 passengers, and the line says she will be dedicated entirely to Bahamas cruises. Carnival, with huge investments in the Bahamas, recently purchased the cruise line Holland America Line for $625 million. **Premier Cruise Line** has acquired the *Sun Princess,* better known as TV's "Love Boat." She has been renamed *Star Ship Majestic* and will operate between Cape Canaveral and Treasure Cay, Abaco. Premier has also bought the *Atlantic,* which has started three- and four-day cruises between Port Canaveral and Nassau. The cruise ship *Tropicale* is operating daily cruises between Miami and Bimini.

A 500-seat theater is just one of the new treasures in store for visitors to **Treasure Island,** until recently a deserted island near Treasure Cay, Abaco. A multimillion-dollar dredging operation in 1988 and 1989 now makes Treasure Island accessible for cruise ships. The work is being undertaken by the Treasure Cay Company. The open-air theater will feature Bahamian performers.

Delta, TWA, and Pan Am are expected to offer more seats out of the Boston–New York gateways to Nassau for the 1990 season. Majestic Air, previously Pacific Interstate Airlines, is to provide charter flights to Carnival's Crystal Palace resort in Nassau from Fort Lauderdale and other gateways. During 1989 Bahamasair, and its charter arm Bahamas Express, are scheduled to add charter services from Newark, Hartford, and Nashville. Late in 1988 Bahamasair began scheduled service from Washington, DC, and discontinued service from Atlanta, where it was competing with Delta and Eastern. A Bahamas Ministry of Tourism spokesman said: "We are in advanced stages of negotiations with other major carriers which will result in new services from other U.S. gateways and also from Europe."

Looking further ahead, the Bahamas Government has already set up a **Quincentennial Commission** in readiness for celebrations to mark the 500th anniversary in 1992 of Christopher Columbus's landing in San Salvador in the southern Bahamas. As part of the "getting ready" program, many tour operators are planning special Discovery Season discounts in the fall of 1990. This Discovery Season will last until December 15 with special prices in hotels, stores, and restaurants. Several bars in Freeport already have planned a special two-for-the-price-of-one drink—the Discovery Colada!

FACTS AT YOUR FINGERTIPS

FACTS AT YOUR FINGERTIPS

FACTS AND FIGURES. The Bahamas are in the North Atlantic Ocean, not in the Caribbean Sea. They lie between the longitudes of 72° 42' W and 80° 45' W, and the latitudes of 20° 45' N and 28° N. The 500-mile-long archipelago extends between southeast Florida and northern Hispaniola (Haiti and the Dominican Republic). The land area of the Bahamas is less than 5,400 square miles.

By accident of geography, the ocean waters of the Bahamas are among the most beautiful, clearest, and least polluted waters in the world. In the entire archipelago there are no rivers or streams to carry silt or sewage to the ocean depths or shallows. The islands are made of coral and limestone, which act as a natural filtering system for man-made wastes, and there are no smoke-belching factories creating acid rain to pollute land or water.

The islands are surrounded by vast areas of shallow water, huge underwater plateaus called the Great Bahama Bank and the Little Bahama Bank. Rising from the Great Bahama Bank are the islands of Andros, Eleuthera, New Providence, and the Exuma chain. The Little Bahama Bank fringes the northern shores of Grand Bahama Island and surrounds the islands of the Abaco chain. Separating the shallow banks are deep subterranean chasms. On the west are the Straits of Florida, through which flows the mighty Gulf Stream. On the north, separating Grand Bahama and Andros, is the Northwest Providence Channel, used by the sleek white cruise ships that ply the sea lanes between Florida and the Bahamas. The Northeast Providence Channel separates the Abacos from Eleuthera, the Berry Islands, and New Providence. TOTO, or the Tongue of the Ocean, an even deeper underwater canyon that bisects the Great Bahama Bank, extends the entire length of Andros (largest island in the Bahamas chain), fringes Lyford Cay at the southwestern tip of New Providence, and sweeps by Chub Cay in the Berry Island chain.

The islands of the Bahamas barely rise above the shallows of the vast Bahama banks. They are low-lying, generally only 20 to 50 feet high; the highest point in the entire chain is 206-foot Mount Alvernia on Cat Island. Because the soil tends to be thin and rocky, the natural vegetation of the islands is primarily small bushes and stubby palmetto shrubs interspersed with stands of graceful casuarina pines whose swaying branches and lacy needles whisper constantly in the soft island breezes. Here and there you'll see a grove of coconut palms, remnants of plantation days, or a stray coconut washed ashore with the tide. And everywhere you'll find the most beautiful white-sand beaches and spectacularly colored ocean waters.

The combination of clear, unpolluted water, the shallows and depths, and the brilliant tropical sunshine gives Bahamian waters their unique clarity and coloring. The inky, midnight blue of the subterranean chasms contrasts with the turquoise, emerald, and aquamarine that mark the vast Bahama banks and the reefy shallows that fringe the beaches and shores of nearly every island.

For a memorable first glimpse of the multiple colors of Bahamian waters, ask for a window seat on the right side of the aircraft flying you into the Bahamas. If you are flying from Nassau down through the Exuma chain, *demand* that window seat on the right side of the aircraft.

PLANNING YOUR TRIP. Planning a trip to the Bahamas can be as easy as hopping on any one of the dozens of daily direct flights from major American cities to Nassau and Freeport. Except during peak travel periods, such as holidays and midwinter, it is not always necessary to have a hotel reservation. Most airlines serving the Bahamas offer package programs that can be booked when you make your flight reservation. Or you can call Bahamas Reservation Service, toll free from anywhere in the U.S. or Canada, (800) 327–0787, for information on hotel vacancies and instant reservations. Reservations can even be made when you arrive. The Ministry of Tourism operates information booths at the international airports in Nassau and Freeport that offer up-to-date listings of hotel vacancies, with telephones available so you can make on-the-spot reservations. However, this is a technique for the sophisticated and adventurous; you could find yourself stranded or taking more expensive accommodations than you had planned.

Thousands of Floridians and Florida vacationers take advantage of the proximity of the Bahamas and pop over for a long weekend or a week-long holiday whenever the spirit moves them. Several airlines offer casino junkets to Nassau or Freeport, departing from Florida cities in the evening and returning in the early hours of the morning. Day trips to the Bahamas aboard a cruise ship are available from the Port of Palm Beach, just north of West Palm Beach; and from Miami.

If you are traveling from other parts of the U.S., Canada, or abroad, it is best to plan your vacation well in advance, so you can be sure to have your choice of travel dates and resort accommodations. The Bahamas Tourist Offices located throughout the United States, Canada, and Europe provide a wealth of information on request. (For addresses, see Tourist Information Services.)

Most Bahamas hotels and resorts offer package programs with significant savings over standard room rates; be sure to ask about them. Many airlines also offer package programs with significant savings.

TRAVEL AGENTS AND TOUR OPERATORS. If you prefer to have a professional do your vacation planning, consult your travel agent. Most travel agents in the United States, Canada, and Europe are knowledgeable about the Bahamas, will suggest island destinations that best suit you, and can offer a wide range of package programs from tour operators worldwide who specialize in Bahamas holidays. Your travel agent can book your airline or cruise trip, arrange transfers to and from the airport, book your hotel accommodations, and even arrange for rental cars and sightseeing tours. In most cases, the services of a travel agent will cost you nothing.

Most Bahamas tour packages include round-trip airfare, airport–hotel transportation, accommodations, one to three meals daily, a welcoming cocktail, and perhaps a sight-seeing tour or cruise, a T-shirt, a travel bag, a few casino chips, or some other gimmick. Some packages are geared specifically to the needs of honeymooners, golfers, or divers.

Tours Operators (USA). The following offer a variety of Bahamas vacation plans:

Adventure Tours, Inc. (301) 922–7000 or (800) 638–9040. Two-, three-, and seven-night land-only packages to Nassau/Freeport and the Family Islands.

American Express Vacations. (800) 241–1700. Three- and seven-night land-only packages to Nassau/Freeport.

Bahamas Express. (800) 722–4262. Day trips, casino junkets, and one-to seven-night land and air packages to Nassau/Freeport and the Family Islands via charter or Bahamasair from Newark, Atlanta, Miami, Orlando, Tampa.

Cable Beach Vacations. (305) 576–9296 or (800) 832–7529. Three-, four-, and seven-night land and air packages to Cable Beach resorts from Florida cities via scheduled air carriers.

Cavalcade Tours. (212) 695–6400. Three-, four-, and seven-night land-only packages to Nassau/Freeport. Golf and honeymoon packages.

Certified Tours. (305) 522–1440 or (800) 872–7786. One- to seven-night land and air packages to Nassau/Freeport and the Family Islands via Delta (Delta Dream Vacations).

Flyfaire. (212) 661–3100 or (800) 367–1036. One- to seven-night land and air packages to Nassau/Freeport and the Family Islands from major U.S. cities via scheduled air carriers.

Funway Holidays/Funjet. (414) 351–3553 or (800) 558–3050. Three-, four-, and seven-night land and air packages to Nassau/Freeport from Chicago and other midwest cities via United Airlines. Land-only packages to the Family Islands.

Go-Go Tours. (201) 967–3000 or (800) 666–9999. Three-, four-, and seven-night land and air packages to Nassau/Freeport from most U.S. gateways via scheduled air carriers. Golf and honeymoon packages.

GWV International. (617) 449–5450 or (800) 343–1215. One- to 14-night land and air packages to Nassau/Freeport and the Family Islands from New York, Boston, and Washington via TWA and charters.

In Style Tours. (718) 224–4100 or (800) 252–7791. Two- to seven-night land and air packages to Nassau/Freeport from northeast, midwest, and Florida cities via scheduled air carriers. Kosher programs.

Paradise Island Vacations. (305) 891–3888 or (800) 722–7466. One- to seven-night land and air packages to Paradise Island resorts from Atlanta, Miami, and other southern cities. Casino, golf, and honeymoon packages.

Piedmont Vacations. (800) 233–6660. Three- to 14-night land and air packages to Nassau from cities served by Piedmont.

Princess Casino Vacations. (800) 545–1130. Junkets to the Freeport resort from Florida, midwest, and southern gateways via Braniff charters. Casino, golf, and honeymoon packages.

Tour Operators (Canada). The following offer a variety of Bahamas vacation plans:

Americanada International Tours. (416) 967–1112. Seven- and 14-night land-only packages to Nassau/Freeport and the Family Islands.

Golf Holidays. (514) 871–8453, (416) 656–6700, or (800) 268–1820. Seven- and 14-night land and air packages to Nassau/Freeport from Montreal and Toronto. Golf tours.

Holiday House. (416) 364–2433 or (514) 842–8115. Seven- to 14-night land-only packages to Nassau/Freeport and the Family Islands from Canadian cities via scheduled air carriers.

Thomson Vacations. (416) 673–8777. Three- to 14-night land and air packages to Nassau, Freeport, Abaco, and Eleuthera from Chicago and from Toronto and other Canadian cities. Three and four-day cruises on the MTS *Jason,* Nassau to Freeport, are available.

Touram. (514) 876–4141 or (416) 975–8004. Seven- to 14-day land and air packages to Nassau/Freeport from Toronto and Montreal via Air Canada.

TIPS FOR BRITISH VISITORS. Passports. Citizens of the United Kingdom do not need passports for visits of less than three weeks. A birth certificate or some similar form of identification is acceptable (but don't forget you *will* need a passport to reenter Britain). Citizens of Commonwealth countries do not require visas. All visitors are required to have onward or return tickets and a document that will permit them to enter another country.

Customs. You may take into the Bahamas, provided you are over 17 years of age, 200 cigarettes or 100 cigarillos or 50 cigars or 250 grams of tobacco; one liter of wine or one liter of spirits over 22% by volume; and 50 grams of perfume.

Returning to Britain, if you are 17 or over, you may bring home (1) 200 cigarettes or 100 cigarillos or 50 cigars or 250 grams of tobacco; (2) two liters of table wine and, in addition, (a) one liter of alcohol over 22% by volume (most spirits), (b) two liters of alcohol under 22% by volume (fortified or sparkling wine), or (c) two more liters of table wine; (3) 50 grams of perfume and one-quarter liter of toilet water; and (4) other goods up to a value of £32.

Insurance. We heartily recommend that you insure yourself to cover health, loss of luggage, trip cancellation, and motoring mishaps. Contact *Europ Assistance,* 252 High St., Croydon CRO 1NF (01–680–1234).

Bahamas Tourist Office. For information on the Bahamas, visit, call, or write the London BTO at 10 Chesterfield Street, London W1X 8AH. (629–5238).

Tour Operators. The following offer holidays in the Bahamas:

Albany Travel, (Manchester) Ltd., 190 Deansgate, Manchester M3 3WD (061–833–0202).

Club Méditerranée, 106–108 Brompton Rd., London SW3 1JJ (581–1161).

Dream Islands of the World, 30 Union Ct., Richmond, Surrey TW9 1AA (948–6117).

Harlequin Holidays, 146 West St., Sheffield, South Yorkshire S1 4ES (0742–750508).

Jetsave, Sussex House, London Rd., East Grinstead, West Sussex RH19 1LD (0342–312033). 14-night two-center vacations in Orlando and the Bahamas from £695.

Kuoni Travel, Kuoni House, Dorking, Surrey RH5 4AZ (0306–885044). Seven-night packages from £552.

Speedbird Holidays, Alta House, 152 King St., London W6 0QV (741–8041).

Tradewinds Faraway Holidays, 81–83 Fulham High St., London SW6 3JP (731–8000). Seven-night packages from £598 to £1,182.

Air Fares. We suggest that you explore the current scene for budget flight possibilities. APEX and other fares are offered by airlines at a considerable saving over the full price. Quite frankly, only business travelers who don't have to watch the price of their tickets fly full price these days—and find themselves sitting right beside APEX passengers! An APEX round-trip ticket to Nassau cost about £429 in the spring of 1989.

Cruise Lines. *Costa Line Cruises,* 324–326 Regent St., Albany House, London W1R 5AA (637–9960).

Dolphin Cruiselines, 168 Sloane St., London SW1X 9LF (235–0168).

Equity Cruises, 77–79 Great Eastern St., London EC2A 3HV (729–1929).

Norwegian Caribbean Lines, 3 Vere St., London W1M 9HQ (493–6041).

Yacht Charter Agencies. *Camper & Nicholsons (Yacht Agency), Ltd.,* 31 Berkeley St., London W1X 5FA (491–2950).

Halsey Marine, Ltd., 22 Boston Pl., London NW1 6HZ (724–1303).

Sun Days Charters, Linden House, Crapstone, Yelverton, Devon PL2O 7PS (0822–853–375).

Worldwide Yachting Holidays, c/o Liz Fenner, 35 Fairfax Pl., London NW6 4EJ (328–1033).

TOURIST INFORMATION SERVICES. The Bahamas Ministry of Tourism operates a network of information offices in the United States, Canada, and Europe that will answer your questions and provide you with brochures and rate sheets for all hotels and resorts in the Bahamas for all seasons. BTO offices have brochures and directories on sports such as golf, tennis, scuba, sailing, fishing, and private flying in the Bahamas, a year-round Calendar of Events, and flyers on Goombay Summer Festival, Student Breakaway months, and the year-round People to People program. The BTO staffs are friendly and anxious to help.

The following are *Bahamas Tourist Offices* in the U.S. and Canada:

Atlanta: 2957 Clairmont Rd., Suite 150, Atlanta, GA 30345; (404) 633–1793.

Boston: 1027 Statler Office Bldg., Boston, MA 02116; (617) 426–3144.

Chicago: 875 North Michigan Ave., Chicago, IL 60611; (312) 787–8203.

Dallas: World Trade Center, Box 581408, Dallas, TX 75258; (214) 742–1886.

Detroit: 26400 Lahser Rd., Southfield, MI 48034; (313) 357–2940.

Houston: 5177 Richmond Ave., Suite 755, Houston, TX 77056; (713) 626–1566.

Los Angeles: 3450 Wilshire Blvd., Los Angeles, CA 90014; (213) 385–0033.

Miami: 255 Alhambra Circle, Coral Gables, FL 33134; (305) 442–4860.

New York: 150 E. 52nd St., New York, NY 10022; (212) 758–2777.

Philadelphia: 437 Chestnut St., Philadelphia, PA 19106; (215) 925–0871.

St. Louis: 555 N. New Ballas Rd., St. Louis, MO 63141; (314) 569–7777.

San Francisco: 44 Montgomery St., Suite 503, San Francisco, CA 94104; (415) 673–0426 or 398–5502.

Washington, D.C.: 1730 Rhode Island Ave., N.W., Washington, D.C. 20036; (202) 659–9135.

Montreal: 1255 Phillips Square, Montreal, Quebec H3B 3G1; (514) 861–6797.

Toronto: 121 Bloor St. E., Toronto, Ontario M4W 3M5; (416) 968–2999.

Vancouver: 470 Granville St., Vancouver, British Columbia V6C 1V5; (604) 688–8334.

The Bahamas promotion boards representing three destinations, Nassau/Paradise Island, Freeport/Lucaya, and the Family Islands, operate offices abroad that offer helpful information, brochures, and rate sheets.

Nassau, Cable Beach, and Paradise Island Promotion Board, 255 Alhambra Circle, Coral Gables, FL 33134; (305) 445–3705. In Chicago, 628 Martin Ln., Deerfield, IL 60015; (312) 541–6250. In Dallas, 1717 Lakewood Blvd., Euliss, TX 76039; (214) 263–9437. In New York, 191 Amity St., Brooklyn, NY 11201; (718) 921–4722. In London, 79 Dean St., London W1V 6HY; 01–437–8766.

Cable Beach Resort Association, 6501 N.W. 36th St., Suite 390, Virginia Gardens, FL; (305) 633–8464.

Grand Bahama Island Promotion Board, 255 Alhambra Circle, Coral Gables, FL 33134; (305) 448–3386.

The Family Islands Promotion Board, 255 Alhambra Circle, Coral Gables, FL 33134; (305) 446–4111.

Bahamas Reservation Service (800) 327–0787 (in Miami, 443–3821) represents more than 100 hotels and resorts with 11,000 rooms. BRS provides information on rates and availability and will make instant confirmed reservations for you free of charge (Mon.–Fri., 9 A.M.–6 P.M. Eastern Time). The BRS number in London is 01–491–4800.

WHEN TO GO. Winter is high season, when hotel rates, airfares, and charter packages are at their peak. The winter season begins in mid-December, usually a week before Christmas, and extends through April or the week after Easter. The second season, known as Goombay Summer, lasts the rest of the year.

Winter season attracts many wealthy visitors from around the world. It also attracts hundreds of thousands of ordinary Americans and Canadians eager to escape the freezing cold and blizzards of northern climes. The weather in winter months is almost ideal, ranging from 65 to 80 degrees F, with a sea temperature of 70–75 degrees, some seven hours of bright sunshine daily, and almost no rain. However, an occasional "norther" can move in, usually the last vestiges of a severe winter blizzard in the north, and skies can cloud over for a day or two and temperatures drop into the low 50s.

During the winter season vacation styles tend to be slightly more formal than during the summer. There are gala charity balls, local theater productions, and name entertainers at famous nightclubs. Most of the fine restaurants, lounges, casinos, and nightclubs require a jacket and tie for men, and women often dress in long skirts, cocktail dresses, or elegant pantsuits. Rarely, however, are evening gowns and black tie appropriate.

In general, during winter season, hotels and resorts enjoy the highest occupancy levels of the year, and prices are somewhat higher across the board for everything from restaurant meals to city tours, from greens fees to shopping bargains. Winter sees the biggest, noisiest, most colorful festival of the year: the Junkanoo masquerade on Boxing Day (December 26) and New Year's Day. Book well in advance for airline tickets and your first choice of hotel or resort, particularly at the peak periods: the week between Christmas and New Year's, George Washington's Birthday week, and Easter week.

Goombay Summer is the season of low prices and high spirits in the Bahamas. It lasts for eight months, and rates for everything are the lowest of the year, usually 20 to 30 percent, sometimes as much as 50 percent, lower. Paradoxically, this may be the most fun and most interesting time of the year to visit the Bahamas. The Goombay Summer calendar is filled with exciting social, cultural, and sporting events such as golf, tennis, and fishing tournaments, and the islands are a riot of color with tropical flowers and magnificent foliage in full bloom.

The drawbacks are that it tends to be warmer and more humid during Goombay Summer, and it is the rainy season. However, the rain comes in swift tropical showers rarely lasting more than an hour and almost never causing gray skies—as a matter of fact, the sun usually shines through the rain. Some rain falls nearly every day in the summer months, usually in late afternoon. It clears the air of the sultry humidity, leaving the evenings fresh and cooler. Hurricanes also arrive in Goombay Summer, about once every eight or ten years. (Most likely months are August, September, and October.)

Temperatures average 80 to 90 degrees during midsummer months, lower in the spring and fall. Humidity averages 77 to 82 percent year-round, with 78 to 82 percent common in summer and fall; sea temperature peaks in summer at around 80 degrees. Because of the higher temperatures and humidity during Goombay Summer, both Bahamians and visitors dress more casually and coolly. Restaurants, nightclubs, and casinos are less formal, and dressy sportswear is accepted almost everywhere in the evenings, although many visitors still enjoy dressing up a bit.

YEAR-ROUND WEATHER CHART

	Mean temperature (F)	Mean relative humidity (%)	Mean hours of bright sunshine	Mean rainfall (inches)
Jan.	69.6	79	7.2	1.90
Feb.	70.0	78	7.9	1.57
Mar.	72.0	78	8.4	1.38
Apr.	74.5	77	8.9	1.89
May	77.0	77	8.5	4.83
June	80.1	79	7.5	9.23
July	81.5	78	8.9	6.08
Aug.	81.9	79	8.5	6.30
Sept.	80.7	82	7.1	7.52
Oct.	78.0	81	6.7	8.31
Nov.	74.2	79	7.4	2.29
Dec.	70.9	78	7.1	1.52

SEASONAL EVENTS. The Bahamas calendar is packed with special events, year-round, and all are open to visitor participation. The official holidays celebrated in the Bahamas, and some of the most popular annual events held month by month, are listed below:

January. The New Year is greeted with the biggest, noisiest, most colorful, and most exciting event on the calendar, the annual *Junkanoo Parade,* a centuries-old masquerade and Goombay music festival, which features exotic sheared crepe-paper costumes and a primitive African beat. The most elaborate parades are held in Nassau and Freeport, with miniparades in the Family Islands. New Year's Day also brings the *Staniel Cay Regatta* in the Exumas. The *Supreme Court Assizes* open with pomp and pageantry on the second Wednesday of the month in Parliament Square; the *Red Cross* holds its annual charity ball in Nassau. Nassau hosts the annual *North American Backgammon Championships,* which attract the "class" of world backgammon enthusiasts, at the Paradise Island Resort and Casino, which also hosts the *PGA-Bahamas Golf Classic.* The annual *International Windsurfing Championships* are held at the Nassau Beach Hotel, and the annual *Princess 10K Road Race* is held in Freeport.

February. In Nassau, the *Annual Heart Ball* (near Valentine's Day) attracts international socialites as well as Who's Who in the Bahamas. Late in the month, yachting takes center stage, as the last two races in the prestigious Southern Ocean Racing Conference annual series are sailed in Bahamian waters: the *Miami-Nassau Race* and the *Nassau Cup Race.*

March. *Student Breakaway* programs in Nassau and Freeport offer daily activities and special events for college students on spring break. In Nassau, the *Snipe Winter Championships* have attracted the international Snipe racing set for decades, hosted by the Royal Nassau Sailing Club. Social highlight of the month is the annual *Red Cross Fair* in the beautiful tropical gardens of Government House, Nassau. In the Family Islands, the annual big game fishing tournament season gets under way on Bimini with the *Bimini Benefit Tournament* at Bimini's Blue Water Resort and the *Bacardi Tournament* at Bimini Big Game Fishing Club. Also at Bimini's Blue Water is the *Hemingway* kickoff tournament for the famed *Bahamas Billfish Championship,* a series of six tournaments that attract top anglers on the international big-game fishing circuits.

April. The fun-filled annual Bahamas workboat racing series, the *Family Island Regatta,* takes place in George Town, Exuma; and major fishing tournaments are scheduled on several islands. In the Abacos, there is the *Abaco Angling Tournament;* Chub Cay Club in the Berry Islands sponsors the *His and Hers Tournament* and annual *Members Tournament;* and Walker's Cay offers the second leg of the *Bahamas Billfish Championship,* followed by the third leg of the series held at the Bimini Big Game Fishing Club. In Nassau, the quarterly *Supreme Court Assizes* opening ceremonies are colorful and interesting. *Easter* is celebrated with a long weekend encompassing two official holidays, *Good Friday* and *Easter Monday. Student Breakaway* programs for college students continue through the month.

May. The fishing tournament season is in full swing. On Bimini and Cat Cay, anglers go after the giant bluefin tuna that migrate along the Gulf Stream each spring to their summer feeding grounds off Nova Scotia. Major *Tuna Tournaments* are held at the Cat Cay Club and Bimini's Blue Water. The fourth leg of the *Bahamas Billfish Championship* is hosted by the exclusive Cat Cay Club, their only tournament open to the public. Chub Cay Club holds its *Blue Marlin Tournament,* and in the Abacos, Green Turtle Yacht Club offers a week-long *All Fish Tournament.* Freeport Rotary Club sponsors an air show at West End Airport. Trials for the *Caribbean Amateur Golf Championship* take place at various golf courses in Nassau and Freeport.

June. Two public holidays fall on the first weekend. June 1 is *Labor Day* and June 4 is *Whit Monday.* In golf, the *Final Trials Medal Singles* take place on Paradise Island. The *Long Island Regatta* takes place at Salt Pond, Long Island, and it's *Regatta Time in Abaco* from the last week in June until July 4. Fishing tournaments take place in Cat Cay and the Xanadu Resort in Freeport. In Nassau and Freeport, the four-month-long

Goombay Summer Festival begins, offering a full calendar of social, cultural, and sporting events scheduled daily (and repeated weekly) for visitors. There are beach parties and boat cruises, art fairs and street dances, Junkanoo parades and Goombay music festivals.

July. One of the year's major holidays is *Independence Day,* which occurred July 10, 1973, marking the end of 300 years of British rule. In Nassau two golf tournaments are scheduled, the *Pepsi Cola Independence Open* at Divi Bahamas and the *Lyford Cay Classic* at Lyford Cay. The annual *Commonwealth Fair,* an exhibition of Bahamian accomplishments in trade, industry, and commerce, is held at the Gibson Primary School, Nassau. *Goombay Summer Festival* continues and the opening of the *Supreme Court* takes place on the first Wednesday. In the Abacos, yacht racing continues with the *Green Turtle Cay Independence Regatta* race week beginning July 4 and continuing through July 10. On Bimini, the Bimini Big Game Fishing Club *Blue Marlin Tournament* winds up the big time tournament season; and the Bimini Blue Water Resort sponsors the *Jimmy Albury Memorial All-Billfish Tournament.*

August. A national holiday is celebrated on the first Monday in August, *Emancipation Day,* marking the freedom of slaves on August 1, 1834. *Fox Hill Day* follows a week later, with residents of an ancient slave village near Nassau putting on an old-fashioned country fair featuring picnics and barbecues, down-home Bahamian cooking, arts and crafts booths, and gospel-singing concerts. In the Family Islands, Emancipation Day is celebrated with picnics, parties, and workboat regattas at Cat Island; Mangrove Cay, Andros; and Black Point, Exuma, near Staniel Cay. On Bimini, the most popular fishing tournament of the year takes place during Emancipation Day celebrations: the *Bimini Native Tournament* offers a week of rivalry and revelry, attracting hundreds of anglers. It is sponsored by the Bimini Blue Water Resort and has been held annually for more than 30 years. In Nassau and Freeport, *Goombay Summer Festival* events continue weekly.

September. *Goombay Summer Festival* continues to the end of the month. In Nassau, the *Bahamas Grand Prix* powerboat races, sponsored by I.P.P.I., are held in the harbor, pitting European and American Formula I in stiff competition for circuit honors and the coveted Champion of Champions Cup. On Bimini, the *B.O.A.T.* (Bimini Open Angling Tournament) is designed for small boats, two-angler teams, and is open to most kinds of fishing, sponsored by the Bimini Big Game Fishing Club.

October. A public holiday is celebrated on October 12, *Discovery Day,* marking the anniversary of Christopher Columbus's discovery of the Bahamas in 1492. In Nassau, the final quarterly *Supreme Court Assizes* open, with ceremonial splendor in Parliament Square, on the first Wednesday.

November. On two consecutive weekends, the Bahamas Humane Society holds its annual fund-raising fetes in Nassau—the *Humane Society Horse Show* at Camperdown Stables, when the horsey set show off their equestrian skills; and the *Humane Society Dog Show and Mini-Fair,* where everything from mutts to pedigrees show their tricks, held at Nassau Botanic Gardens. At North Andros, the *Thanksgiving Bonefish Championship Tournament* is held. In George Town, Exuma, the Hotel Peace 'n Plenty hosts the *Bonefish Bonanza.* At the Bimini Big Game Fishing Club the competition is *The Wahoo.* For private aviators there is the *Bahamas Invitational Fly-In* from Fort Pierce, Florida.

December. In Nassau, the *Marlborough Tennis Tournament,* held at the Ocean Club, attracts big-name stars. In Freeport, the *Grand Bahamas Vintage Grand Prix* features classic racers, such as Ferrari, Aston Martin, Lotus, and Porsche, dating from pre-World War II to the 1970s, an annual attraction for racing buffs and celebrities as well as ordinary visitors. In Bimini, anglers compete in the *Adam Clayton Powell Memorial Wahoo Tournament,* named for the late New York congressman who made Bimini his second home. The calendar of events for the year winds up with *Christmas Day* and the day after, *Boxing Day,* both national holidays. Boxing Day, a traditional English holiday, received its name from the ancient custom of landlords to box up leftover Christmas goodies and present them as gifts to their tenants and serfs. Here it marks the opening of the traditional *Junkanoo* celebrations. At dawn, hundreds of masked revellers parade through the streets in elaborate crepe-paper costumes to the beat of primitive African drums. The rivalry and revelry is surpassed only by the goings-on on New Year's Day, when a whole new set of costumes are paraded for even grander prizes and prouder acclaim.

People to People Program. In Nassau and Freeport, hundreds of Bahamian volunteers participate in the Ministry of Tourism's *People to People Program,* which brings visitors and islanders together in informal social and cultural activities. Visitors may be invited home for a party or Bahamian meal; taken on a personally guided tour of the city; invited to participate in a local club meeting or sporting or cultural event, or attend a church service. There is no set format, tourism officials simply introduce visitors to Bahamians who share similar interests or hobbies, professions or clubs; plans and itineraries are left up to the volunteers and their visitors. There is no charge to visitors, and most activities involve no expense, but it is wise to have money with you for incidentals. The program has operated successfully for many years, and visitors who participated have been enthusiastic about the experience and the opportunity to meet Bahamians and to learn something of their lifestyle and culture. It could be the highlight of your Bahamas holiday. To sign up, have your travel agent arrange with the Ministry of Tourism in advance, join through the service desk at your hotel, or contact any Tourist Information Office in Nassau or Freeport. In Nassau, you can contact the People to People division at 326–5371 or 322–7500; in Freeport, call 325–8044.

Year-round. The Bahamas calendar offers dozens of events for anglers, yachtsmen, scuba divers, aviators, golfers, and tennis buffs in addition to fine opportunities to watch cricket, soccer, and rugby matches. For complete details on sports events in the Bahamas, including entry fees, requirements, and regulations, contact the *Bahamas Sports Hot Line,* (800) 327-7678, Mon.–Fri., 9 A.M.–5 P.M. For a *Calendar of Events,* published in December and June each year by the Ministry of Tourism, contact any Bahamas Tourist Office.

HOW TO GET THERE BY AIR. Dozens of flights leave major U.S. cities daily for Nassau and Freeport on *Bahamasair, Braniff Express, Caribbean Express, Chalk's International, Delta, Eastern, Midway, Pan American, Piedmont,* and *TWA. Air Canada* has two flights weekly to Nassau from Toronto and Montreal. *British Airways* offers flights to Nassau from London; Bermuda; and Kingston, Jamaica.

Miami's proximity to Nassau (35 minutes flying time) and the frequent service (10 to 12 flights daily) between the two cities on *Bahamasair* and

Eastern make Miami International Airport a logical jumping-off place for the Bahamas.

Bahamasair offers frequent scheduled service to 19 Family Islands from the Nassau hub. In addition, several small commuter airlines operate dozens of scheduled flights daily to Nassau, Freeport, and the Family Islands from Miami, Fort Lauderdale, Tampa, Orlando, and Palm Beach. For the most convenient carrier, flights, and connections on the major airlines, check with your travel agent or directly with the carrier. For Bahamasair, call (800) 222–4262 in the U.S. Telephone numbers for Florida commuter airlines: *Chalk's International,* in the U.S. (800) 327–2521, in Fla. (800) 432–8807. *Florida Express,* in the U.S. (800) 327–8538. *Piedmont Shuttle,* in the U.S. (800) 251–5720. *Aero Coach International,* in the U.S. (800) 327–0010, in Fla. (800) 432–5034. *Gull Air,* (305) 684–1247, in Fla. (800) 222–4855. *Caribbean Express,* in the U.S. (800) 351–0104, in Fla. (800) 223–7652. *Walker's Cay Airlines,* in the U.S. (800) 327–3714, in Fla. (800) 432–2092.

Where luggage is concerned, major U.S. airlines treat Nassau as a domestic destination and allow passengers to check two pieces of luggage and carry on a third piece small enough to fit under a seat. However, many of the small commuter airlines that serve the islands from Florida cities have weight limitations of 44 pounds (20 kilos) per person; excess baggage is permitted, at an additional charge per pound, but that extra luggage may follow on a later flight—which might be the next day or even the next week.

HOW TO GET THERE BY SEA. There is an entire fleet of sleek, luxury cruise ships that sail twice weekly from Florida ports *only* to the Bahamas. They generally depart each Friday on three-night cruises, calling at Nassau and a Family Island; and each Monday on four-night cruises, calling at Nassau, Freeport, and a Family Island. Each offers a wide range of cabins and price categories with seasonal ups and downs, and most offer greatly discounted airfares from cities across the U.S. on widely advertised "Fly-Cruise" programs.

A cruise is an easy, interesting, and fun-filled introduction to the Bahamas, and many cruise passengers return later to spend longer holidays at their favorite island or resort. Ships are likely to be at their fullest, and highest priced, at vacation times, and these cruises should be booked well in advance. Cruise bargains are often available during post-vacation periods, such as fall to mid-December, the first few weeks after New Year's, and after spring vacations. Christmas–New Year's holidays are almost always sold out in advance and command a premium rate.

The following is a selected listing of cruise ships sailing from **Florida** every week on two-, three-, and four-night cruises. Rates quoted are based on minimum and maximum charges per person, double occupancy, were in effect at press time, and are subject to change.

Carnivale. 1,206 passengers. Three nights to Nassau every Friday ($375–$885); four nights to Nassau and Freeport every Monday ($495–$1,025). Departs from Port of Miami. *Mardi Gras.* 1,108 passengers. Three nights to Nassau every Thursday ($375–$895); four nights to Nassau and Freeport every Sunday ($495–$1,025). Departs from Port Everglades. Both Carnival Cruise Lines, 5225 N.W. 87th Ave., Miami, FL 33166; (800) 327–7373, U.S.; (800) 325–1214, Fla.

Discovery I. 1,300 passengers. Day trips to Freeport/Lucaya from Port Everglades every Monday, Wednesday, Friday, and Sunday. From $89 per person includes meals, port and service charges; cabins are extra. One-to three-night ship-and-shore vacations available. Discovery Cruises, 8751 W. Broward Blvd., Suite 300, Plantation, FL 33324; (305) 476–9999.

Dolphin IV. 566 passengers. Three nights to Nassau and Blue Lagoon every Friday ($425–$795); four nights to Nassau, Freeport, and Blue Lagoon every Monday ($545–$915). Departs from Port of Miami. Dolphin Cruise Line, 1007 N. America Way, Miami, FL 33132; (305) 358–2111, or (800) 222–1003, U.S.

Emerald Seas. 920 passengers. Three nights to Nassau and Little Stirrup Cay every Friday; four nights to Nassau, Freeport, and Little Stirrup Cay every Monday, ($395–$1,065). Departs from Port of Miami. Admiral Cruises, Inc., 1220 Biscayne Blvd., Miami, FL 33101; (305) 373–7501, or (800) 327–0271, U.S.

Galileo. 539 cabins. Two nights to Nassau every Friday ($189–$395). Departs from Port of Miami. Chandris-Fantasy Cruises, 4770 Biscayne Blvd., Miami, FL 33137, (305) 576–9900 or (800) 423–2100, U.S.; (800) 432–4132, FL.

Sunward II. 674 passengers. Three nights to Nassau and a Family Island every Friday ($345–$845); four nights to Nassau, Freeport, and a Family Island every Monday ($495–$915). Departs from Port of Miami. Norwegian Cruise Lines, 2 Alhambra Plaza, Coral Gables, FL 33134; (305) 447–9660 or (800) 327–7030, U.S.

SeaEscape. Two ships sail day cruises to Freeport, daily from Miami and daily except Saturday from Fort Lauderdale, departing 8:30 A.M., returning by 11 P.M. $99; $89 senior citizens; $59 ages 12–17; $39 under 12. SeaEscape Ltd., 1080 Port Blvd., Miami, FL 33132. (305) 379–0000 or (800) 327–7400, U.S.; (800) 432–0900, FL; (800) 327–2005, Canada.

S.S. Royale (772 passengers) and *S.S. Oceanic* (1,200 passengers) cruise together, three nights to Nassau and a Family Island every Friday ($355–$880), four nights to Nassau, a Family Island, and a day at sea every Monday ($355–$1,055). The four-day cruise includes a stay in Orlando at Walt Disney World. Departures from Port Canaveral. Premier Cruise Lines, Box 573, Cape Canaveral, FL 32920; (305) 783–5061 or (800) 327–7113, U.S., (800) 432–2545 FL.

Many other cruise ships sailing on seven- and 14-day itineraries from Florida, New York, and other U.S. ports call at Nassau and/or a Family Island on their Caribbean cruises. Among these are Carnival Cruise Lines' *Festivale Jubilee* and *Holiday;* Costa Lines' *Costa Riviera;* Norwegian Cruise Lines' SS *Norway, Skyward, Southward,* and *Starward;* Royal Caribbean Line's *Nordic Prince, Song of America, Sun Viking;* Sitmar Cruise's *Fairwind;* Sun Line Cruise's *Stella Solaris;* Home Lines' *Homeric;* and Holland America's *Noordam.*

GETTING AROUND THE BAHAMAS. Nassau is the point of departure for all scheduled inter-island travel, whether by plane or by boat. A visitor to Freeport, for example, must return to Nassau to go on to another island destination.

By Plane. *Bahamasair* flies from Nassau to 20 islands with varying frequency (three daily 737 flights Nassau to Freeport and return; two weekly flights aboard 44-passenger HS-748s, Nassau to San Salvador). For reservations and information in Nassau call (809) 327–8511; in Freeport, (809) 352–8341; and in the U.S., (800) 222–4262.

Charter airlines offer inter-island service that for families or small groups can be less expensive and more convenient than scheduled air service. Charter services in Nassau include *Bahamasair,* (809) 327–8316; *Pinder's Charter Service,* (809) 327–7320; and *Trans Island Airways,* (809) 327–8329. In Freeport, *Helda Charters,* (809) 352–8832, and *Lucaya Air Service,* (809) 352–8885.

Private plane fliers should contact any Fixed Base Operator (FBO) in Florida for information on regulations and the necessary equipment for flying to and through the Bahamas. If you are flying your own plane, your U.S. or Canadian Airman's Certificate will be recognized as your official flying credential. (But you may need an extension of your aircraft insurance for over-water travel to the Bahamas.) Most FBOs will have the excellent *Bahamas Flight Planner Chart,* or it may be obtained from any Bahamas Tourist Office. Another valuable publication is the annual *Pilot's Bahamas Aviation Guide,* $19.95 (plus $2 postage) from Pilot Publications, Box 3190, Ocala, FL 32678; (800) 521–2120.

By Boat. No cruise ships or ferry services operate between the islands (except for short runs with small boats that link such islands as Nassau and Paradise Island, or Treasure Cay and Green Turtle Cay or between Marsh Harbour, Elbow Cay, and Man-O-War Cay). The only seagoing inter-island transportation is by the government-operated mailboats that depart from Potter's Cay Dock in Nassau, calling at Family Island ports on a weekly schedule.

Mailboats are an interesting and adventuresome way to travel—for the intrepid visitor who does not mind limited passenger accommodations with diesel smells and the company of fruit and vegetables, an automobile or two, and perhaps a few chickens and goats along with the mailbags. Tickets are sold only on sailing day, on a first-come, first-served basis, and all sailings are subject to weekly, daily, and sometimes last-minute revision. One-way rates range $16–$45. For a schedule of sorts, drop by the dockmaster's office on Potter's Cay, under the Paradise Island Bridge in Nassau, or call him at (809) 323–1064. Each island chapter of this guide gives the relevant mailboat services and sailing days.

At most marinas in Florida, private yacht owners can find information about sailing to the Bahamas, and charts can be purchased at marine stores. An invaluable aid in sailing to and through the Bahamas is the annual *Yachtsman's Guide to the Bahamas,* with charts of every harbor, tide tables, VHF and radio facilities, wind and weather guides, a resorts index, and more. An official publication of the Ministry of Tourism, it is available for $16.95 (plus $4 postage) from Tropic Isle Publishers, Box 610935, North Miami, FL 33161; (305) 893–4277.

Private yachts and private planes arriving from foreign ports must clear customs at an official port of entry. Once cleared, yachtsmen and fliers are issued a cruising permit or a flying permit that allows them to sail to any port or land at any airstrip in the Bahamas.

The official ports of entry in the Bahamas are:

Abaco: Walker's Cay, Green Turtle Cay, Marsh Harbour, Sandy Point. **Andros:** Nicholl's Town, San Andros, Fresh Creek, Mangrove Cay, Congo Town. **Berry Islands:** Great Harbour Cay, Chub Cay. **Bimini:** Alice Town, North Bimini for yachts, South Bimini airport for planes. **Cat Cay:** Cat Cay Club. **Eleuthera:** Harbour Island, Hatchet Bay, Governor's Harbour, Rock Sound, Cape Eleuthera. **Exuma:** George Town. **Grand Bahama:**

West End, Freeport, Lucaya. **Inagua:** Matthew's Town. **New Providence–Nassau:** any yacht basin or Nassau International Airport. **Ragged Island:** Duncan Town. **San Salvador:** Cockburn Town.

Yacht charter fleets will be found in the Abacos at Marsh Harbour and Hope Town on Elbow Cay. A variety of sail and power yachts, with or without captain and crew, are offered by two operators: *Abaco Bahamas Charters,* Hope Town, Abaco, (800) 626–5690; and *Bahamas Yachting Services,* Marsh Harbour, Abaco, (800) 327–2276.

Bare boats or yachts with captain and crew may be chartered at several marinas in Nassau and on Grand Bahama Island. Each island chapter of this guide gives specifics on the rental of cruising and fishing boats.

By Car. In Nassau and Freeport you'll find Avis, Hertz, National, and Budget Rent-A-Car, all with fleets of new or late-model automobiles for rent by the day, the week, or longer, and you can arrange for a rental in advance through your travel agent. Car rental agencies are located at the airports, at the cruise ports, and in town; free pickup and delivery at your hotel or the airport is standard practice.

Car rental rates do not include gasoline (about $1.50–$1.60 a gallon), but all rates include unlimited mileage. A $150 deposit is generally required. In 1989, Avis rates for air-conditioned models were $66–$85 per day, $379–$479 per week. National offered a rate of $270 per week for a non air-conditioned car. Some rental agencies may have occasional bargain rates, particularly during low season, and the smaller, locally owned agencies may give you a considerable saving on a slightly older car.

Caution. A drawback to driving in the Bahamas is the left-right confusion factor: All traffic keeps to the left (in the British style), yet virtually all cars, rental or privately owned, have the steering wheel on the left (in the American style).

PACKING. In choosing your wardrobe for a Bahamas vacation, think in terms of being cool, comfortable, and casual for day wear, and slightly dressy but not formal for evenings on the town, particularly in the cities of Nassau and Freeport.

Women should pack several changes of shorts, slacks, jeans, or casual cotton dresses and skirts with lightweight blouses, tank tops, or T-shirts for day wear. Laundry and dry cleaning tends to be expensive, so wash-and-wear choices are ideal. Skimpy bikinis are acceptable on any beach (no nude bathing, please), but you must have a beach robe or cover-up for walking through lobbies, in shops or restaurants, or along the streets. (Bahamians frown on "overexposure.") Men should follow the same general rules—cool, comfortable, and casual for daytime with jeans, slacks, shorts, short-sleeved shirts, and T-shirts in cotton or Dacron, a jacket and tie for evenings.

For sailing, fishing, boat cruises, or just an early morning walk along the beach, you will want a lightweight jacket or sweater to protect you from the sun's rays and occasional cool breezes. And if you plan to explore or shop, be sure to bring comfortable walking shoes.

Particularly during the winter season, both men and women dress well at the elegant restaurants, nightclubs, and casinos. Summers are more casual, but most visitors enjoy dressing up a bit at night. Women may need an evening sweater, shawl, or dressy jacket for dining out, nightclubbing, or casino hopping. Air conditioners run at full speed practically everywhere.

Pack sunglasses, plenty of film, sun lotion, insect repellent, shampoo, and other personal items, as these tend to be rather expensive in the Bahamas. You might bring along a few paperbacks to read, as they also have a higher price tag. Don't bother bringing a sun hat; dozens of styles are available in the strawmarkets, handmade, handwoven, and inexpensive.

U.S. and Canadian electrical appliances—hair dryers, hot rollers, travel irons, electric razors—will operate on the Bahamian electrical current (120V), which is identical to that in the U.S. and Canada. British and European visitors should bring their own adapters for 220V appliances, as they are often not available even in large resorts and hotels in the cities.

PASSPORTS AND VISAS. U.S. citizens do not need a passport or a visa to visit the Bahamas for periods not exceeding eight months. A birth certificate, voter registration card, or the United States Alien Registration Card for noncitizens residing in the U.S. is accepted as proof of citizenship. Bahamas immigration officials sometimes accept a driver's license with photograph as identification for Americans entering the Bahamas. However, visitors should be aware that on occasion travelers have had difficulty reentering the United States without proof of citizenship.

Canadian citizens and citizens of the United Kingdom do not need passports or visas to enter the Bahamas for periods not exceeding three weeks. Identification similar to that required for Americans is accepted as proof of citizenship. Citizens of all other countries are required to have passports, although there are few visa requirements.

CUSTOMS. If you plan to travel with foreign-made articles, such as cameras, binoculars, and expensive timepieces, it is wise to put with your travel documents the receipt from the retailer or some other evidence that the item was bought in your home country. If you bought the article on a previous trip abroad and have already paid duty on it, carry the receipt. Or register such items with customs prior to departure. Otherwise, on returning home, you may be charged duty (for British residents, Value-Added Tax as well).

Entry formalities. All visitors to the Bahamas must complete and sign a Bahamas Immigration Form collected upon entry. All carriers provide this form, which has a carbon duplicate that will be returned to you. The duplicate is surrendered upon departure, so be sure not to lose it (tuck it in with your airline or cruise ticket so it will be handy when you leave). All visitors must also have return or onward tickets upon entering the Bahamas.

Customs requires only a verbal baggage declaration, but luggage is subject to customs inspection. There is no restriction on the amount of foreign currency you may bring into the country.

Each adult is allowed 50 cigars or 200 cigarettes and one quart of spirits free of customs duty, in addition to personal effects.

Cautions: Firearms may not be brought into the Bahamas without an official Bahamian gun license. Animals may not be brought into the Bahamas without an official import permit from the Ministry of Agriculture, Fisheries, and Local Government. The possession of marijuana or other narcotic drugs is a serious offense, and offenders are subject to heavy fines and/or imprisonment.

Departure formalities. Departure formalities are simple. All visitors departing for U.S. destinations through either Nassau International Airport or Freeport International Airport clear U.S. Customs and Immigration in the Bahamas (thus avoiding long lines and hassles at stateside airports). Customs forms, available at the airports, must be filled out before departure and presented to the U.S. officials, and luggage is subject to inspection. Visitors departing from other destinations or traveling to countries other than the United States clear customs on arrival in the U.S. or the country of debarkation.

Duty-free allowances. U.S. residents may bring home $400 worth of foreign merchandise as gifts or for personal use without having to pay duty, provided they have been out of the country more than 48 hours and provided they have not claimed a similar exemption within the previous 30 days. Every member of a family is entitled to the same exemption, regardless of age, and the exemptions can be pooled. Included for travelers over the age of 21 are one liter of alcohol, 100 (non-Cuban) cigars, and 200 cigarettes. Only one bottle of perfume trademarked in the U.S. may be brought in. Beyond the first $400, there is a flat tax of 10 percent of the fair retail value on the next $1,000 worth of merchandise. After $1,400, duty is at the discretion of the customs agent, depending on the type of goods you wish to bring in.

Note also that the Bahamas qualify fully for GSP (Generalized System of Preferences), which permits U.S. residents to bring home an unlimited amount of Bahamian-made products without paying duty. Such products include goods that have 35 percent of their value in Bahamian labor, anything manufactured in the Bahamas, and items made from material imported into the Bahamas but significantly altered before sale. Specific items include jewelry made from shells, straw products, clothing and gift items crafted in the Bahamas, local wood carvings and art objects, 100-year-old (or older) antiques, and locally made liqueurs (although U.S. alcohol tax must be paid on the latter). Simply list such items as GSP on your customs form, and ask that GSP rating be applied. *Caution: Turtleshell products, plants, and fruits cannot be taken into the U.S.*

Gifts valued at less than $50 may be mailed to friends or relatives at home, but not more than one per day (of receipt) to any one addressee. These gifts must not include perfumes costing more than $5, tobacco, or alcohol. Mark package "Unsolicited Gift—Value Under $50."

Canadian residents may bring in 50 cigars, 200 cigarettes, two pounds of tobacco, and 40 ounces of liquor duty free, provided they are declared in writing to customs on arrival and accompany the traveler in hand or checked-through baggage. These are included in the basic exemption of $150 a year. Personal gifts should be mailed as "Unsolicited Gift—Value under $25." Canadian customs regulations are strictly enforced; check your allowances and make sure you have kept receipts for whatever you have bought abroad. For further details, ask for the Canada Customs brochure "I Declare."

AIRPORT TAXES AND OTHER CHARGES. The departure tax from the Bahamas is $5 for adults and children over 12 years; $2.50 for children 2–12 years; children under 2 are exempt. International airline and steamship tickets issued in the Bahamas are subject to a $2 government tax.

A 6 percent government tax/resort levy is collected by all hotels in the Bahamas, based on European-plan room-rate charges. In addition, many hotels add a 10–15 percent service charge to cover gratuities for food and beverages; some add a housekeeping charge (in lieu of a tip to the room maid). Be sure to ask about all charges when you make your reservation or check in to your resort or hotel, so you will not be surprised when presented with your final bill. There is no sales tax on any item purchased in the Bahamas.

MONEY. The Bahamian dollar is held at par with the U.S. dollar, and the two currencies are used interchangeably. You can expect to receive change in either currency or both. The Bahamian dollar is divided into 1-, 5-, 10-, 25-, and 50-cent coins, and an unusual 15-cent coin. Other coins are: $1, $2, and $5, with special issues of larger denominations in gold and silver. Favorite coin souvenirs are the scalloped-edge 10-cent piece and the square-shaped 15-cent piece. Paper currency is issued in the same denominations as U.S. currency, $1, $5, $10, $20, $50, $100, etc. In addition, there are two unusual paper bills, the 50-cent note and the $3 note—both favorites of collectors. All paper currency is colorful and appropriate for souvenirs.

Visitors from outside the United States may want to convert their currency into U.S. dollars before arrival. Currency exchange is handled by banks in the Bahamas, although some hotels will convert limited amounts of certain foreign currency at relatively high commission rates. Bank conversion rates are lower, but banking hours are limited. In Nassau and Freeport, banking hours are 9:30 A.M.–3 P.M. Monday to Thursday, 9:30 A.M.–5 P.M. Friday. All banks, including the airport branches, operate on the same schedule and are closed weekends and holidays. In the Family Islands, exchange conversion can be even more difficult, as many islands have very small branch banks open only for a few hours or a few days each week; others have no banks at all.

Personal checks are rarely accepted, even with passport identification. However, traveler's checks are accepted by most large hotels, fine restaurants, and stores; credit cards are accepted almost everywhere in the major resort centers, including restaurants and stores. An American Express card holder may cash a personal check at the American Express agencies in Nassau and Freeport. Visa card holders may obtain a cash advance of up to $1,000 by presenting their card at one of several major banks in Nassau and Freeport.

WHAT IT WILL COST. Since we are covering more than a dozen islands and half a dozen offshore cays, we have studied each area individually and given a projected daily estimate (based on winter- or high-season rates) for two persons within each island grouping. This daily rate includes a double room at a beach hotel, and three meals a day with tips, but it does *not* include 6 percent room tax/resort levy, service charges, or surcharges. In addition, we have listed separately the approximate rate for a one-day sightseeing tour with a taxi driver/tour guide or a 24-hour car rental.

New Providence—Nassau, Cable Beach, and Paradise Island

Standard, double room at a beach hotel	$145
Breakfast at your hotel	$15
Lunch at an *inexpensive* native restaurant	$25
Three-course dinner at an *expensive* restaurant (without liquor)	$60
Room, meals, gratuities	$245

One-day sightseeing with taxi driver/tour guide $60
or 24-hour car rental

Total: $305

Grand Bahama—Freeport, Lucaya, West End

Standard, double room at a beach hotel $115
Breakfast at your hotel $15
Lunch at an *inexpensive* native restaurant $25
Three-course dinner at an *expensive* restaurant (without liquor) $60

Room, meals, gratuities $215

One-day sightseeing with taxi driver/tour guide $60
or 24-hour car rental

Total: $275

The Family Islands

Standard, double room at a beach hotel $100
Breakfast at your hotel $15
Lunch at an *inexpensive* native restaurant $15
Three-course dinner at an *expensive* restaurant (without liquor) $50

Room, meals, gratuities $180

One-day sightseeing with taxi driver/tour guide $60
or 24-hour car rental

Total: $240

HOTELS AND OTHER ACCOMMODATIONS. The Bahamas offer an exceptionally broad range of visitor accommodations to fit almost any vacation lifestyle and budget. More than 180 guest houses, hotels, resorts, and apartment or cottage complexes offer over 13,000 rooms for vacation rentals on some 20 islands throughout the Bahamian archipelago. Most types of vacation accommodations are included in this wide range, with the exception of campgrounds, as camping is illegal anywhere in the Bahamas.

Most of the high-rise, luxury, oceanside resorts that offer round-the-clock activities, casinos, gourmet dining, elaborate theater revues, and a broad spectrum of sports activities including tennis and golf are located in the resort centers of Nassau, Cable Beach, and Paradise Island on New Providence, and Freeport/Lucaya on Grand Bahama Island. Both islands also offer simple seaside cottages; attractive and modern apartments, townhouses, and villas for self-catering vacations; small, modest hotels with 100 rooms or less offering personalized service and informal atmosphere; charming inns with a dozen rooms or less, some in well-preserved historic homes; and sports enclaves, large and small, that cater to golf, tennis, and diving enthusiasts. On these islands, the range of accommodations is matched by the range of rates. Even the most luxurious international resorts offer a broad range of rates within the hotel complex. Throughout the year, hotel and resort rates on Grand Bahama tend to be somewhat lower than comparable accommodations in Nassau, Cable Beach, and Paradise Island on New Providence.

In the Family Islands, there is almost as broad a range of vacation accommodations as in the resort capitals of Nassau and Freeport, with the exception of large high-rise resorts with casinos and other sophistications. Sports enclaves are particularly popular in the Family Islands. Bimini, Chub Cay, and Walker's Cay are favorites of big game fishermen; scuba divers head for Andros, Harbor Island, Spanish Wells, the Exumas, Rum Cay, and Long Island. For golfers, there are luxurious country club resorts on Eleuthera at Cotton Bay and in the Abacos at Treasure Cay. Rates at Family Island resorts tend to be significantly lower than comparable accommodations in Nassau, with a few famed, world-class exceptions in the deluxe range.

Particularly good rates are offered throughout the Bahamas during the off-season, Goombay Summer (June–Aug.), and the Discovery Season (Sept.–mid-Dec.), when rates can be anywhere from 20 to more than 40 percent lower than in the high-season winter months.

Most hotels in Nassau and Freeport offer optional EP (European Plan—no meals) or MAP (Modified American Plan—breakfast and dinner). Due to limited outside dining facilities in small villages and island settlements in the Family Islands, many hotels and resorts offer only MAP or FAP (Full American Plan—all meals). Often, these meal plans can provide significant savings over paying for three meals a day separately.

Hotels and resorts are arranged into five categories: *Super Deluxe, Deluxe, Expensive, Moderate,* and *Inexpensive.* Price is the basic criterion, although other factors, such as comfort, convenience, atmosphere, and facilities, are taken into consideration. Because there is a broad diversity of rates from island to island, the price range for each category varies and is listed in the *Practical Information* section for each island.

Apartment-rental and time-sharing opportunities are also listed in the island-by-island *Practical Information* sections.

DINING OUT. In Nassau and Freeport, there is a large variety of dining options, from elegant gourmet dining rooms in the luxury hotels to fast-food franchises. Most food served in American- and Continental-style restaurants tends to be rather expensive, as everything from fresh vegetables to steak is imported. Excellent native restaurants, which are lower priced, are abundant in Nassau, Freeport, and in nearly every small village and settlement in the Family Islands. (Note: For liquors and liqueurs, wines and beer, the legal drinking age is 18 years.)

The island chapters provide detailed lists of dining options. As with hotels and resorts, restaurants are arranged into five categories, defined in each *Practical Information* section: *Super Deluxe, Deluxe, Expensive, Moderate,* and *Inexpensive.* Price is the basic criterion, although other factors are taken into consideration, such as quality of food, ambience, and service. We have also indicated which restaurants accept credit cards. For those that do, we have used the following abbreviations: AE, American Express; BA, Bank America; DC, Diners Club; MC, MasterCard; V, Visa.

TIPPING. Most Bahamas hotels and restaurants have adopted the European custom of adding a service charge to your bill—usually 15 percent, sometimes as little as 10 percent. Use your own discretion when tipping over and above that for exceptional services rendered. Where no fee is added, tip is based on services delivered. In restaurants and nightclubs, and for room, beach, or poolside hotel service, 15 percent is standard. A 15 percent tip is also standard for taxi and surrey drivers, barbers and beauty operators, and even bartenders. Porters and bellmen are tipped 50 cents per bag and something extra for unusually heavy items such as golf clubs.

Many hotels add on a housekeeping charge or "maid's gratuity" of $2 per person per day to your bill. Be sure to ask about all such automatic charges when you check in, so you won't be surprised when you check out.

CASINOS. There are currently five casinos in the Bahamas. Visitors must be 21 years of age or over to gamble; Bahamians or Bahamas residents are not permitted to gamble. Dress code is informal during the day, more formal at night. On New Providence, there is the new Carnival's Crystal Palace Casino on Cable Beach and the new casino at the Divi Bahamas Resort at the southwestern end of Nassau, scheduled to open in 1989. On Paradise Island is the more formal and elegant Paradise Island Casino, operated by Resorts International. On Grand Bahama, there is the opulent Princess Casino, operated by Princess Hotels, and the Lucayan Beach Hotel's friendly and attractive Monte Carlo Casino.

All offer virtually round-the-clock gaming action, croupiers with favorite games of chance: roulette, blackjack, baccarat, craps, wheel of fortune, and acres of state-of-the-art slot machines with payoffs up to $100,000 or more. The casinos also offer a choice of bars, restaurants, and entertainment, as well as theaters featuring elaborate floor shows and bare-bosomed stage-girl revues to rival Paris and Las Vegas.

TELEPHONES, TELEGRAMS, AND TELEX. Direct distance dialing is available from the U.S. and Canada to many Bahamian islands, and service is expanding rapidly. You may dial direct to Nassau; Grand Bahama; Abaco; Andros; Berry Islands; Bimini; Eleuthera; Harbour Island; Spanish Wells; George Town, Exuma; and Stella Maris, Long Island. The area code is 809. From the Bahamas, direct dialing is available to the U.S., Canada, South America, Europe, and the Orient from Nassau, Grand Bahama, Bimini, parts of Andros, George Town in the Exumas, Governor's Harbour and Rock Sound on Eleuthera, and Marsh Harbour, the Abacos. To call abroad from other islands, dial the operator for assistance. Visitors should be aware that many hotels add a service charge to long-distance telephone calls placed from the hotel, typically 25 percent plus $2.50 for credit card or collect calls. Whenever possible, expensive long-distance calls should be placed through public telephone centers, which are open during normal business hours; the operator will place your call at regular international rates.

Telex service is available through most major hotels, and there are public telex services in Nassau and Freeport. Telegraph service is also available. To place a telegram by phone, dial 910.

Emergency numbers are listed in each of the island chapters.

POSTAGE. Bahamian postage stamps are readily available from post offices throughout the islands and are often sold at hotels and shops. Airmail postage rates to the U.S. and Canada are: first-class letters, 45¢ each ½ ounce; second-class letters, 35¢ each ½ ounce; post cards, 40¢. Airmail rates to other destinations are: first-class letters, 50¢ each ½ ounce; second-class letters, 40¢ each ½ ounce; post cards, 40¢. Air letters to all foreign destinations are 40¢. Parcel post packages (weight limit 22 pounds) to the U.S. are $3.50 for the first pound, $2.25 each additional pound; to Canada, $4 for the first pound; to the U.K., $7 for the first pound. Post offices are open Mon.–Fri. 8:30 A.M. to 5:30 P.M. and Sat. until 12:30 P.M. in Nassau and Freeport. Family Island post offices are sometimes open only a few hours and days each week.

LANGUAGE. English is the universal language in the Bahamas. Accents will range from clipped British "upper clawss" to West Indian calypso, from early American Scots and Irish brogues to English cockney or a southern drawl.

TIME ZONE. The Bahamas are on Eastern Time. When it's noon in the Bahamas, it's 9 A.M. in Los Angeles and Vancouver, 10 A.M. in Phoenix, 11 A.M. in Chicago, noon in New York and Toronto, and 5 P.M. in London, England. The Bahamas observe Daylight Time, like the U.S., from the first Sunday in April to the last Sunday in October.

What Bahamians call Bahamian Time is a slow, leisurely pace, more of a ramble than a rush, and it's a way of life in the Bahamas. It affects everything from hotel and restaurant service to telephone calls and business appointments. Relax, slow down, and enjoy it!

ELECTRIC CURRENT. Electricity is normally 120 volts, 60 cycles, providing compatibility with all American appliances. Occasional brown-outs occur in Nassau, more rarely in Freeport/Lucaya. In the Family Islands, many resorts rely on their own generators for electricity, and occasional breakdowns are not uncommon. However, candles are provided in most hotel rooms, guests take the minor inconvenience caused with good-natured patience, and repairs are soon under way.

TRAVELING WITH PETS. We recommend leaving your pets with friends at home or boarding them at an appropriate facility. Bringing pets out of and back into the country—whatever your point of origin—can involve quarantine time and considerable hassles, and resort hotels rarely have facilities for animals.

If you absolutely must bring your pet, plan at least a month in advance. Request permission from the Ministry of Agriculture, Trade, and Industry, Box N–3028, Nassau, Bahamas. State the type of pet and your port of entry into the Bahamas. Then await an official permit. Upon entering the Bahamas you must present your permit, a Veterinary Health Certificate issued within 24 hours of your departure from home, and proof of a Rabies Vaccination issued not less than ten days nor more than nine months prior to arrival.

TRAVELING WITH CHILDREN. Most resorts and hotels offer free accommodation for children under 12 years of age sharing a room with parents, guardians, or other adults. Some hotels raise the age limit to 16. Hotels and resorts that do not offer free accommodation generally have substantial discounts for children sharing a room with adults. There are no commercial baby-sitting services in the Bahamas, but most hotels and resorts will make arrangements for such services when given adequate notice. If you are traveling with children, check with your travel agent or directly with the resort to determine the availability of services. A visit to any resort destination with children is often more convenient and less expensive when you take an apartment or a villa complex with kitchen facilities and two or more bedrooms. Dozens of such resorts exist in the Bahamas in a broad price range, and these self-catering resorts are listed under each of the island chapters in this guide.

STUDENT AND YOUTH TRAVEL. There are no youth hostels in the Bahamas. Most hotels and resorts do offer deep discounts for a third or fourth person sharing a room, however, so several students traveling together can reduce their per-person costs for accommodations.

Student Getaway programs are offered each spring in Nassau and Freeport, generally from mid-February to late April, to coincide with spring breaks at U.S. and Canadian high schools and colleges. The programs, a promotion of the Ministry of Tourism, offer events for each day of the week—Goombay music sessions, street fairs, beach parties, sporting events. Many events are free, and big discounts are offered at attractions, sight-seeing tours, discos, and nightclubs. All a student needs to participate is his or her own official student identity card (with photo).

HINTS TO THE DISABLED. The major airlines and cruise lines can usually accommodate wheelchair passengers when notified in advance. An excellent brief guide to airline travel for people confined to a wheelchair or with other handicaps is available free from TWA, 605 Third Ave., New York, NY 10016. The Air Transport Association (1700 New York Ave. N.W., Washington, DC 20006) also publishes a free pamphlet, titled *"Air Travel for the Handicapped."*

Toilet facilities accessible to the handicapped will be found at all international airports and at most hotels and shopping plazas in the Bahamas. A chart of all resorts and hotels providing special facilities for the handicapped, compiled by the Bahamas Paraplegic Association, is available at any Bahamas Tourist Office and at most travel agencies. In Nassau, contact Phyllis Alridge at 322–2393 or 323–1392 for further information on facilities for the physically disabled.

HEALTH. Few real hazards threaten the health of a visitor to the Bahamas. The water is safe to drink everywhere, there are no endemic tropical diseases to guard against, and the ocean waters are among the least polluted in the world. Poisonous snakes are nonexistent, and the small lizards you seem to encounter everywhere are harmless. The worst problem may well be a tiny predator, the "no see 'um," a small sand fly that tends to appear after a rain, near wet or swampy ground, and around sunset. If you feel particularly vulnerable to insect bites, bring along a good repellent.

The most serious hazard to health may well be the sunshine; the gentle breezes make lying in the sun such a pleasure that one forgets how strong the sun is. Even people who are not normally bothered by strong sun should head into this area with a long-sleeved shirt, a hat, and long pants or a beach wrap. These garments are essential for a day on a boat and advisable for midday at the beach. Also carry some sun-block lotion for nose, ears, and other sensitive areas such as eyelids, ankles, etc. Be sure to take in enough liquids. Above all, limit your sun time for the first few days until you become used to the heat and the tropical sunshine.

Medical facilities are considered excellent for an island group so small in population and so diverse in distribution. Physicians, dentists, and surgeons in private practice are readily available in Nassau and Freeport. Nassau has the 505-bed Princess Margaret Hospital, government operated, and the 24-bed Doctor's Hospital, privately operated. In Grand Bahama, there is a government-operated hospital and two privately operated clinics. In the Family Islands, there are 13 health centers and 36 clinics. Where intensive or urgent care is required, patients are brought into the nearest major hospital facility by emergency flight service. There are several 24-hour emergency aircraft services operating from South Florida, among them the *Airborne Ambulance Service* (305) 949–6301, and *Air Ambulance Network* (305) 387–1708, from Miami or Fort Lauderdale. Medical facilities are listed, along with emergency numbers, under each island grouping in the following chapters.

SECURITY. Don't be fooled by the appearance of paradise when you visit the Bahamas. New Providence Island, especially Nassau and Paradise Island, requires the same precautions you would take in visiting any other cosmopolitan area. The same goes for Freeport, Grand Bahama Island. Women should not walk unescorted after dusk, and all visitors should avoid deserted nighttime streets. Lock your car doors, and no matter where you are staying, do not leave valuables unattended on the beach or in hotel rooms. Most major resorts and hotels offer safety deposit boxes for your cash and jewelry. Take advantage of this complimentary service. The Family Islands are generally quieter and safer, but you'll always be wise to take precautions and secure your valuables no matter where you travel.

THE BAHAMAS:
FIRST STOP
IN THE NEW WORLD

THE BAHAMAS

First Stop in the New World

Christopher Columbus, searching for a new route to the ancient world of the Far East, discovered instead a New World in the West, a populated world of which Europeans had no knowledge. Everyone knows the date, October 12, 1492, and the names of the three small caravels that made up his fleet, the *Niña,* the *Pinta,* and the *Santa María.* The place was the island of Guanahani, easternmost in the Bahamas chain, which Columbus called San Salvador and claimed for Spain.

On Guanahani, Columbus found a peaceful Arawak Indian village of thatched huts, with friendly natives who had fled to these islands to escape the warlike cannibal tribes of the Caribee. They called themselves Lucayans ("island people") and welcomed Columbus and his great-winged boats as messengers from heaven. They presented him with fresh water, green parrots, and the handwoven *hamacas* in which they slept. (Hammocks would be the Arawaks' greatest gift to civilization; within a decade they were standard gear on ships around the world—until the U.S. Navy began to phase them out in 1942.) Columbus was more interested in the bits of gold the natives wore. In sign language he asked where the gold could be found. They pointed to the southwest, to a great island they called Cobla (Cuba). Perhaps he heard "Kublai" in their cries, because he was more convinced than ever that the land of the great Kublai Khan was nearby.

For the next two weeks, he "harbor hopped" from island to island in the southern Bahamas, discovering and naming Santa Maria de la Concepcion (Rum Cay), Fernandina (Long Island), Isabella (Crooked Island), and Islas de Arena (the Ragged Island chain). He crossed the treacherous shallows and rocks of the Great Bahama Bank and called them Baja Mar, or "shallow sea," which became the name for the entire archipelago, Bahamas. On October 27, Columbus left Bahamian waters and went on to discover Cuba, Hispaniola, and most of the islands of the Caribbean.

Although Columbus never returned to the islands of the Lucayans, the Spanish colonists and conquistadores who followed him returned again and again on slaving raids. Between 1500 and 1520, the entire population of the Bahamas was carried off to work the fields of Cuba, the mines of Hispaniola, and the pearl beds of Margarita and Trinidad.

English Colonization

It wasn't until 1629 that Britain's king, Charles I, claimed the Bahamas for the English crown and granted proprietary rights to his attorney general, Sir Robert Heath, for "the area of the American mainland he allowed to be called Carolina . . . and also all those our islands of Bahama." Unfortunately, the king lost both his throne and his head, and Heath died in exile. No previous attempt had been made to settle the Carolinas or the Bahamas.

Religious and political dissension rocked England, and a growing group of dissenters challenged the burning issue of a state church. They were ridiculed and persecuted, and thousands were driven into exile. The most famous among them were the Pilgrims, who founded Massachusetts Colony in 1620. Others fled to Bermuda, seeking religious freedom, and then had to flee again. Under the leadership of William Sayle, former governor of Bermuda, they set sail for the Bahamas.

They called themselves the Company of Eleutherian Adventurers, named for the Greek word meaning "freedom," and drew up a remarkable document, destined to become the first constitution of the Bahamas. It guaranteed religious freedom, equal justice for all, and a republican form of democracy—the first in the new world. In 1648, they settled on the island of Cigatoo and renamed it Eleuthera. The small colony of 70 barely managed to survive, making their homes in huts and caves at the northern end of the island and the small cays offshore, Spanish Wells and Harbour Island. Many of their blond, blue-eyed descendants live there today.

When Charles II was restored to the throne lost by his father, in 1660, religious dissension diminished, yet the stream of colonial settlers to America continued. By 1670, there were just 1,100 settlers in the Bahamas. Some remained on Eleuthera, but most were living on an island where Sayle had once found shelter in a storm, and which he had named New Providence. Life was hard for the handful of settlers. The thin, rocky soil produced few crops, and most of the people earned their living from the sea. Good times came only when Spanish treasure ships were wrecked on their shores and the settlers salvaged the cargoes. Wrecking became a way of life; some of the unscrupulous planted false lights to lure the Spanish ships to destruction, others turned to piracy.

Pirates and Buccaneers

The Lord Proprietors, more concerned with the vast plantations they were creating in the Carolinas, paid little attention to the Bahamas, sending out a string of incompetent and unscrupulous governors who encouraged piracy. In 1684, infuriated by the activities of the wreckers, the Spanish governor in Havana sent ships and troops to attack and burn the settlement at Nassau. The few remaining honest settlers fled to Jamaica and the Carolinas.

For the next 40 years, Nassau became the headquarters for countless pirates, buccaneers, and the scum of the seven seas. They ruled the Spanish Main, attacking the treasure galleons bound for Spain and the merchant ships bound for colonies in America and the Caribbean. Nassau was ideal. It lay astride the trade routes between the old world and the new, and its strategic natural harbor, formed by the barrier of Paradise Island, was shallow and open at both ends, perfect for eluding the cumbersome warships that were brave enough to give chase. There were as many as 2,000 pirates operating out of New Providence in those days, and among them were famous names that have survived in history and legend for nearly 300 years. There was Captain Avery, who had captured the treasure ship of the Great Mogul in the Indian Ocean and run off with his daughter; the arch pirate Edward Teach, better known as Blackbeard; Charles Vane, Peter Hynd, Stede Bonnet, Benjamin Hornigold, and Calico Jack Rackham and his infamous crew—two buxom young women, Anne Bonney and Mary Read, who reportedly boarded their prize ships stripped to the waist and brandishing cutlasses.

British colonial authorities were besieged with complaints from governors of every maritime colony in America and threats from France, Holland, and Spain. Proprietary government had failed, and King George I appointed a national hero, Captain Woodes Rogers, to the post of Royal Governor. Rogers was a bit of a rogue himself, and the pirates knew him well. During the War of the Spanish Succession, he had sailed around the world as a privateer. Daniel Defoe told Rogers's story in *Robinson Crusoe* (1719).

When Woodes Rogers arrived in Nassau at daybreak on July 26, 1718, the whole town turned out to greet him, and pirates cheered him. He read the Royal Proclamation of Pardon for pirates who surrendered and hanged those who refused. Within weeks, he had seized control of Nassau and restored law and order. He even converted pirates to "privateers" and sent them off in their own vessels to repel the French and Spanish warships that continued to threaten the islands. He saved the Bahamas from both the pirates and the Spanish, and the Crown granted him a crest that read "Expulsis Piratis, Restituta Commercia" (Pirates Expelled, Commerce Restored). It would become the motto of the Bahamas for more than 250 years.

Despite the best efforts of Woodes Rogers and the Royal Governors who followed him, the islands remained impoverished and sparsely settled. Privateering flourished briefly during the on-again, off-again wars between England and Spain; between conflicts the settlers turned to wrecking, the perennial standby.

The Bahamas and the American Revolution

While the British colonies in America were seething with revolt, the colony of the Bahamas was quiet, peaceful, calm, and loyal. When the rebellious American colonists declared their independence in 1776, George Washington was named commander in chief of the ragged army of farmers, but he had no navy. His army was desperately short of guns and ammunition, so he commandeered eight small merchant ships, fitted them with cannons, and sent them off to Nassau. The new American Navy captured Nassau without firing a shot and sailed home two weeks later with most of the arms and ammunition and the Bahamas' governor as hostage.

In retaliation, the British outfitted Nassau as a privateering base to attack rebel ships trading with their French and Spanish allies in the Caribbean. The operations were so successful, and so many American prisoners were captured, that the governor complained that he could not "keep nor victual them" but had to transport them to the nearest American port and set them free.

On May 6, 1782, a combined fleet of some 80 American, Spanish, and French warships aimed at the fort at Nassau, and the city once more surrendered without a shot being fired. The Spanish occupied the Bahamas for more than a year, until the American Revolutionary War ended with victory for the rebels. When the peace treaty was finally signed in September 1783, the 13 American colonies had gained their independence, Spain had been granted Florida, and, as a consolation prize, the Bahamas were returned to the British Crown—a transaction Parliament considered a mixed blessing at best.

Following the revolution, the Americans turned their wrath on the traitors at home, the loyalists. Plantation owners in Virginia and the Carolinas fled to Florida to begin their lives anew. When they learned that Florida would be ceded to Spain, the Bahamas became their last hope for protection under the British flag. But 700 Spanish troops still guarded the harbor at Nassau, and a Spanish nobleman occupied the governor's mansion. Undaunted, a group of hearty adventurers, under the leadership of Colonel Andrew Deveaux of South Carolina, set out to "liberate" Nassau from the Spanish.

They had less than a hundred men, half of them unarmed, two small ships, and half a dozen fishing boats filled with volunteers they had recruited on Eleuthera and Harbour Island to help the cause. By a series of tricks and ruses, they gained the high ground behind the fort and Government House, dragging a couple of cannons with them to the top of the hill. At dawn, they fired a warning shot at the governor's house and boldly demanded that he surrender, claiming they had more than a thousand troops surrounding the town. Caught by surprise, the Spanish capitulated. When the governor returned to Havana, he was tossed into prison as punishment for his humiliating defeat.

After Deveaux's astonishing success, he was hailed as a hero by the Bahamians and became a prominent member of the newly revived House of Assembly. Loyalists by the thousands followed him to the Bahamas, from New York and New England, from Virginia, Florida, and the Carolinas, bringing with them their families and their slaves. From 1784 to 1789, the population of the Bahamas tripled to 11,300, nearly 8,000 of them black slaves.

The aristocratic loyalists thrived in the sunny Bahamas, dominating the colonial legislature and the trade and commerce and rebuilding Nassau into a city of southern charm, with great mansions, schools, churches, and public buildings, many of which survive today. One of the most prominent refugees, Lord Dunmore, who had been the last Royal Governor of Virginia, became governor of the Bahamas. He erected massive defenses, Fort Charlotte and Fort Fincastle, but neither would ever fire a shot in anger, and no foreign flag would fly over the Bahamas again. Peace and prosperity seemed assured.

The boom did not last long; by 1800, the thin, rocky soil was exhausted and a tiny insect had wiped out most of the crops. Gradually, the loyalists gave up their plantations and fled back to the mainland or to richer British colonies to the south. The emancipation of slaves in 1834 wiped out the last vestiges of a plantation system. The remaining settlers once again turned to the sea for their livelihood, and wrecking became a thriving industry.

Tourism Roots and the Civil War

A trickle of visitors had been coming to the islands for nearly a century, invalids looking for a rest cure in the sunny Bahamas. In the 1850s, the Bahamas legislature passed the first Tourism Encouragement Act, contracted with Samuel Cunard to provide steamship service between New York and Nassau, and authorized the building of a grand hotel to attract winter visitors from northern climes. The Royal Victoria Hotel would welcome guests for more than a century—even though its debut in 1861 was a near disaster.

The tourism plan collapsed with the opening guns of the Civil War on the U.S. mainland. The North launched a blockade against southern ports, Wilmington, Charleston, and Savannah. Nassau was the nearest neutral port to the south, and overnight blockade-running became the Bahamas' biggest industry. The Royal Victoria became its headquarters. Fortunes were made by many Bahamians, and the government treasury benefited hugely from import and export duties imposed upon war supplies arriving from Britain and the Continent and cotton flowing through the blockade from southern ports. Not since the days of pirates and buccaneers had Nassau seen such a boom. But when the war ended, poverty returned once again to the islands, and even the perennial standby, wrecking, failed when the Imperial Lighthouse Service erected great oil-burning lights throughout the Bahamas chain. Poverty would be a way of life for Bahamians from the Civil War to the end of World War I.

Temperance Folly and Tourism Boom

In 1919, "Prohibition" became the 18th Amendment to the U.S. Constitution, and from 1920 to 1933 bootlegging and rum-running were a rich Bahamian industry in the tradition of the privateers and blockade-runners of earlier days. During the "Roaring Twenties," the islands enjoyed a tourism boom unprecedented in history. Nassau's picturesque harbor was crowded with opulent private yachts, some of the most powerful names in industry and high finance at their helms: William K. Vanderbilt, Vincent Astor, J. P. Morgan, and E. F. Hutton, as well as Whitneys, Armours, and Mellons. Nassau Harbour was deepened. The grand old Royal Victoria was refurbished; a new Colonial Hotel was built on the ashes of one that had burned in 1921; and the great, sprawling Fort Montagu Beach Hotel made its debut. On January 2, 1929, a fledgling airline named Pan American launched daily air service from Miami to Nassau, operating eight passenger Sikorsky seaplanes—the latest word in comfort and luxury for that early era of commercial flight. Suddenly the islands were hours instead of days from the U.S. mainland, and they became the international playground for wealthy visitors. The Bahamas had finally found a basic industry that could survive good times and bad.

War and the Windsors

In the early months of World War II, the Bahamas enjoyed another tourism boom as wealthy refugees flocked to the islands from Britain and Europe. Most prominent of the new arrivals were the former King of England and his American bride, the Duke and Duchess of Windsor. After the abdication the Windsors had lived a life of luxury at their Paris mansion and their estate on the Riviera. When the Nazis marched through France, they fled to neutral Portugal, a hotbed of Axis intrigue. There they became the victims of a plot hatched by German and Portuguese diplomatic officials to lure the Duke into the German orbit—if necessary, by kidnapping.

The lure would be nothing less than the British throne! The Duke and Duchess would be declared King and Queen in exile, and once Britain was defeated, they would ascend the throne. If they agreed, unlimited money would be put at their disposal in a Swiss bank account. After the war, cables from German and Portuguese diplomats in Lisbon to Von Ribbentrop and Hitler himself were made public and the plot revealed.

Winston Churchill, Britain's wartime prime minister, learned of the kidnapping plot and determined to send the Duke as far from the war zone as possible. The Duke of Windsor was ordered to the post of governor and commander in chief of the Bahama Islands, that tiny outpost of the empire 5,000 miles away from the war—a post he held from 1940 to 1945. After Pearl Harbor, when the U.S. entered the war, the Bahamas became an important Royal Air Force base. The fighter planes and bombers that poured off American production lines were flown to Nassau, where Allied pilots were trained to fly them before delivery to war command posts around the world.

When the war ended in 1945, tourism began again. The war left the Bahamas a legacy of two modern airports, and a new invention called air-conditioning kept the hotels open year-round. For more than 40 years, since the end of World War II, tourism has been the mainstay of the Bahamas' economy, with visitor arrivals increasing each year in a steady upward curve.

The Quiet Revolution

In the 1960s, a "quiet revolution" occurred in the Bahamas. After more than 300 years of rule by the white minority, a young London-educated black lawyer, Lynden O. Pindling, led his Progressive Liberal Party to victory in the 1967 elections, bringing a black majority government to the Bahamas for the first time in history. He guided his nation to full independence from the British Crown on July 10, 1973. Prince Charles, heir to the English throne, presided over the impressive ceremonies, and the Bahamas chose to remain within the Commonwealth of Nations, continuing their historic friendship and cultural ties with Great Britain. The Bahamas replaced Woodes Rogers's motto with a proud new crest: "Forward, Upward, Onward Together," but they retained his greatest legacy, a strong parliamentary democracy that has thrived for more than 250 years.

The Bahamas Today

The 1960s and 1970s saw another revolution in Bahamas tourism. The vintage Royal Victoria Hotel and the Prohibition-era Fort Montagu Beach Hotel quietly closed, too dated and too expensive to convert to modern year-round, air-conditioned resorts. Of Nassau's original grand hotels, only the 1920s British Colonial stands today under the wing of Sheraton, which maintains the venerable harborside hotel as a moderate-priced, updated resort. New hotels rose along Nassau's famed Cable Beach and in town. Hog Island across the harbor, an enclave of private mansions for decades, was rechristened Paradise Island with glittering high-rise hotels and a glamorous gaming casino and linked to Nassau by a soaring bridge. On Grand Bahama Island, the new city of Freeport and its suburb Lucaya were carved from the pine forests; modern hotels and sprawling beach resorts appeared, two Continental casinos made their debut, and thousands of acres of tropical greenery were tamed for several world-class golf courses. In the Family Islands, small inns, cottage colonies, and country-club resorts sprung up along the beaches on a dozen different islands, bringing the benefits of tourism to most Bahamians.

Bahamians are friendly and gracious hosts, and visitors are warmly welcomed. English is the universal language, spoken with a variety of accents and lilts. Pockets of poverty remain here and there throughout the islands, but most Bahamians manage to earn a decent living. Tourism facilities are among the most modern and luxurious of any sun, sand, and sea destination in the world, and well-educated young Bahamians, both black and white, are becoming increasingly involved on the highest levels of the tourism industry as owners, managers, planners, and decision-makers.

The Sporting Life

From gambling in the casinos to gamboling on the beaches, the Bahamas offer a kaleidoscope of sporting activity. Year-round, near-perfect weather guarantees something for everyone from anglers to divers, from fliers to windsurfers, from parasailors to water-skiers, from golfers to tennis buffs, from horseback riders to beachcombers. Among the biggest drawing cards for the outdoor sportsman is nearly a dozen world-class, championship 18-hole golf courses in Nassau and on Paradise Island, Grand Bahama, Abaco, and Eleuthera. For those more interested in indoor sports, there's gambling till dawn in Continental casinos, dancing to a merengue or a goombay beat, disco and limbo, fire dances and goat-skin drums, and French-style revues acclaimed by sophisticates as better than Las Vegas or the Lido.

The Underwater World

The Bahamas are the favorite gathering spot for international divers among any tropical island destination in the world. The more than 700 islands and 2,000 cays are surrounded by living reefs, with waters so clear that visibility ranges to 200 feet or more. Colors vary from pale turquoise to brilliant aquamarine with ever-changing tones of purple, green, and blue, and water temperatures are warm year-round. For the sport diver from novice to expert, it is an underwater wonderland waiting to be explored.

There are spectacular drop-offs that begin in 20 feet of water and plummet vertically thousands of feet, while nearby there are shallow coral gardens abounding in colorful plant life and waving sea fans. There are mysterious ocean blue holes and fascinating historic wrecks dating from the days of the Spanish Main and the Civil War. There are reefs with thousands of brilliantly colored tropical fish, giant stingrays and moray eels, and reefs where sharks gather in great schools, lurking for prey; plus giant underwater caverns, labyrinths of winding coral tunnels, and steep-walled canyons. The opportunities for underwater adventures are nearly limitless, and divers from every continent return year after year in quest of new thrills and excitement. Throughout the islands dozens of dive resorts and dive operators offer trips to nearby reefs and underwater attractions; and many dive resorts offer full courses of instruction for beginners through experts, including professional training and certification.

Big Game and Light-Tackle Fishing

Some of the finest big game fishing in the world can be found in Bahamian waters, and the record books prove it. Anglers here have set more than 50 world records, according to the International Game Fishing Association, and new records are set or broken nearly every year.

Each year from March through July, anglers from all over the world gather for the annual big game fishing tournament season in quest of world-record-setters and the prestigious Bahamas Billfish Championship. They spare no effort or expense in their quest. Half-million-dollar fighting machines, Hatteras and Hinckleys, Bertrams and Burgers line the docks, bursting with gleaming tackle and manned by professional crews.

Competitors follow a tradition launched in the 1930s when Ernest Hemingway, Howard Hughes, and Zane Grey "discovered" the Bahamas and tracked the massive tuna and blue marlin that make their annual migratory runs along the edge of the Gulf Stream and the fathomless depths of the Tongue of the Ocean.

But you needn't be a tournament angler to enjoy the fishing scene in the Bahamas. The season lasts 365 days a year, and virtually every hotel and resort in the islands offers deep-sea, drift, or reef fishing charters, from their own dock or nearby marinas. Rates are around $200 to $300 a half day aboard a fully equipped fishing yacht with captain and mate; when two or three couples share a charter, the costs are well within the average vacationer's budget. Many charter-boat captains are happy to line up other anglers for charter sharing, and hotel managers often arrange fishing groups to spread the costs.

Most awe-inspiring of the big game fish common to the Bahamas are the giant blue marlins, ranging in size from 250 pounds to well over 1,000 pounds. They roam Bahamian waters throughout the year, but in record numbers in spring and summer months from April to mid-September. Best hunting grounds are along the edge of the Gulf Stream off Bimini, Grand Bahama, and Walker's Cay; at the Tongue of the Ocean off Andros and Chub Cay; and from Eleuthera north to Green Turtle Cay, Abaco. Another monster frequenting these waters is the tackle-busting bluefin tuna, weighing up to 1,000 pounds. They appear in massive schools each spring from early May to mid-June on their migration northward to the rich her-ring grounds off Nova Scotia. Their favorite route is at the edge of the Great Bahamas Bank off Bimini and West End, Grand Bahama.

During the fall and winter seasons, the streamlined, speedy wahoo is found throughout Bahamian waters. Weighing up to 130 pounds, they are among the world's fastest and most challenging game fish. During the late winter months through early spring, one of the most popular billfish is abundant, the scrappy white marlin, weighing up to 150 pounds and found in deep channels from Bimini east to Eleuthera, from Walker's Cay in the north to the Exuma Cays in the south. Another popular billfish appears during late summer and early autumn, the high-leaping sailfish, which cruises the depths around Chub Cay, Bimini, Grand Bahama, the Abacos, and the Exumas.

Other possibilities for Bahamas-bound anglers include fishing from a dock with a handline, stalking bonefish from a small boat, fly-fishing, plug-casting, spinning in the bays, and trolling or drift fishing over the miles of coral reefs that fringe the islands' shores.

Among the favorite light-tackle fighting fish found in these waters are the Allison tuna, found during the summer months, and the blackfin tuna, found during the autumn and winter months. Year-round, amberjacks roam the reefs and wrecks, the multicolored dolphin cruises the deeper waters, and snapper, grouper, and snook are found in all reefy areas throughout the island chain—a piscatorial grab bag to satisfy almost any angler.

Around-the-World Shopping

The Bahamas have been known to generations of visitors for bargains on luxury goods from around the world. Although there are no duty-free shops on the islands, and no free ports, the savings are substantial over comparable U.S., Canadian, and European prices because import duties on luxury items are kept low to compete with other Caribbean destinations such as the U.S. Virgin Islands and the Dutch Antilles. The Bahamas have no sales tax or value-added tax, which results in increased savings, particu-larly on "big ticket" luxury items.

Best buys on imported goods, and the widest selection, are found in Nas-sau's Bay Street shopping district and in the International Bazaar in Free-port. Particularly good bargains are German and Japanese cameras and optics; Swiss and designer watches; English and European bone china, such as Royal Doulton, Wedgwood, Crown Derby, Royal Copenhagen, and Coalport; French, Irish, German, and Scandinavian crystal, such as Baccarat, Lalique, Daum, Waterford, and Orrefors; collectible porcelain figurines such as Hummel, Lladró, and Royal Doulton; French perfumes bottled and packaged in France; Scottish cashmeres and tartans; Irish lin-ens and English woolens.

Native handicrafts are found everywhere in the great sprawling straw-markets in Nassau and Freeport, along the roadsides, on the grounds of the grand hotels, and beneath the shade of old silk-cotton trees in dozens of tiny villages in the Family Islands. Most famous of the Bahamian handi-crafts is strawwork, which is painstakingly woven by hand from palm fronds and shaped into hundreds of items from straw hats of every shape and size to purses and totes, place mats and floor mats, picnic baskets and wall hangings, dolls and toy animals. All are gaily decorated with brilliant raffia flowers and figures, seashells, and bits of calico. Other handcrafted items found in the strawmarkets are wood and coconut carvings, polished seashells, and jewelry made from coconut shell, seed pods, berries, seashells, and shark's teeth. There are also delightful island fashions, with men's shirts and ladies' skirts of cool cotton in bold tropical designs and primitive African patterns. Many Bay Street stores and shops in the International Bazaar feature native handicrafts such as exquisite jewelry crafted from tortoise, conch, and whelk shells, pink and the rare black coral; original island fashions and fabrics such as Androsia, hand-batiked cottons in gay colors from the island of Andros; and Bahama Hand Prints, silk-screened cotton blends in delightful Bahamian patterns and prints made in Nassau.

Bargaining is a way of life in the strawmarkets of the Bahamas. The straw workers enjoy it nearly as much as the visitors, and they rarely, if ever, expect to receive the first price quoted for their wares. Offer half and then negotiate the rest. Don't try to bargain with the merchants and sales staff of the elegant and sophisticated shops along Bay Street and in the International Bazaar, however; their prices are fixed.

Gourmet Dining and Conch Cuisine

In Nassau and Freeport the dining options range from elegant gourmet dining rooms in the luxury hotels and posh restaurants in historic mansions to fast-food franchises—Kentucky Fried Chicken, Tony Roma's Ribs, and McDonald's. The cuisine is just as varied, from Caribbean to Continental, with choices ranging from Japanese kobe steak to homemade Italian pastas; Polynesian delights to English pub food and steak and kidney pie; from French haute cuisine to American rib roast, and just about everything in between. Most food served in American and Continental-style restaurants tends to be rather expensive, for everything from fresh vegetables to steak is imported to this island nation. However, there is a lower-priced alternative, which Bahamians have enjoyed for generations and visitors have applauded for years: *going native*.

Excellent native restaurants are abundant in Nassau and Freeport and in nearly every small village and settlement in the Family Islands. They are mostly Bahamian-owned and Bahamian-run family establishments, simple and unpretentious in decor, neat, and serving good down-home Bahamian cooking at reasonable rates. Much of the food served is raised locally and bought fresh daily at the farm markets and fishermen's wharfs, and Bahamian cooks work magic with simple ingredients from the land and the sea.

Here are some favorite island dishes to try; some are served everywhere, even at exclusive restaurants, while others can be found only by going native.

Conch, pronounced "konk," is the muscular meat of the beautiful pink conch shell found everywhere in the Bahamas. It is a staple of the Bahamian diet, may not be exported, and is served many ways. Most popular are conch salad, chopped raw and marinated in lime juice and spices (similar to seviche); scorched conch, fresh and raw, which is scored, sprinkled with lime juice and hot pepper sauce; conch chowder, diced with potatoes, vegetables, tomatoes, and spices, and simmered into a thick soup; conch-burger, ground up, formed into a patty, fried, and served on a bun like a hamburger; pounded flat and fried or steamed, called fractured conch and steam conch; and, perhaps most popular of all, conch fritters, diced and combined with flour and eggs, deep-fried into crispy, chewy, bite-sized hors d'oeuvres.

Grouper is a local fish that abounds in all Bahamian waters. It is firm and mild-tasting, with few bones, and is cooked in many different ways. It is served batter-dipped and deep-fried as grouper fingers; baked, broiled, or fried as grouper steaks or cutlets; and cooked with potatoes and onions in a hearty, spicy stew called boil fish, a favorite Bahamian breakfast treat, served with hot johnnycake (delicious) and hominy grits. Another favorite is stew fish, grouper steamed in a browned flour gravy with spices.

Peas 'n' rice replaces potatoes in Bahamian cuisine and is served with everything. It is a tasty blend of white rice and chick-peas or pigeon-peas, with tomatoes, onions, and spices, plus a touch of salt pork or bacon.

Bahamian lobster is the spiny, clawless lobster or crayfish, with tender, delicious tail meat (similar to South African rock lobster tails). It is served boiled or broiled with drawn butter, in popular recipes such as lobster Newburg or cream soups, and chilled in lobster salad, which is often stuffed in a melon or avocado half.

Many varieties of *turtle* thrive in Bahamian waters, and the meat is used for turtle soup, patés, stews, and steaks. Occasionally you can find a restaurant that will cook turtle pie (to order only, as it takes hours), which is a whole turtle baked in the shell with a marvelous, spicy stuffing.

Two varieties of *crab* are native to the Bahamas: the saltwater stone crab and the land-dwelling blue crab. Stone crabs have large, succulent claws (when caught, only one claw is removed and the crab returned to the sea where he grows another one!) that are delicious boiled and served hot with drawn butter, or chilled and served with a creamy mustard sauce. Land crabs are served almost exclusively in native restaurants, usually diced and mixed with a tasty stuffing, returned to the shell, and baked. One of the most famous dishes is crab and rice, where crab is boiled with rice, tomatoes, and onions.

Desserts. Bahamians have a special way with the fresh fruits that grow abundantly on their islands, using them in cakes, pies, puddings, and ice cream. Look for a few of these delights in native restaurants: guava duff, sweet potato pie, coconut soufflé or mango soufflé, banana fritters, dilly bavarois, pineapple gumbo, yam bread, carrot cake, rum and raisin or soursop ice cream.

Beverages cover all popular international brews and vintages, and some have a special Bahamian flair. Water is potable everywhere, although it does have a distinctive, slightly salty taste. If you prefer bottled water, it is readily available in most hotels and restaurants on all islands. Although Bahamians prefer tea, the American-style coffee served is good and strong, and European espresso is served in many restaurants. Soft drinks include all international favorites in bottles and cans, plus a Bahamian speciality, Goombay Punch, a carbonated soda with a pineapple flavor. As virtually all liquor, except rum, is imported with relatively high duty paid, cocktails, beer, and wine tend to be expensive everywhere in the islands in lounges and restaurants. However, excellent buys are available in liquor stores on imported liquors and liqueurs. Rum, which is distilled on Grand Bahama (coconut rum), Eleuthera (pineapple rum), and in Nassau (all Bacardi products), is generally the best buy whether purchased by the bottle in a liquor store or in a drink at a restaurant or lounge. Bahamians do wonders with rum—here are some island specialties: *Bahama Mama,* orange

juice, crème de cacao (or coconut rum), and light rum; *Goombay Smash,*
pineapple juice, coconut rum, sugar, dash of lemon, and Galliano; *Bahamas Sunrise,* half champagne and half fresh-squeezed orange juice; *Yellow
Bird,* banana liqueur, orange juice, Triple Sec, Galliano, and light rum;
and *Nassau Royale,* an excellent coconut-rum liqueur, made by Bacardi,
and used as an after-dinner drink, as flambé over fruit or ice cream, and
mixed with hot black coffee with a dollop of whipped cream for Bahamian
Coffee (superb!). Other fruity, tropical favorites include Planter's Punch,
Banana Daiquiri, Cocoloco, Piña Colada, Rum Punch, and dozens more.

The Bahamas' Beat: Goombay and Junkanoo

Goombay is the beat of the Bahamas, primitive, pulsating, and sensu-
ous, almost pure rhythm with virtually no melody. Its cultural roots go
deep into an African past, and its origins can be traced to the dance, music,
and mask traditions of West Africa and to the ancient harvest festivals
celebrated by tribes of the Ivory and Gold Coasts. It was imported to Bermuda, the Bahamas, and the Caribbean with slavery. It is called "gombey"
in Bermuda and "gombay" in Jamaica, where it is still heard, but it seems
to have survived and thrived in its purest and most primitive form in the
Bahamas.

The word "goombay" derives from the Bantu language and means both
rhythm and goatskin drum. For centuries, the universal instrument in the
Bahamas has been the goatskin drum, which is handcrafted from wooden
kegs or steel cans and covered with taut goatskin or sheepskin hides. Small
fires are built inside the drum to shrink the leather to maximum tautness,
essential for achieving the basic goombay beat. Today the goombay drums
are still made in the age-old, traditional way.

The goombay beat is heard in its most basic form in the music and dance
that accompany the annual Junkanoo masquerades, which are held on the
day after Christmas, New Year's Day, and during the Goombay Summer
Festival from June through September. The Junkanoo parades and the
goombay beat of the goatskin drum have been inextricably linked throughout Bahamian history, with written records and descriptions going back
nearly two centuries. The costumed Junkanoo paraders dance a slow,
rhythmic shuffle, which Bahamians call "rushin," accompanied by the
constant, pulsating beat of the goatskin drums, punctuated with the clank
of cowbells; the shrill of tin whistles; the blare of brass bugles; the shaking
of poinciana pods, which sound like maracas; and the clicking of lignum
vitae sticks imitating castanets.

Year-round, the goombay beat is heard wherever Bahamians gather:
beach parties, country fairs, street dances, hotel galas, and, especially, native nightclubs, where the goatskin drums are backed up with guitars.
Much of the Bahamas' contemporary music, composed by young Bahamian musicians, features the unmistakable goombay beat as well.

Bahamian music and dance have been deeply influenced by other West
Indian rhythms, Jamaica's reggae, Martinique's merengue, Trinidad's calypso, and Latin bongo and conga drummers. Favorites are ring dances
and jump-in dances, accompanied by Bahamian calypso folk songs that
tell of unrequited love and poke good-natured fun at Bahamian family life.
(Ask almost any balladeer to sing "Love, Love Alone," which tells the
story of the King of England's romance, his abdication, and his marriage
to Wallis Simpson, or the delightful "Shame and Scandal in the Family.")

In recent years the major influences on Bahamian music and dance have been American, with everything from folk to rock, rhythm and blues, country western, and disco heard everywhere—flavored a bit with the goombay beat.

NEW PROVIDENCE ISLAND

Nassau, Cable Beach, and Paradise Island

New Providence Island is best known for the busy, bustling city of Nassau, hub of the island nation. Its modern jet-age airport is served daily by a dozen international airlines, and its sheltered deep-water harbor is one of the world's most famous ports of call, hosting more than 20 sleek luxury liners weekly, from Florida, New York, and Europe. Its glittering resorts and casinos along Cable Beach and on Paradise Island attract more than a million and a quarter visitors each year, making Nassau the single most popular destination in all of the Bahamas and the Caribbean.

Although it is one of the smallest islands in the archipelago, some 65 percent of the Bahamian population live on New Providence. Nassau boasts over 135,500 residents, out of a total population of around 225,000.

The 320-year-old capital city was originally named Charles Town, after King Charles I. In 1695 it was renamed Nassau in honor of King William III, who had been Prince of Orange-Nassau before ascending the English throne. Its colorful history includes Spanish invasions and pirates bold, who used Nassau as their headquarters during raids along the Spanish Main. And it includes old forts seized and occupied by the brave new American Navy in 1776, when the Americans won a comic-opera victory without firing a shot. They occupied Nassau for two weeks before sailing home in triumph.

The cultural and ethnic heritage of old Nassau includes southern charm imported by British loyalists from the Carolinas and reflected in its architecture, African tribal traditions of freed slaves, and a bawdy history of blockade-running during the Civil War and rum-running in the Roaring

Twenties era of Prohibition. Over all is a subtle layer of civility and sophistication, derived from three centuries of British rule and law.

Reminders of the British heritage are everywhere in Nassau. Court jus-
tices sport scarlet robes and bottom wigs, the police wear colonial garb
with starched white jackets, red-striped navy trousers, and tropical pith
helmets, traffic keeps to the left, and the language is distinctly English,
though softened by an easy island-calypso drawl. Much of the Caribbean's
charm can be found in old Nassau as well. The colorful harborside market,
with out-island sloops bringing catches of fish and conch, open-air tropical
fruit and exotic vegetable stalls, street hawkers vending guava juice and
soursop ice cream, and straw ladies weaving their magic on hats and baskets, brings to sophisticated Nassau the flavor of the Caribbean, the es-
sence of the West Indies—side by side with the glamour and glitter of international resorts and Continental casinos.

Exploring Nassau

The centuries-old city of Nassau lies on a sun-splashed hillside overlooking the bustling harbor and busy Bay Street. Its narrow sidestreets climb
the gentle slope and wander along the crest of the hill for less than a mile
in either direction, making the most historic sections of the city easy to
explore. Along the way, you'll find many old colonial sites reminiscent
of pre-Revolutionary America. There are colonnaded government buildings, reminders of the old South; an unusual octagonal-shaped library that
once was Nassau's "gaol" (jail); centuries-old churches; an ancient fort;
and many charming historic mansions surrounded by walled tropical gardens. Government House, on the hilltop, is the finest example of Bahami-
an-British, colonial-American-influenced architecture. Its graceful col-
umns and broad, circular drive could be in Virginia or the Carolinas, but
its pastel pink color and distinctive quoin corners painted white are typically Bahamian. Quoins are a common architectural embellishment, found
on many old Bahamian homes and public buildings. For another unique
old-Bahamas architectural touch, look for the Bahama Shutters, the
wooden louvers that completely enclose large upper and lower verandas
on many well-preserved old mansions and are designed to keep out the
tropical sun and encourage the tropical breezes.

Old Nassau

Two or three hours and a pair of comfortable shoes are all you need
to take a walking tour of old Nassau. (*Caution:* Many of the narrow streets
have no sidewalks, and traffic may move in both directions. Whenever possible you should walk facing the flow of traffic.)

To begin your tour, hop in a taxi, the hotel courtesy bus, or the public
jitney service, and head for the Strawmarket on Bay Street. Leave your
rental car or scooter behind; traffic is heavy and parking is very difficult
in downtown Nassau.

The Strawmarket, sprawled through the arched, open-air Market Plaza
on Bay Street, is lively from early morning till evening, seven days a week.
Stroll for a while among the hundreds of stalls and bargain with the straw
ladies for a hat and perhaps a woven bag for toting home your purchases.

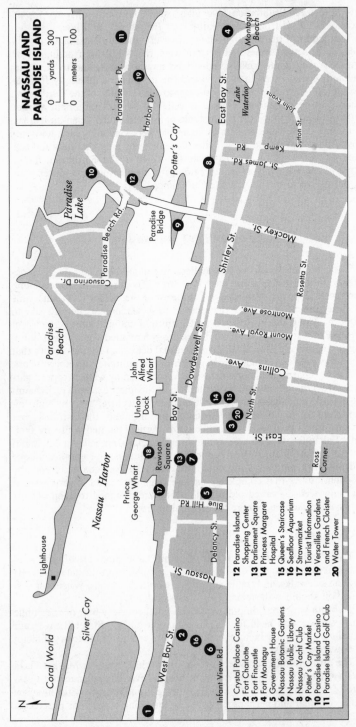

NASSAU AND PARADISE ISLAND

0 yards 300
0 meters 100

Coral World
Silver Cay
Lighthouse
Nassau Harbor
Paradise Beach
Paradise Lake
Paradise Bridge
Potter's Cay
Montagu Beach
Lake Waterloo

West Bay St.
Infant View Rd.
Nassau St.
Delancy St.
Blue Hill Rd.
Bay St.
Prince George Wharf
Union Dock
John Alfred Wharf
Rawson Square
Dowdeswell St.
Collins Ave.
North St.
East St.
Ross Corner
Mackey St.
Shirley St.
Mount Royal Ave.
Montrose Ave.
Rosetta St.
East Bay St.
St. James Rd.
Kemp Rd.
John Evans
Sutton St.
Casuarina Dr.
Paradise Beach Rd.
Paradise Is. Dr.
Harbor Dr.

1 Crystal Palace Casino
2 Fort Charlotte
3 Fort Fincastle
4 Fort Montagu
5 Government House
6 Nassau Botanic Gardens
7 Nassau Public Library
8 Nassau Yacht Club
9 Potter's Cay Market
10 Paradise Island Casino
11 Paradise Island Golf Club
12 Paradise Island Shopping Center
13 Parliament Square
14 Princess Margaret Hospital
15 Queen's Staircase
16 Seafloor Aquarium
17 Strawmarket
18 Tourist Information
19 Versailles Gardens and French Cloister
20 Water Tower

Exit the Strawmarket on the harborside, and stroll eastward along Woodes Rogers Walk for a fine view of the busy harbor and cruise ship wharf.

At Rawson Square cut across the causeway to Prince George Wharf, where the great white ocean liners tie up. Along the way, you'll see the lively seagoing life of old Nassau, a picturesque mix of small island sloops, inter-island freighters crowded with cargo and produce, glass-bottom tour boats, oceangoing yachts and sailing schooners, and the Bahamian ferry-boats that ply back and forth across the harbor to Paradise Island every 15 or 20 minutes. Here, you will also find a Ministry of Tourism Information Centre well stocked with booklets, brochures, maps, and expert advice from Bahamahosts, and if it is Goombay Summer or Discovery Season, you can join a walking tour conducted by well-trained guides.

To proceed on your own, cross back over the causeway to Rawson Square, the heart of old Nassau. Here you'll find shady benches and a fountain, a handsome bust of Sir Milo Butler, first Bahamian governor general of the Bahamas, and a colorful signpost, with dozens of bright signs pointing the direction to every island in the Bahamas. You'll find the straw-hatted surrey horses, their quaint fringe-top carriages, and their friendly drivers eager to carry you off on a ride through the old city and past some of the nearby historic sites. Across from the surrey ranks, you'll find a row of luxurious, air-conditioned limousines, Nassau's fleet of tour cars. If you plan a guided tour of the island, this might be a good time to negotiate the rate and the date with the drivers.

Directly across Bay Street from Rawson Square is Parliament Square, a cluster of pink, colonnaded, and quoined government buildings dating from the early 1800s and patterned after the southern colonial architecture of New Bern, early capital of North Carolina. In the center of the square is a statue of the young Queen Victoria on her throne, which was dedicated after her death in 1901. The statue is flanked by a pair of old cannon, and to the right is the Bahamas House of Assembly. Each session of the House is opened with great pomp and pageantry, in the British tradition, then settles down to day-to-day sittings that are sometimes raucous, often lively, and always interesting. Sessions are open to the public, but the chamber is small, and arrangements to attend must be made ahead of time through the Clerk of the House. Behind the statue of Queen Victoria is the Senate Chamber, and to the left of the statue is the old Post Office building (1812).

To the left of Parliament Square is a narrow street called Bank Lane, still known by its earlier name, Gaol Alley, to many Bahamians and antiquarians. Here you'll find the Central Police Station and Roselawn, a delightful restaurant. If you're ready for lunch, try it or the Terrace Café on Parliament Street, which runs along the right side of Parliament Square. Between Gaol Alley and Parliament Street, the old Treasury and the Supreme Court overlook the Garden of Remembrance and the Cenotaph, which honors Bahamian war dead from both world wars.

At the top of the square, facing Shirley Street, you'll find a unique old octagonal building, once the gaol of Gaol Alley. Built in 1799, the structure served as a jail until 1879, when it was converted to the Nassau Public Library. You can have a quiet look around at the small prison cells, which are now lined with books, and examine its excellent collection of historic prints and old colonial documents. Across the street from the library are the remains of the Royal Victoria Hotel and Gardens. The hotel, the first ever built in the Bahamas, opened in 1860, just at the outbreak of the Civil War in the United States. It became the headquarters for the colorful blockade runners, Confederate officers and English textile tycoons who traded guns for cotton. The charming old hotel stands abandoned and in disrepair, after welcoming guests for more than a century until 1971. However, the lovely old gardens are still worth a stroll, with a botanical wonderland of more than 300 varieties of tropical plants, palms, and a beautiful centuries-old spreading ficus tree.

On leaving the Royal Victoria Gardens, turn east and continue along Shirley Street. As you pass East Street, you might drop down toward the harbor for a look at Cascadilla, at Millar's Court, a lovely house set in a tropical garden. It was the residence of the late Sir Harold Christie, a prominent citizen. Head back to Shirley Street and continue east. Just beyond East Street, you'll see another lovely old Bahamian mansion with broad verandas and Bahama shutters, set in beautiful grounds: Addington House. Built in the 1880s, it is now the home of the Right Reverend Bishop Michael Eldon, the first Bahamian to be named Anglican Bishop of the Bahamas.

Continue along Shirley Street to Elizabeth Avenue, where the small National Historical Museum shows collections of maps and prints, Arawak artifacts, and shells (open Tuesday and Thursday). At the head of Elizabeth Avenue is the Queen's Staircase, a famous Nassau landmark. Its 66 steps, hewn from the coral limestone cliff by slaves in 1793, were designed to provide a direct route from the town to Fort Fincastle at the top of the hill. The staircase was named more than a hundred years later, in honor of the 66 years of Queen Victoria's reign. Climb the staircase to reach Fort Fincastle, another historic Nassau landmark. The fort, shaped like the bow of a ship, was built in the early 1790s by the loyalist governor, the Earl of Dunmore. He named the fort for one of his former titles, Viscount Fincastle. The fort never saw a shot fired in anger but served as a fine lookout and signal tower, guarding Nassau's harbor. The fort is in reasonable repair and can be explored; there is a fine view over the city and the harbor. But for a really spectacular panoramic view of the island of New Providence, climb the nearby Water Tower. (If you are not quite up to the steep, winding stairs, for 50 cents you can take an elevator to the top—there's no charge for the view.) The great white tower rises 126 feet, more than 200 feet above sea level, and is the highest point on the island.

From the grounds of the fort, follow Prison Lane back to East Street, where you'll find Mortimer's Candy Kitchen and the Best-Ever Candy Company, the oldest candy factory in the Bahamas. They are famous for hot peppermint candies and peppermint balls, Bahamian sesame-seed candy called "benny cakes," coconut creams and coconut chews, homemade fudge, and pink popcorn. Follow East Street north a short way to reach East Hill Street, and turn west to Nassau's new Post Office building, the place to shop for exceptionally beautiful stamps. The Post Office's Philatelic Bureau has a wide selection, along with first-day covers and other collectibles.

Across from the Post Office, at the top of Parliament Street, is another notable Bahamian mansion, Jacaranda, built in the 1840s. It is a private home, but you can view it through its graceful wrought-iron entrance gates. Continue down Parliament Street for a block or so toward the harbor to Green Shutters (1865), a charming Bahamian house converted into a famous pub. Dine indoors or out, on anything from "bangers 'n' mash" to Bahamian conch chowder. Return to East Hill Street after your pause to refresh, and continue west.

Along East Hill Street, you'll pass two historic mansions on your left. The first is the East Hill Club, a pink-and-white Georgian colonial built in the 1840s. Once the private winter home of Lord Beaverbrook, it is now a small inn. The second is Glenwood, an impressive private home said to have been built in the 1880s. Opposite Glenwood is Bank House, one of the oldest houses in Nassau, built in the 1780s by Edwin Charles Moseley, founder and publisher of the *Nassau Guardian,* the Bahamas morning newspaper that has been published continuous since 1844.

Just beyond these mansions, on the north side of the street, you will find a broad flight of stairs that will take you down to Prince Street (actually the westward extension of Shirley Street, and sometimes called Duke Street). Here are two historic churches, St. Andrew's Kirk, Presbyterian, built in 1810, and Trinity Methodist, built in 1866. They are open weekdays during the day for a quiet pause and a look around. Nearby is the New Bahamas Central Bank. Its cornerstone was laid by Prince Charles in 1973 during Independence ceremonies, and it was officially opened in 1975 by Queen Elizabeth II.

Continue west along Prince Street. As you pass Market Street, look up the hill for a good view of Gregory Arch, the graceful, picturesque entrance to Grant's Town. Known as the "over-the-hill" section of Nassau, Grant's Town was laid out in the 1820s by Governor Lewis Grant as a settlement for freed slaves. The arch was named for John Gregory, governor from 1849 to 1854.

Proceeding west along Prince Street, you will arrive at Government House, the gracious mansion that since 1801 has been the official residence of the royal governors of the Bahamas. Among the most famous occupants were the Duke of Windsor and his American bride, Wallis Warfield Simpson, who presided over the colony from 1940 to 1945. Entrance from Prince Street is up a broad staircase with an ancient cannon at its base and an impressive 12-foot statue of Christopher Columbus on the midpoint landing. The statue commemorates Columbus's landfall at the tiny island of Guanahani in the southeastern Bahamas. A private residence, Government House is open to the public only for a monthly Government House Tea Party on Friday at 4 P.M. in the tropical gardens. During the summer, several fetes and fairs are held on the grounds of Government House; most are well publicized on local television and radio, in the newspapers, and on posters and flyers in the hotels.

There is pomp and pageantry year-round at the great circular entranceway to Government House, with the colorful Changing of the Guard ceremony scheduled alternate Saturdays at 10 A.M. The Royal Bahamas Police Force Band puts on a fine performance, with music and marching in traditional British colonial precision, style, and ceremony. Their uniforms are superb—crisp white tunics, navy trousers with a red stripe, white tropical pith helmets—and the drummers are decked out in leopardskin tabards. And the music—from stirring marches to Bahamian goombay, from Caribbean calypso to American pop songs—sounds as good as the performers look. During Goombay Summer, they bring Bay Street alive with concerts and marching, and each Wednesday from 8 to 9 P.M. they draw great crowds as they perform the traditional Beat the Retreat.

Back on Prince Street, follow the high Government House wall around the corner to Baillou (pronounced "blue") Hill Road. Here Prince Street becomes West Hill Street and continues westward. Just around the corner on Baillou Hill Road, you will find the side entrance to Government House. Directly opposite this entrance is another famed landmark, Gray-cliff, a superb example of Georgian colonial architecture, dating from the mid-1700s. Legend has it that it was built by a Captain Gray, whose priva-teering vessel was named the *Graywolf;* its colorful history includes use as an officers' mess by the British West Indian garrison and a certain noto-riety during the rum-running days of Prohibition. Until recently it was the private winter home of the Earl and Countess of Dudley. Today the gracious antique-filled mansion is operated as an elegant inn, with a gour-met restaurant and well-stocked wine cellar. Its swimming pool, the first built in Nassau, is still one of the loveliest, surrounded by brilliant tropical flowers and foliage, in a walled garden.

From Graycliff, continue west on West Hill Street. Note the old Baha-mian houses on the north side of the street, swathed in wood-louvered Ba-hama shutters, and more old mansions on the hillside on the south side of the street. Walk along for a block or two until you come to a broad stone staircase on your right, which will lead you down to Queen Street. Queen Street runs for just a block or so, and the large building on your left is the American Embassy. Stop by for information and customs bro-chures, or for a look at an interesting painting of *The Landing at New Prov-idence,* which depicts the American Navy and Marines landing at Nassau in 1776. It usually hangs in the lobby.

Across from the embassy, at 28 Queen Street, is the Deanery (1710), thought to be the oldest house in Nassau. Acquired by the Anglican church in 1800, it serves as rectory for Christ Church Cathedral. The orig-inal kitchen and slave quarters are in the small one-story building to the west.

At the foot of Queen Street you'll meet Marlborough Street, and just ahead, stretching along the harbor, you'll see the Sheraton British Colo-nial, Nassau's oldest resort and one of its most famous. It was built origi-nally in 1899, on the site where Fort Nassau stood from 1696 to 1837. The first wooden structure was destroyed by fire in 1921, and today's huge pink-and-white classical/tropical resort made its debut in winter season 1923. Modernized and up-to-date, it is still one of Nassau's most popular hotels, fondly known to Bahamians and generations of visitors as "the B.C."

In front of the British Colonial is a fine statue of Woodes Rogers, who was appointed first Royal Governor of the Bahamas by George I in 1718. He routed the pirates who had made Nassau their pillaging headquarters, granting the King's amnesty to all who surrendered and hanging those who refused.

Turn east on Marlborough Street, past Cumberland Street (where Marl-borough becomes King Street), to George Street. Here you will find Christ Church Cathedral, built in 1837. The site has been occupied by a church for 300 years, according to records dating to 1684. The simple old church has been the seat of the Anglican Bishop since 1861. In that year Queen Victoria issued Letters of Patent constituting Christ Church a cathedral and ordained that "the whole town of Nassau henceforth be called The City of Nassau." Stop for a quiet look around the church and churchyard.

Just beyond the cathedral, turn toward the harbor on Market Street. On the west side of the street you will see Balcony House, a small Bahami-an home dating from the 1790s. The second-floor balcony of the wooden house hangs over the street, and steps lead directly from the pavement to its front door. Follow Market Street a few steps farther, and you'll be back on Bay Street. Just ahead, you will see the Bahamas Electricity Corporation, a two-story pink-and-white building. The top floor was added at the turn of this century, and if you look carefully at the ground floor, you can see bricked-over arches that once opened onto a roofed, open-air pavilion. For more than half a century, from 1769 until Emancipation, this was Vendue House, Nassau's notorious slave market, where men, women, and children were put on the auction block along with pigs and cattle, coconuts, and fish. Just a few doors away, you'll find yourself back at the bustling Strawmarket, where your walking tour began.

Around the Island

Outside the old city of Nassau, to the west and the east of the downtown center, the interesting sights and areas to explore are easily reached by rental car or motorscooter, taxi tour, or one of Nassau's air-conditioned limousine tour cars. If you are on your own, be sure to pick up the *Bahamas Trailblazer Map,* offered free at most hotel front desks or tour desks. You will find two copies helpful, as there are detailed maps of the city environs and of the island of New Providence on opposite sides. Wear comfortable clothes for exploring, and sturdy walking shoes or sneakers. Be sure to bring your camera and pack a tote with suntan lotion, sunglasses, swimsuits, and towels, in case you are tempted to try the warm, crystalline waters lapping the endless beaches that fringe the island. Plan an early start, as the full tour will take most of a day.

Begin at the grounds of old Fort Charlotte, located on West Bay Street at Chippingham Road. The massive fort is located at the top of the hill, commanding a fine view over the water and Arawak Cay, a small man-made island that holds huge storage tanks for fresh water barged in from Andros Island to serve Nassau during periodic water shortages. There is plenty of parking on the grounds of the fort, and you can easily walk to other nearby attractions such as the Ardastra Gardens, Nassau Botanic Gardens, and Seafloor Aquarium.

Fort Charlotte is Nassau's largest and best-preserved fortification, built by Lord Dunmore between 1787 and 1794. He named it in honor of George III's Queen Charlotte. The fort was dubbed Dunmore's Folly because of the staggering expense of building it. It cost more than £32,000— eight times more than originally planned. Yet in its nearly 200-year history, the fort has never fired a shot in anger. Wander through the grounds of the fort, see its cannons, cross its waterless moat, and walk along its ramparts. Local guides conduct tours and offer commentary on the history of the fort, and they will guide you through the fort and its underground dungeons. There is no charge, but tips are expected.

The Nassau Botanic Gardens, located directly behind Fort Charlotte, has 18 acres of tropical gardens with flowering trees, shrubs, and exotic tropical plants. Many trails wander through the gardens, delightful for strolling and identifying the hundreds of species along the way. There are two freshwater ponds with lilies and water plants, along with many varieties of colorful tropical fish. You'll also find a small cactus garden with many rare plants, leading to a charming grotto made of local quarry stones and roofed over with conch shells. On the grounds there is an enclosed playground for children, and there are many shady spots for relaxing.

Ardastra Gardens, west of the Nassau Botanic Gardens on Chippingham Road, are known to generations of Nassau visitors for the famed "marching flamingos." Here are five acres of tropical greenery and flowering shrubs, a fine aviary of unusual and rare tropical birds, and many species of animals that call the gardens home. Highlight of the garden tour is a unique attraction that has delighted visitors for decades: the parading of a flock of brilliant pink flamingos, national bird of the Bahamas. Drillmaster Joseph Lexion barks commands to his colorful long-legged charges; they respond with amazing discipline and seem to enjoy it as much as their trainer, who accompanies the show with a running commentary and amusing if occasionally bizarre lectures.

Seafloor Aquarium is a wonderful showcase of underwater life located just beyond the Nassau Botanic Gardens, where Chippingham Road becomes Columbus Avenue. Huge tanks hold a vast variety of tropical sea life, including sharks, manta rays, giant turtles, living coral reefs, and the exotic fish that inhabit them. Every two hours a special show is put on, with delightful performing dolphins and trained sea lions. On the grounds are a small factory that makes beautiful conch-shell, coral, and tortoiseshell jewelry and a gift shop that sells a broad selection of these typical Bahamian souvenirs.

Leaving the area of Fort Charlotte, return along Chippingham Road to West Bay Street and turn right toward the old city of Nassau. On your right you will pass Clifford Park, the site of holiday celebrations and the public ceremonies on the occasion of a royal visit, with a large reviewing ground, playing fields, and grandstands. Here you can watch the local soccer, rugby, cricket, and field hockey teams in action on weekends. On your left is the beautiful Western Esplanade Beach, also known as Lighthouse Beach for the stunning view across the harbor to the great Nassau Light at the tip of Paradise Island.

Just beyond Clifford Park you will see the 125-foot observation tower of Coral World soaring above the ocean waters. (The tower's crow's nest affords spectacular panoramic views.) A bridge links it to Silver Cay, site of the new Coral World Marine Park.

Coral World

The Coral World park occupies the entire island of Silver Cay, with its landscaped boardwalks, trails, bridges, waterfalls, and reflecting pools. A winding staircase leads to the underwater observatory, with 360-degree views of a living coral reef, thousands of tropical fish, and hundreds of species of coral. The Reef Tank shows you a living underwater reef; in the Shark Tank denizens of the deep prowl and are fed by scuba divers twice daily; the Sea Turtle Pool allows the giant ocean creatures their own island on which to bask in the sun and a lagoon for swimming. There are two huge Marine Garden aquariums and the Flamingo Haven, where a flock of the colorful birds make their home in a salty lagoon and nest along the shore. At the western end of the island the nautical yet rustic Clipper restaurant and bar offers Bahamian and American dishes and splendid views of the ocean, the neighboring islands, and Cable Beach. (Look for the elusive "green streak" just as the sun sets.)

As you approach downtown, at the Sheraton British Colonial Hotel, West Bay Street becomes Bay Street, one-way in the opposite direction. Traffic is routed up Baillou Hill Road, on your right, to Shirley Street.

This street runs parallel to Bay Street, with one-way traffic traveling eastward through town. (If you have skipped the walking tour of Old Nassau, you may want to read that section now, for this drive will take you past many of the "not to be missed" sights detailed there, as you travel eastward along Shirley Street.)

Just a block or two before you reach the main traffic intersection at Mackey Street (with a traffic light), look for two small lanes on your left. Lover's Lane and Church Street run on either side of St. Matthew's Anglican Church, the oldest church in the Bahamas. Turn down either lane to find a convenient parking spot because you will want to explore the lovely old church and ancient cemetery.

St. Matthew's Church, built between 1800 and 1804, was designed by a transplanted American loyalist, Joseph Eve. The church is a well-preserved example of the neoclassic forms and gothic proportions popular during this period. Within the same block on Shirley Street are two other sights of interest. There is the small, beautifully maintained Jewish cemetery surrounded by an ornamental iron fence—the only Jewish cemetery in the Bahamas. On the opposite side of the street is the Sacred Heart Roman Catholic Church. On the next block, on the right side of Shirley Street, is another of Nassau's landmark churches, surrounded by a cemetery: Ebeneezer Methodist Church, built in 1840 of wood and rebuilt of native stone in 1848.

If your morning of exploring ancient forts, tropical gardens, and old churches has built up your appetite, try a hearty Bahamian lunch at one of the excellent native restaurants nearby, such as Marietta's, a small hotel just off Mackey Street on Okra Hill, where the stew fish with johnnycake and grits or peas 'n' rice is delicious.

To do a bit of shopping after lunch, drop into Bahamas Hand Prints at Mackey and Shirley streets. Here you will find an interesting workshop producing delightful handcrafted silk-screened fabrics and fashions in lovely island prints. Another famous Nassau shop, just half a mile south on Mackey Street, is the Nassau Art Gallery, which offers an excellent selection of Bahamian artworks, including oils, watercolors, and prints. Across the street from St. Matthew's is Maura's Lumber, an old-fashioned general store that has served Bahamians for generations. Here you will find hardware and lumber, a wonderful collection of toys, and surprising bargains in fine European china and crystal. A block or two away, on East Bay Street, a marvelous old gingerbread house is the Temple Gallery, owned by the artist Brent Malone. Offerings include works by Malone and other Bahamians, with frequent art shows and exhibitions. Visitors are welcome.

Follow Mackey Street to Bay Street and the harbor. They meet at the roundabout at the foot of the Paradise Island Bridge. Cross to the foot of the bridge, and turn onto the narrow lane that runs under the bridge to Potter's Cay, one of the most picturesque spots on the island. Here are the open-air fruit-and-vegetable market and the docks for the Family Island sloops that bring fresh fish and wares to market. Almost any time of day the tiny cay is alive with activity. Fishermen hawk their wares from the decks of their colorful out-island sloops—one of the last wind-powered commercial fishing fleets in the world. Women and children set up stalls and sell dozens of varieties of exotic fruits and vegetables. Virtually everyone in Nassau stops by this native marketplace at least once a week to shop, so don't be surprised to see everything from chauffeur-driven limousines to pickup trucks.

Look for the great mounds of conch shells that form artificial islands in the harbor and the out-island freighters and government mail boats with decks loaded with everything from automobiles and refrigerators to crates of live chickens and perhaps a few goats, along with the passengers. If you are considering an adventurous mail boat trip to one of the Family Islands, drop by the Dock Master's Office here on Potter's Cay; he'll be able to give you sailing dates and times.

Potter's Cay is a photographer's delight, but some Bahamians, like other people around the world, may object to being photographed. It's a good idea to ask politely and respect their wishes. Generally you will find the people genial, warmly welcoming, glad to chat, and proud to exhibit their wares. Don't leave without sampling a few. Look for Pearline, who makes delicious, crispy conch fritters; pick up a tiny Eleutheran pineapple, delicately flavored and delightful—most vendors will slice it for you, so you can eat it while strolling—or pick out a bagful of sugar apples, tiny finger bananas, mangos, and a papaya or two to eat at leisure back at your hotel.

Paradise Island

For a complete change of pace, go "over the bridge" to Paradise, a glittering international resort and casino center. The bridge toll is $2 per car or scooter, 25 cents for walkers. On Paradise Island, the hotels are widely spaced, set amid acres of landscaped gardens, and overlook a half-mile of broad ocean beach. Linking the hotels are well-paved roads winding through tropical forests, shady riding trails, and biking, hiking, and jogging paths.

As you cross the bridge, you will find yourself on Casino Drive, leading directly to the Paradise Island Resort and Casino (which includes the Britannia Towers and Paradise Towers) and, nearby, the Sheraton Grand Hotel. Turn right at the first intersection and bear left to Paradise Island Drive, which will take you to the Paradise Island Shopping Village, where there are delightful stores and branches of some exclusive Bay Street shops, all in a compact shopping mall. Continue along the drive until you reach the parking area for the Versailles Gardens at the Ocean Club, one of the loveliest spots on the island.

The Versailles Gardens and French Cloister stretch across the island from harborside to oceanside. On a rise overlooking the harbor are the handsome French cloisters, once a monastery in Montrejau, France, built in the fourteenth century. The classic stone cloisters were purchased by William Randolph Hearst in the 1920s, dismantled and shipped to California, and stored for decades. Huntington Hartford, heir to the A & P fortune, who first developed Hog Island and renamed it Paradise, purchased the mass of stones in the 1960s and had the cloisters reconstructed as a showcase for his resort island. The views from the rise are across the harbor to old Nassau, and the spot is a favorite for weddings. Wander through the gardens and admire the plants and flowers and the highly eclectic collection of statuary and fountains.

Exit the gardens near the Ocean Club on the ocean side of the island. The main clubhouse was once Huntington Hartford's private home. Drop in and make reservations for dinner at the Courtyard Terrace, one of the most romantic settings in the islands. The many diversions on Paradise

Island include the Ocean Club's fine tennis courts, and just beyond the Versailles Gardens lies the Paradise Island Golf Course. Nearby, you can rent horses for an hour or two for a canter along the beach or through the shady island trails. Or take a quiet stroll along the beach, which runs for more than a mile in either direction.

If you'd prefer to check out the casino on your tour of Paradise, pick up your car and retrace your route to Casino Drive and the world-famous Paradise Island Casino. In the afternoons the casino is less formal and considerably less crowded, so if you are not too casually dressed (shirtless, barefoot, or otherwise scantily covered sightseers are not welcome), try your luck at the slot machines, roulette wheels, or blackjack tables. Even if flirting with Lady Luck is not your style, stroll through the shopping arcades and the handsome casino and pause to watch the action. If you've planned to attend the lavish casino show, whose stage-girl revue rivals the best of Paris or Las Vegas, now is a good time to make your reservations.

Walk through the landscaped grounds of the resort. Be sure to stop at the narrow wooden bridge across the Paradise Lagoon. Here you'll find a troupe of trained porpoises who love to show off for visitors. Check out the feeding times, when they put on an especially delightful show. Or rent a paddle boat for an hour and pedal your way around the lagoon. If you'd like to experience one of the most beautiful beaches in the world, head back to your car and drive toward the Paradise Island Bridge. At the roundabout (traffic circle), turn to the right, toward the western end of the island, along Paradise Beach Road, which winds through shady pine and palmetto forests.

Along the way, you'll cross the Lagoon and see Club Land 'Or on the right, an attractive apartment resort and time-sharing complex. A little father along, on your left, is the entrance to Chalk's seaplane base. If you've never seen the classic old seaplanes take off from and land in the water, stop in at Chalk's. The airline operates more than a dozen flights a day to Miami, Fort Lauderdale, Palm Beach, and Bimini.

Continuing westward along Paradise Beach Road, turn right at Casuarina Drive to the Paradise Beach Inn. Turn left on the lane that leads to the Paradise Beach Pavillion. This is the entryway to Paradise Beach, one of the most beautiful crescent-shaped strips of white sand in the islands and a favorite of visitors to Nassau since the 1890s. The $3 entry fee includes towels, changing rooms, lockers, and showers, along with a welcoming cocktail for adults. Dotting the beach are "chickees," palm-thatched umbrellas that provide shelter from the sun between dips in the warm, gin-clear sea. If you've arrived at sunset, the westward view is unforgettable.

Exploring New Providence

Plan to spend at least five or six hours driving around the island. Although New Providence is just 22 miles long and 7 miles wide, there are several stops you may want to make along the way.

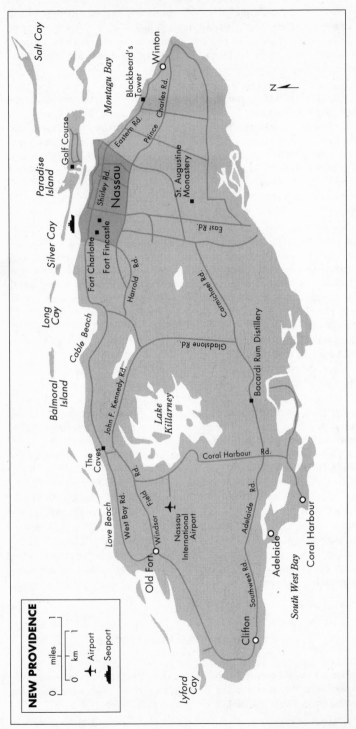

NEW PROVIDENCE

miles
km
✈ Airport
⚓ Seaport

Salt Cay
Montagu Bay
Blackbeard's Tower
Winton
Prince Charles Rd.
Eastern Rd.
N
Golf Course
Paradise Island
Silver Cay
Shirley Rd.
Nassau
St. Augustine Monastery
Fort Charlotte
Fort Fincastle
Harrold Rd.
East Rd.
Long Cay
Cable Beach
Carmichael Rd.
Gladstone Rd.
Bacardi Rum Distillery
Balmoral Island
John F. Kennedy Rd.
Lake Killarney
The Caves
Coral Harbour Rd.
Love Beach
West Bay Rd.
Field Rd.
Windsor Field
Old Fort
Nassau International Airport
Adelaide Rd.
Adelaide
Coral Harbour
Southwest Rd.
South West Bay
Clifton
Lyford Cay

Fort Montagu and Blackbeard's Tower

From the Paradise Island Bridge, drive eastward along East Bay Street (two-way traffic). On the harbor side, you will see several marinas, gathering spots for international yachtsmen cruising Bahamian waters. The first marina is Nassau Yacht Haven, directly across the street from one of Nassau's oldest and finest small hotels, the Pilot House. A little further along are the Bayshore Marina, Brown's Boat Basin, and the Nassau Harbour Club, a small hotel and extensive marina catering to the yachting set. On the right is Waterloo Lodge, a palatial mansion once the home of the Bahamas' first minister of tourism, Sir Stafford Sands. The house and gardens overlook a small inland lake known as Lake Waterloo, and the mansion houses a fine Polynesian restaurant, the Mai Tai, and a swinging new nightspot, the Waterloo Discotheque. Just beyond, on a spit of land overlooking the harbor, you'll see Fort Montagu.

The diminutive fort overlooking the eastern end of Nassau Harbor is the island's oldest fortification, built in 1741 of native limestone. Although the smallest of Nassau's forts, it saw more action than the other two combined, and it has the distinction of having been occupied by the American rebels for two weeks during 1776. George Washington ordered the new American fleet of eight small merchant ships to "proceed to Nassau and possess themselves of His Majesty's powder, artillery and other stores in His forts in New Providence." At daybreak on March 3, 1776, Commodore Ezekial Hopkins and his young first lieutenant, John Paul Jones, captured Fort Montagu without firing a shot and ran up America's first official flag. The "war" lasted two weeks, and the Americans sailed off with everything movable from Nassau's forts.

Today the little fort is well maintained and easy to explore. The broad public beach that stretches for more than a mile beyond the fort is one of Nassau's most popular meeting places, with a good beach bar selling thick, juicy burgers and frosty beers. The beach's broad shallow waters before the drop-off make it a pleasant one for children and inexperienced swimmers. Sunday afternoons are lively, with a good "rake and scrape" band and a large local crowd. It overlooks Montagu Bay, where many of the international yacht regattas and colorful Bahamian workboat races are held annually. The Fort Montagu Beach Hotel, the huge, pink 1920s-vintage hotel along the shore, once one of Nassau's grandest, is now abandoned and derelict.

At the great curve of the island beyond Fort Montagu, East Bay Street becomes the Eastern Road, and the area is known as the Montagu Foreshore, site of some of the island's impressive oceanside mansions. One of the most notable is the Hermitage, built by Lord Dunmore in 1787 as his summer residence and later rebuilt and expanded in the early 1920s. It is made entirely of Bermuda stone and local hardwoods. It serves as the official residence of the Catholic Bishop of the Bahamas.

Near the intersection of Fox Hill Road and the Eastern Road, a winding trail leads to the ruins of an old tower on the hillside. This is known as Blackbeard's Tower. Legend has it that it was the lookout for Edward Teach, the notorious pirate known as Blackbeard, who ruled the motley band of buccaneers that operated from the "Pirate's Republic" of Nassau between the 1690s and 1720s. The old stone ruins are much more likely to be a water tower of the 1890s than a pirate's lookout of the 1690s, but the legend persists, and the view from the top is splendid.

Continuing along the Eastern Road, you'll pass more oceanside mansions and a rather eccentric private home built as a replica of a lighthouse. Off to the right a narrow lane leads to Camperdown, gathering spot for the local "horsey set." If there are horse shows or dressage or jumping exhibitions scheduled, you will see posters or read about them in the newspapers.

Fox Hill Village, St. Augustine's Monastery

As the Eastern Road curves along the eastern end of the island, it links up with Prince Charles Avenue, which cuts off to the right. Follow Prince Charles Avenue to the first traffic light and you will be in the heart of Fox Hill Village, one of the oldest slave settlements on the island. It was once the vast Sandilands Estate, but after emancipation in 1834 the British divided up the land generously among the freed blacks. The second Tuesday of August each year is Fox Hill Day, a highlight on the Bahamian calendar. It is an old-fashioned country fair, alive with goombay music, gospel singing, arts-and-crafts booths, and fine down-home cooking. Legend has it that Fox Hill celebrates Emancipation Day (a public holiday on the first Monday of August each year) eight days later, because in 1834 it took more than a week for the news of emancipation to reach the residents of Fox Hill.

From the village, turn right on Fox Hill Road to Bernard Road, and turn left. Here you will find St. Augustine's Monastery, the home of the Benedictine monks in the Bahamas. The great Romanesque monastery, built in 1946, was designed by John Hawes, better known as Father Jerome, who also designed and built the two great churches on Cat Island.

The impressive buildings of the monastery overlook beautiful grounds and gardens, and the monks of St. Augustine are happy to show visitors around. Be sure to drop into the little bakery—the pastries and bread are excellent, and a favorite souvenir is a jar or two of the homemade guava jam.

Continue along Bernard Road, across the intersection of Village Road, and onto Wulff Road, continuing west. If you are ready for lunch, stop off at the Three Queens' restaurant for one of its outstanding Bahamian specialties.

Continue west on Wulff Road to Mackey Street and turn right, heading north. Turn left at the light onto Madeira. This area, known as Palmdale, is a small but thriving middle-class business and residential community. Look for the United Book Shop, which has an excellent selection of books about the Bahamas and books by Bahamians. A good history of the islands is *The Story of the Bahamas,* by the late Dr. Paul Albury, Bahamian dentist, author, and historian.

Continue west on Madeira, passing St. Thomas More's Catholic Church and School, crossing Montrose Avenue, where Madeira becomes Gibbs Corner. Continue west to East Street, and turn left to Young Street. Here you will find the Hardecker Children's Clinic, a successful American project that helps deprived Bahamian children.

Go west on Young Street to Baillou Hill Road, turn left, and continue to the traffic circle, which links up with Harrold Road. You will pass a low-income housing development known as Yellow Elder, easily distinguished by the distinctive round African-style architecture of the houses. Still traveling west, you will pass Angelo's Art Centre and Museum, well worth a stop. It is owned and operated by Angelo Roker, a noted Bahamian artist and printer, and offers a good selection of local artworks, along with Angelo's own paintings and prints. Old Bahamian and West Indian prints and maps are available as originals and reproductions.

Continue west on Harrold Road to Prospect Road, and turn left to Prospect Ridge Road. This heavily wooded area, called Prospect Heights, is one of the most prestigious residential communities on the island. Follow Prospect Ridge Road to Skyline Drive, where the several magnificent houses include the private residences of high government officials. The large pink-and-white house with the sentry box in the front yard is the home of the prime minister.

Cable Beach, Love Beach, and Lyford Cay

Retrace your route to Prospect Bridge Road, turn left to Prospect Road, and left once again to the traffic circle that links with West Bay Street. Here West Bay Street becomes a dual carriageway (the Bahamian name for a divided highway). Turn left and continue west along the Cable Beach hotel strip.

Here you will see some of Nassau's most celebrated hotels, most beautiful oceanside homes, and vistas of turquoise and emerald Bahamian waters. You'll pass the Ambassador Beach Hotel, the Nassau Beach Hotel, and Carnival's Crystal Palace Hotel. The casino here offers the Bahamas Rhythms Theatre, with an elaborate French-style revue. If you plan to catch the show during your vacation, now is a good time to make reservations. You'll find the casino casual, friendly, and informal day or night. In late afternoons, the dealers and croupiers offer free lessons in all of the games, teach you the rules, and tip you off on the odds. Great fun for novices—and for some regular players who could use the advice.

After checking out the casino, stroll through the shopping arcade. On the upper level, notice particularly the large showcases exhibiting superb examples of Junkanoo Art, a unique Bahamian craft. This is one of the few places in the islands where you can get a close-up view of this colorful, creative art form except during the lavish Junkanoo Masquerades held annually at Christmas and New Year's, when hundreds march and cavort in the fantastic handcrafted costumes—some as wide as a street and ten feet tall.

Continue westward along Cable Beach. The dual carriageway ends at Delaporte Point, an attractive condominium apartment complex on a peninsula overlooking the sea. Continuing west, you will pass the Caves on your left, large limestone caverns carved by the wind and the sea, reputedly hiding places for seventeenth-century pirates and their booty. Opposite is a long, winding stretch of sand known as Caves Beach. A short way farther along is a spit of land on the ocean side called Conference Corner. Here three trees were planted by heads of state attending the Nassau Conference in December 1962, held at Lyford Cay. Participating were U.S. President John F. Kennedy, Prime Minister John Diefenbaker of Canada, and Prime Minister Harold Macmillan of Britain.

A few miles farther you will pass Traveler's Rest, a famous Bahamian restaurant featuring hearty native fare. Across the street is Gambier Beach, fine for swimming and beachcombing, and nearby is Gambier, a small country village originally settled by freed slaves.

Beyond Gambier the island is less populated and settlements are few as the road winds along remote, deserted beaches and through pine and palmetto forests toward the western end of the island. On the right you will pass Love Beach, with an attractive apartment and condominium colony, the International Sports Club. At Northwest Point, West Bay curves slowly to the south and continues southwesterly, inland from the sea. A few miles down the road you will see the walled and guarded entrance to Lyford Cay, one of the most exclusive residential clubs in the world.

Lyford Cay is a posh haven for international socialites, financiers, the titled, and the famous. Britons, Canadians, French, Swiss, Greeks, Brazilians, Spaniards, Germans, and Americans mingle at the yacht club and golf course with old Bahamian families.

Lyford Cay is actually a peninsula; 4,000 acres of verdant greenery overlook the sea, intersected by navigable canals and dotted with more than 220 magnificent private homes. The club was founded in the 1950s by the Canadian developer E. P. Taylor. Second and third generations of the original Lyford Cay members still live on the cay or return each year for holidays at their island hideaway. Unless you are a member or the guest of a member, you won't be permitted beyond the gates, but there is a delightful little shopping center at the entranceway that is fun to explore. Keep your eye on the daily newspapers; there are frequent charitable events held at Lyford Cay, and some are open to the public.

The South Shore

After Pleasant Bay, West Bay Street makes a great arc at Clifton Point, the western tip of the island, and continues eastward, where its name changes to Southwest Road. You will pass the Bahamas Electricity Corporation plant and the huge desalinization complex, where much of Nassau's drinking water is converted from sea water. The new Commonwealth Brewery nearby produces Guinness lager, Vita Malt, and Kalik, a Bahamian beer named for the sound of Junkanoo bells. Heading east, you will see the Divi Bahamas Beach Hotel, a completely self-contained country-club resort and time-sharing complex. Guest golfers are welcomed and golf clubs, racquets, and scuba gear can be rented.

The road winds easterly through miles of untamed forest known as the Pine Barrens. Both sides of the road are fringed by thousands of acres of casuarina pines, palmetto and cycads, flowering shrubs, wildflowers, and many varieties of wild orchid. Look for a narrow lane that leads off to the right, toward the sea. This will take you through Adelaide Village, one of the oldest and most picturesque of the early slave settlements on New Providence.

Here time seems to have stood still for 150 years. Only 15 or 20 families remain in the village, many living as their ancestors did in cottages made of stone with thatched roofs woven from palm fronds. They cultivate small gardens, growing pumpkins, sweet potatoes, and melons; raise chickens and a few goats; and fish in homemade boats along the shore. The villagers are friendly and welcoming, although tourists seldom touch their small world. Unlike Fox Hill and Gambier, Adelaide was settled by blacks who had never been slaves. Their ancestors were captured from their African homes and loaded aboard slave ships bound for the New World, but they were rescued on the high seas by the British Royal Navy. In September 1832, the first cargo of rescued slaves reached Nassau. Some were given plots of land at Adelaide; others were settled at Carmichael, a few miles away. Stroll through the village or drive down to Adelaide Beach, one of the most remote and unspoiled beaches on the island.

Circle back to the main road, turn right, and continue eastward. Here the road's name changes to Adelaide Road. In a few miles you will cross an intersection with Coral Harbour Road. A left turn will take you to Nassau International Airport, and a right turn leads to the Coral Harbour development. Back in the 1960s this area was slated for major tourist development and the luxurious Coral Harbour Club and Golf Resort was opened. However, the area did not thrive, and today the hotel is headquarters for the Royal Bahamas Defense Force and its fleet of swift patrol boats. The Happy Trails riding stables nearby are the only public riding stables in Nassau. One-hour trail rides with a guide are $30, with pickup at and return to your hotel. There are renewed development plans for the Coral Harbour area, and a new luxury Ramada Renaissance Hotel and Casino is planned for a beachfront site.

A few miles farther along Adelaide Road, look for another road leading off to the right toward the sea. This leads to the Bacardi Rum Distillery, which produces nearly half a million cases of rum and liqueurs each year, including Nassau Royale, a delightful Bahamian cocoa-rum liqueur (the base for Bahamian coffee, which rivals Irish coffee as an after-dinner treat). Drop by the Visitor's Bar, open each weekday until around 4 P.M., for complimentary samples of Bacardi products.

Continuing eastward, Adelaide Road becomes Carmichael Road as it passes through another country village settled by rescued slaves, Carmichael. Beyond, the Pine Barrens are left behind, and the road curves through built-up areas of villages and housing developments, ending at Blue Hill Road. Turn left and travel north along Blue Hill Road.

Blue Hill Road bisects two of Nassau's oldest neighborhoods, Bains Town on the left and Grants Town on the right, both known for generations as "over the hill" because of their location just over the ridge from downtown Nassau. These "country villages" within the city were also settled by rescued slaves, along with emancipated blacks who had worked the Bahamian plantations. Both villages today are poor but picturesque, with tiny wooden homes painted in bright tropical colors, often surrounded by bougainvillea and tropical greenery. There are many Baptist and fundamentalist churches in the area, and even more bars, shops, and small grocery stores serving the local population.

At the intersection with Meeting Street (traffic light), turn left to Nassau Street, then right for one block and right on Delancey Street. Here you will pass a Bahamian home that's now one of Nassau's finest restaurants, Buena Vista. It also operates as a small inn.

Just beyond Buena Vista is the intersection with West Street. On the corner is St. Francis Xavier Cathedral, the oldest Catholic church in the Bahamas, constructed in 1885. In 1893 the church purchased the stately mansion next door to use as a priory. The house, known as Dunmore House, was built by Lord Dunmore in 1787 as his official residence and was used by eighteenth-century governors until today's Government House was completed in 1803. Today, Dunmore House is a beautifully preserved example of early British colonial architecture.

Turn left on West Street, toward the harbor. West Street ends at Bay Street, between the Sheraton British Colonial Hotel and old Fort Charlotte, where your tour of Nassau and the island began.

PRACTICAL INFORMATION FOR
NEW PROVIDENCE ISLAND

HOW TO GET THERE. By air. Nassau International Airport is served directly from the U.S. mainland by more than a dozen nonstop international flights daily from American cities such as Miami, Fort Lauderdale, Palm Beach, Tampa, Atlanta, Chicago, Boston, Philadelphia, Washington, D.C., Newark, and New York. It is linked conveniently to most major cities around the world by a brief 35-minute jet hop from the Miami gateway. Airlines serving Nassau include *Bahamasair, Braniff, Delta, Eastern, Midway, Pan American, TWA, Piedmont, United, Chalk's International, Air Canada,* and *British Airways. Aero Coach International* and *Caribbean Express* are among the commuter airlines that fly daily between Nassau and Florida cities. In addition, there are frequent charter flights to Nassau from U.S. cities, Toronto, and Montreal. Taxi fare from the airport to downtown Nassau is about $14.

By sea. Half a dozen cruise ships sail once or twice weekly to Nassau from Miami, Fort Lauderdale (Port Everglades), or Port Canaveral. The following ships sail each Monday and Friday to Nassau on three- and four-night cruises (four-night cruises also call at Freeport, Grand Bahama): Carnival Cruise Line—*Carnivale* and *Mardi Gras* (Thursday and Sunday); Admiral Cruiseline—*Emerald Seas;* Norwegian Cruise Line—*Sunward II;* Dolphin Cruiseline—*Dolphin IV;* and Premier Cruiseline—*Royale* and *Oceanic.* Friday-only sailings to Nassau by Chandris Line—*Galileo* or *Britannis.* For more details on Bahamas cruises, see "How to Get There by Sea" in *Facts at Your Fingertips.*

TELEPHONES AND EMERGENCY NUMBERS. The area code for Nassau is 809. Dial direct from anywhere in the U.S. or Canada. Hotels generally charge 25¢ for local calls and add a substantial service charge for long-distance calls.

Emergency numbers on New Providence Island. Fire, 919; Police, 322–4444; Ambulance, 322–2221; Bahamas Air Sea Rescue, 322–3877; Hospital, 322–2681.

HOTELS. Nassau, Cable Beach, and Paradise Island offer the widest range of vacation accommodations on any island in the Bahamas chain, and the broadest price range to match almost any budget. There are small historic inns, clusters of cottages, homey or sophisticated apartment and villa complexes, budget in-town hotels, sprawling country-club resorts, and glittering high-rise beach hotels with nonstop sports and entertainment, casinos, and stage revues—nearly 70 different properties, offering close to 4,000 rooms for rent.

Hotel price categories per room for two people in winter season are: $200 and up, *Super Deluxe;* $185–$199, *Deluxe;* $150–$184, *Expensive;* $120–$149, *Moderate;* under $119, *Inexpensive.*

Rates in goombay summer season tend to be 10 to 20 percent lower, and year-round packages can be as much as 20 to 40 percent lower than winter rates. We have indicated whom to contact for reservations, and you'll note that most may also be booked through Bahamas Reservation Service, tel. 800–327–0787, toll-free from anywhere in the U.S. or Canada. It is abbreviated below as BRS.

Cable Beach

Meridien Royal Bahamian. *Super Deluxe.* Reserve direct: 5775 N.W. 11th St., Suite 350, Miami, FL 33126; tel. 305–262–1397; in the U.S. 800–543–4300; or through BRS. This grand old hotel, formerly the Balmoral Beach, became the top Bahamian hotel when the Meridien chain, a subsidiary of Air France, took over the management for the 1988–89 winter season with promises of the finest in French service and cuisine coupled with Bahamian tradition. The hotel boasts elegant architecture, fountained terraces, 200 spacious high-ceiling rooms overlooking the sea, and 16 Georgian villas in the gardens. Featured are English country-house decor, afternoon tea in the lounge, elegant dining at *Baccarat* (a name change is expected), concierge service, fluffy terry robes, and dozens of other amenities, including a pool, tennis courts, a beach, water sports, and an exclusive health spa complete with masseurs and mud baths. And to top it off, the hotel is on a private island across the bay.

Carnival's Crystal Palace Hotel. *Deluxe to Super Deluxe.* Reserve direct: 5225 N.W. 87th Ave., Miami, FL 33166; tel. 305–599–2600 or through BRS. With the final rooms due to open early in 1990, Carnival's Crystal Palace Hotel and Casino becomes the biggest resort in the Bahamas, with over 1,550 rooms. At the end of 1988, Carnival bought the neighboring Cable Beach Hotel for $82.5 million and merged the two properties. It was not certain at press time how the two properties would be managed. The combined hotels boast a 2,000-foot-long private beach; an 18-hole, par-72 golf course; a health club; and a sports center with ten tennis, three indoor squash, and three racquetball courts. The casino—the Bahamas' biggest—has 750 slot machines and 51 blackjack, seven craps, and nine roulette tables as well as one mini baccarat and one big six table. The 1,000-seat *Bahamas Rhythms Theatre,* which is between the two hotels, features a French-style show girl revue. Alongside it is a New York-style delicatessen and a gourmet Italian restaurant. All water sports are available at the beach concession stand, including small-boat sailing, parasailing, and fishing expeditions.

Nassau Beach Hotel. *Deluxe to Super Deluxe.* Reserve direct: 500 Deer Run, Miami, FL 33166; tel. 305–371–1820 or through BRS. This 425-room oceanside resort has recently been completely refurbished and refurnished. There are four fine restaurants with a variety of menus, and two lounges offer good local entertainment. All rooms are attractively furnished, are air-conditioned, and have private balconies overlooking courtyard gardens or the sea. One wing is reserved for Palm Club members, whose luxury package includes limousine, concierge, gourmet dining, and sports facilities. There is an Olympic-size swimming pool, 3,000 feet of beach, a multitude of water sports, and nine tennis courts (six lighted). Rates include all taxes and charges.

Cable Beach Inn. *Expensive.* Box N–4920, Nassau; tel. 327–7341 or through BRS. (Formerly Bahamas Beach Hotel.) This elegant resort has 120 rooms, each air-conditioned, with bath or shower. Good dining and entertainment; English-style pub and new state-of-the-art dance club, *Inn Spirations.* Two tennis courts, two pools, ocean beach, bikes, and water sports. Three popular barbecues weekly, with live entertainment.

Wyndham Ambassador Beach. *Expensive.* Reserve direct: 5775 N.W. 11th St., Miami, FL 33126; tel. 305–264–5925; in the U.S. 800–327–3305. A classic Bahamas resort, low-rise and U-shaped, overlooking 1,800 feet of beach. All rooms are carpeted and have a balcony, cable TV, and a dial telephone. The spacious lobby abounds with tropical greenery and has an attractive bar/lounge. *The Pasta Kitchen,* a pretty, intimate restaurant with oak-paneled walls and country-French chairs, serves homemade Italian specialties. The *Flamingo Cafe* dining room and the *Pelican Bar and Game Room* are among the other attractions. Huge pool and water sports are available at oceanside. There are four all-weather lighted tennis courts and golfing at the Cable Beach golf course.

Downtown Nassau

Graycliff. *Deluxe.* Box N–10246, Nassau; tel. 322–2976/7. A charming and historic inn on a hillside off Bay Street, next to the governor's mansion. The great house is a 230-year-old Georgian colonial mansion set in a walled tropical garden, once headquarters for Nassau's West Indian Regiment. In more recent years it was the private winter home of the Earl and Countess of Dudley, hosting British royalty and notables. Converted to a small inn and gourmet restaurant half a dozen years ago, Graycliff still has much of the charm of an English country house, with antique-filled rooms and personalized attention from the staff. There are 12 air-conditioned rooms and a poolside cottage that overlooks a magnificent walled swimming pool surrounded by tropical greenery.

Sheraton British Colonial. *Moderate to Expensive.* Box N–7148, Nassau; tel. 322–3301 or 800–325–3535. At 1 Bay Street, Nassau's most famous address, you'll find the great sprawling, tropical pink resort known to generations of visitors as the B.C. Host to the titled and famous during its heyday in the 1920s, the British Colonial remains one of Nassau's most popular resorts, with the highest year-round occupancy rate in the Bahamas. Its modestly priced, attractive packages appeal to large and small tour groups, value-conscious vacationers, and college students on spring break. The grand old resort has been given a new breath of life. The old wing (dating from the 1920s) has been completely refurbished. The east wing (built in the 1960s) had been given its face-lift earlier. The British Colonial has 325 rooms and suites, a broad harborside beach, three lighted tennis courts, and a shopping arcade. The *Patio Bar* offers live entertainment nightly, the *New Blackbeard's Forge* restaurant prepares steaks and lobster to order at your table, and the spacious *Bayside Buffet* offers unlimited salad fixings and the best harbor view in Nassau.

Buena Vista. *Inexpensive.* Box N–564, Nassau; tel. 322–2811 or 322–4039. On Delancey Street, overlooking old Nassau, this 200-year-old estate is best known for its gourmet restaurant. Upstairs in the rambling old house the six spacious, high-ceilinged guest rooms are comfortable but not luxurious. Rooms can be noisy as window air conditioners wheeze and late-night diners linger over brandy on the terrace. Attractive gardens for sunning, but no pool; three blocks to the Western Esplanade Beach. Surprisingly inexpensive and usually booked well in advance.

Hotel Corona. *Inexpensive.* Box SS–6396, Nassau; tel. 326–6815 or through BRS. A small, family-run hotel with 21 balconied bedrooms overlooking busy Bay Street. Knotty pine corridors and large but unpretentious rooms, all air-conditioned. The very good, casual restaurant on the street floor (decor: captain's chairs and old brick walls) serves Bahamian specialties and American dishes at modest prices.

Dolphin Hotel. *Inexpensive.* Box N–3236, Nassau; tel. 322–8666 or through BRS. On West Bay Street, a few minutes' walk from downtown, and across the street from Lighthouse Beach (known as the Western Esplanade). Sixty-six modestly furnished and somewhat drab, air-conditioned rooms, each with a private balcony and ocean view. Dining room and dining terrace at poolside offer hearty Bahamian dishes, but service can be erratic.

El Greco Hotel. *Inexpensive.* Box N–4187, Nassau; tel. 325–1121/4. West Bay Street, very near downtown business and shopping. A small, tastefully decorated and Spanish-flavored 26-room hotel with special appeal for business travelers. Rooms are air-conditioned, spacious, and have private telephones. There is an attractive courtyard pool, and Lighthouse Beach is just across the road. The hotel boasts one of the best gourmet restaurants in Nassau, the *Del Prado,* with Continental decor and cuisine.

New Olympia Hotel. *Inexpensive.* Box N–984, Nassau; tel. 322–4971/2/3 or through BRS. Small, casual family-run hotel with 53 air-conditioned rooms, some with private balconies and a splendid ocean view. The popular *Pub Lounge* is a gathering spot for guests, locals, and visitors. The dining room offers Greek, Bahamian, and American dishes, and *Sonny's* on the garden patio is a favorite snack spot. Just a few steps away from Lighthouse Beach and an easy stroll to downtown shopping. Small service charge added.

Pilot House Hotel. *Inexpensive.* Box N–4941, Nassau; tel. 322–8431; in the U.S. 800–223–9815; or through BRS. A favorite of cruising yachtsmen, this charmingly nautical hotel overlooks the marina and the harbor, "Across the Bridge from Paradise," on Nassau's East Bay Street. Each of the 125 spacious rooms is air-conditioned, with private telephone and balcony overlooking a tropical courtyard and sparkling pool. There's island entertainment nightly at the *Windward Mark* or *Captain's Lounge,* and excellent dining in the *Regatta Room* or on the palm-shaded terrace. The resort operates frequent water-taxi service to Paradise Island and downtown Nassau for guests at no charge.

Outside Nassau

Divi Bahamas Beach Resort and Country Club. *Deluxe.* Box N–8191, Nassau; tel. 326–4391; in the U.S. 800–367–3484 or through BRS. The former South Ocean Beach Hotel reopened in 1988 with new carpeting and furnishings in all rooms, an attractive lobby rotunda, and a resurfaced and refurbished pool area. A great, sprawling country-club resort located on the southwestern shore of New Providence Island, overlooking miles of beach and the sea. The resort boasts the only USGA-rated 18-hole championship golf course in the Bahamas. There is an elegant clubhouse, a pro shop, and a fine restaurant and bar at the golf course. The 120-room low-rise hotel offers nightly entertainment, gourmet or casual dining, four tennis courts lighted for night play, a beautiful pool, and 600 feet of private white-sand beach. All rooms are air-conditioned. Sporting amenities include an excellent scuba program, catamaran sailing, snorkeling, and most other water sports. Bicycles, motor scooters, and automobiles for rent, and frequent complimentary bus service to Nassau. A casino (Nassau's third) is planned for 1990.

Paradise Island

Ocean Club. *Super Deluxe.* Box N–4777, Nassau; tel. 326–2501; in the U.S. 800–321–3000. Elegance and luxury in a sophisticated clublike setting. One of the Caribbean's finest tennis resorts. The main house was once Huntington Hartford's mansion, and the resort has hosted the celebrated, the noted, and the notorious over the years. It has two low wings with 70 opulent rooms overlooking a lovely garden courtyard, each with balcony or terrace, telephone, and cable TV. There are five two-bedroom villas with private Jacuzzis, and 12 tennis cabanas adjacent to the courts (best buy!). Tennis amenities include resident pro, instruction, nine Har-Tru courts, and free court time for guests. The resort has a long, lovely ocean beach reached by a staircase, and is next door to the beautiful French cloister and Versailles Gardens. There's an attractive pool and patio, with haute cuisine al fresco in the *Courtyard Terrace.* Golf and casino nearby. Owned by Resorts International.

Paradise Island Resort and Casino. *Deluxe to Super Deluxe.* Box N–4777, Nassau; tel. 326–2000/3000; in the U.S. 800–321–3000; or through BRS. Resorts International's two spectacular oceanside hotels offer elegance, luxury, opulence, and glitter with all the accountrements of an international playground. The 1,200-room resort complex consists of the twin towers of the Britannia Beach Hotel, with 600 rooms, now called the Britannia Towers, and the 500-room Paradise Island Hotel, now called Paradise Towers and boasting a new entryway and a two-story atrium lobby. They are linked by arcades of shops and restaurants leading to the *Paradise Island Casino* and *Le Cabaret Theatre,* and share several miles of beautiful ocean beach. The landscaped grounds include tropical gardens, palm-lined pathways, blue lagoons, and huge swimming pools. There are a dozen gourmet and specialty restaurants, and half a dozen bars and lounges indoors and at poolside. Rooms are attractively furnished, offer private telephones, cable TV, and balconies with ocean, pool, or lagoon views. "Club Paradise" guests occupy a 100-room beachfront tower that opened in 1987; their all-inclusive luxury package includes 24-hour concierge service, a rooftop deck with Jacuzzi, private lounge, gourmet dining, and complimentary sports. The resort includes a full watersports program, 12 tennis courts for day or night play, a Parcourse layout for joggers, health club, and an 18-hole championship golf course.

Sheraton Grand Hotel. *Deluxe to Super Deluxe.* 150 Alhambra Circle (12th floor), Coral Gables, FL 33134; tel. 800–325–3535; through Sheraton worldwide; or through BRS. An elegant new oceanside resort, member of the worldwide Sheraton Hotel chain, with a super-deluxe penthouse that rents for $11,000 a day! There are 350 beautiful ocean-view rooms and suites, each air-conditioned, with telephones and cable TV, set along a broad sandy beach with a terraced pool deck. The atrium lobby features a lovely fountain and lounges overlooking the sea. Top floors are the "Tower" section, reached by keyed elevator, and offer full concierge service, private bar, Continental breakfast, and evening liqueurs, among other amenities—they're very expensive. Sports facilities include scuba, sailing, parasailing, and four tennis courts lighted for night play. Other amenities include a masseur, beauty shop, gift shop, and *Androsia Boutique* (hand-batiked fabrics and fashions from the island of Andros). Located next door to the Paradise Island Casino.

Holiday Inn. *Deluxe.* Box SS–6214, Nassau; tel. 326–2101 or 800–465–4329; or through BRS. High-rise Holiday Inn amenities with a tropical, Bahamian flair. There are 535 attractive rooms in a 17-story tower overlooking a splendid crescent ocean beach. Rooms are air-conditioned and have telephones and cable TV. Huge free-form pool with a "floating" bar (stools are in the water), four tennis courts with instructor, all water sports, dining rooms, and lounges with good island entertainment nightly. There's a full activities program with a cheerful, friendly staff who put on their own delightful show every Friday evening.

Paradise Paradise. *Deluxe.* Box SS–6259, Nassau; tel. 326–2541; through Resorts International, 800–321–3000 in the U.S.; or through BRS. Casual, cozy, and delightful—just 100 rooms along Paradise Beach, the Bahamas' most famous ocean strand. All rooms are modestly furnished, motel-style, and air-conditioned, with telephone and cable TV. A favorite of the younger crowd. Dress code tends to bikinis and jeans, with dress-up time for trips to the casino, cabaret, and nightclubs. A good restaurant, friendly bar/lounge with native show, and an attractive pool. All-inclusive plan with breakfast available, and free sports including sailing, snorkeling, windsurfing, waterskiing, tennis, and biking.

Harbour Cove. *Expensive.* Box SS–6249, Nassau; tel. 326–2561; through Loews worldwide reservation service; or through BRS. Two hundred and fifty newly decorated and attractive rooms, located near the Paradise Island Bridge on the southern shore, overlook the harbor and the island. All are air-conditioned, with telephones, and cable TV; some with private balconies. There is a small man-made crescent beach with a lovely pool and bar. Very attractive public rooms. Fine dining indoors and on the terrace; lounges with native entertainment. The resort operates a water-taxi service to Nassau for shopping and sightseeing.

Club Med Paradise Island. *Moderate.* Box N–7137, Nassau; tel. 800–258–2633. Famous international vacation club for group-fun devotees. The Paradise Club Med offers 300 rooms, newly refurbished with white tile floors and wicker and rattan furnishings, set amid tropical gardens, extending across the island from oceanside to harborside. The clubhouse and pool were once part of a lavish private estate. Informality, French flair, and Bahamian flavor mark the nonstop activities, sports, and entertainment, with special emphasis on "Intensive Tennis." There are 20 Har-True surface courts, nine lighted for night play; instructors; lessons, and ball machines—all free to guests. Other sports include boating and deep-sea fishing expeditions. All-inclusive packages booked direct or through a travel agent.

Yoga Retreat. *Inexpensive.* Box N–7550, Nassau; tel. 326–2902. Swami Vishnu Devananda's rustic retreat offers 35 rooms and cottages with spartan furnishings and contemplative lifestyle. Swimming pool, tennis, private beach. Vegetarian dining only. No credit cards.

APARTMENT HOTELS. Most apartment-rental complexes offering short-term vacation leases operate as apartment hotels, with a clubhouse or dining room, a central pool, and maid service.

Cable Beach

Cable Beach Manor. *Moderate.* Box N–8333, Nassau; tel. 327–7784/5 or through BRS. Thirty-three unpretentious studio, one-, and two-bedroom apartments with kitchens, within walking distance of all Cable Beach attractions and shopping center. All apartments are air-conditioned and have daily maid service. Nicely landscaped grounds, swimming pool, and small private beach. Casual atmosphere—a favorite of families for decades.

Casuarinas Apartment Hotel. *Moderate.* Box N–4016, Nassau; tel. 327–7921/2 or through BRS. Family-owned casual resort with personalized Bahamian service. 74 modern studio, two-room, and three-room apartments and townhouses for up to six people, all air-conditioned with daily maid service. Excellent native cooking at popular *Round House* and *Albrions,* located in the hotel annex across the street. Pool with whirlpool, minipool for children, small private beach.

Henrea Carlette Apartments. *Moderate.* Box N–4227, Nassau; tel. 327–7801 or through BRS. Attractive new apartment hotel complex one block from the beach offering 20 nicely furnished housekeeping units with kitchens. All are air-conditioned, with maid service, and overlook a courtyard and swimming pool. *Androsia* serves Bahamian specialties.

Ocean Side Manor Suites. *Moderate.* Sun Resorts, Box SS–5505, Nassau; tel. 326–2295 or through BRS. A one- and two-bedroom apartment and townhouse complex opposite a quiet beach at the western side of the island, 2½ miles from the Cable Beach hotel strip. The casual, comfortable, spacious units each have kitchen, dining area, and living room; 15 units cluster around a freshwater pool, and there is a small restaurant.

Orange Hill Beach Inn. *Inexpensive.* Box N–8583, Nassau; tel. 327–7157. On West Bay Street, beyond Cable Beach. 18 pleasantly furnished rooms, studios, and a family-size apartment. For breakfast you might pick your own bananas or oranges in the clubhouse orchard. The small dining room and bar are for guests only. The beach is just across the road. With Nassau International Airport nearby, Orange Hill is convenient for those making overnight connections to a Family Island.

Paradise Island

Villas in Paradise. *Deluxe.* Box SS–6379, Nassau; tel. 326–2998. Thirty one-, two-, and three-bedroom single or duplex villas, some with private swimming pools. All are attractively furnished, well equipped with full kitchens and air-conditioning. Within easy walking distance of all Paradise Island attractions, including the beach, golf course, casino, and shopping center.

Bay View Village. *Expensive.* Box SS–6308, Nassau; tel. 326–2555; or through BRS. A stunning apartment, townhouse, and villa complex located near Harbour Cove on a hillside overlooking Nassau Harbour and Montagu Bay. There are two solar-heated swimming pools, walled tropical gardens, and a night-lighted tennis court. Eighty-six one-, two-, and three-bedroom units, each with air-conditioning, telephones, maid service, full kitchen, dining and living areas, and a bathroom with each bedroom. Each unit has a terrace or patio and overlooks the gardens, the pool, or the sea. Five-minute walk from the golf course, casino, and beautiful beach. Vacation rentals or purchase.

Club Land 'Or. *Expensive.* Box SS–6429, Nassau; tel. 326–2400; in the U.S. 800–446–3850 or through BRS. A beautiful apartment complex overlooking the Paradise Island Lagoon amid tropical greenery. Seventy-one attractively furnished apartments have full kitchens and two separate sleeping areas for up to four adults, with terrace or patio overlooking the gardens, the pool, or the lagoon. Within easy walking distance of beach, golf, tennis, and casino. *The Blue Lagoon* serves fine seafood specialties, and there is a relaxing lounge with entertainment. Available for vacation rentals or time share purchase.

Outside Nassau

Paradise Manor Suites. *Deluxe.* Sun Resorts, Box SS–5505, Nassau; tel. 326–2295; or through BRS. An attractive new apartment complex just minutes from the beach and casino. One-, two-, and three-bedroom, town-house-style apartments with kitchens and living rooms are arranged in two-story buildings clustered around two swimming pools.

Sunrise Beach Club and Villas. *Deluxe.* Box SS–6519, Nassau; tel. 326–2678. Stunning new one-bedroom townhouses, two-bedroom apartments, and three-bedroom villas set in tropical gardens with pools and waterfall. The owners are European, the styling Mediterranean. Overlooks two miles of beach. Ideal for families. Vacation rental or time-share purchase.

Orchard Garden Apartments. *Inexpensive.* Box N–1514, Nassau; tel. 323–1297 or 325–9250; or through BRS. Twenty-two rooms in cottages and apartments clustered around a central swimming pool and set in two acres of trees and gardens. Located off East Bay Street on Village Road, near old Fort Montagu and Fort Montagu Beach. Rooms are spacious and clean, with kitchenettes, air-conditioning, and telephone.

TIME SHARING. Studios, one-, two-, and three-bedroom units available by the week, month, or longer for time-share purchase or vacation rental.

Colony Club Resort. Box SS–5420, Nassau; tel. 325–7405 or 325–4824. Located on St. Albans Drive off West Bay Street. Twenty studio apartments with kitchen facilities. Bar, pool, beach nearby. Vacation rental or time share.

Guanahani Village. Guanahani Development Ltd., Box N–3223, Nassau; tel. 323–1331 or 327–8469; in Florida 800–432–8257; in the U.S. 800–327–1584. Luxury three-bedroom, 2½-bath apartment units oceanside on Cable Beach. Time share or vacation rental. RCI affiliate.

Sandpiper Resort. New Providence Development Co., Box N–4820, Nassau; tel. 327–4177. In the South Ocean Beach Hotel complex at the southwestern end of New Providence Island. One- and two-bedroom apartments, pool, tennis, golf, private beach.

Westwind II Club. Box 10481, Nassau; tel. 327–7529; in the U.S. 800–253–7772. Attractive oceanside, two-bedroom townhouse units located on Cable Beach near the Cable Beach Hotel and Casino.

For further information on apartment rentals, purchases, or time-sharing opportunities, contact the *Bahamas Real Estate Association,* Box N–8860, Nassau; tel. 325–4942. In the U.S. contact Vacation Home Rentals, 235 Kensington Ave., Norwood, NJ 07648; tel. 201–767–9393.

HOW TO GET AROUND. Metered taxis meet all incoming flights at Nassau International Airport and at the cruise-ship port. There is no bus service to or from the airport. However, visitors booked on package tours that specifically include airport transfers are picked up at the airport by tour-operator buses and transported to their hotel free of charge. Approximate metered taxi rates to hotels are as follows: Cable Beach hotels, $10; downtown Nassau hotels, $14; Paradise Island hotels, $18. On New Providence Island, jitney service is available between residential areas, hotels, and downtown Nassau. These are inexpensive, run on a semiregular basis, and can be anything from modern nine-passenger vans to air-conditioned

40-passenger buses or a converted school bus lettered by hand, "Rapit Transid."

Transportation to Paradise Island is by metered taxi, with an additional $2 charge for the bridge toll (no charge exiting Paradise Island) or via water taxis (small motor launches seating up to 200 passengers) that criss-cross the harbor every 10 or 15 minutes during daylight hours for about $3 each way. On Paradise Island there is a round-the-island bus service operating every 20 or 30 minutes, making stops at all hotels and attractions such as the casino, beaches, shopping center, golf course, and Chalk's sea-plane ramp.

In addition to the public transportation listed above, many hotels offer regularly scheduled, complimentary bus service (or water-taxi service) to downtown Nassau and Bay Street shopping. Car rentals are available through most hotel desks or at the following locations: *Avis Rent-A-Car,* at the airport, tel. 327–7121; Cable Beach and Nassau, tel. 322–2889; in Paradise Island, tel. 326–2061. *Budget Rent-A-Car,* at the airport, tel. 327–7405/6. *Hertz,* at the airport, tel. 327–8684; Cable Beach, tel. 327–6866. *National Car Rental,* at the airport, tel. 327–7301; at Sheraton British Colonial, tel. 325–3716; at Cable Beach, tel. 327–6000. Car-rental rates average $50–$85 per day, $260–$545 per week, plus gas, depending on type of car, equipment, and season. A deposit of $150 is required with the rental of each car. Insurance is available at all rental locations and is strongly recommended. There are several local agencies that tend to have lower rates. Check them out in the Bahamas Yellow Pages.

Motor scooters are available at many hotels—check with your front desk. Average rental for motor scooters is approximately $30 per day and $20 per half-day, including insurance. Crash helmets are mandatory and included in rental.

TOURIST INFORMATION SERVICES. The Bahamas Ministry of Tourism operates information booths in the arrivals section (tel. 327–6833) and the departure section (tel. 327–6782) of Nassau International Airport; at Prince George Wharf cruise-ship port, tel. 325–9155; at Rawson Square on Bay Street, tel. 326–9781; and at Fort Charlotte, tel. 322–2274. Ministry of Tourism headquarters is located at the Market Plaza (Strawmarket) on Bay Street, tel. 322–7500. The Nassau/Paradise Island Promotion Board has its headquarters in Hotel House on West Bay Street, tel. 322–8381. All locations offer a wide range of colorful brochures, maps, rate sheets covering all hotels for summer and winter seasons, and information on what to do and sights to see, including participation in the popular "People to People" program. For sources of information closer to home, see the "Tourist Information Services" section in *Facts at Your Fingertips.*

SPECIAL EVENTS. *Bahamas Blue Water Run.* Annual half-marathon event with both men's and women's divisions, attracting a large field of international runners. Sponsored by the Bahamas Striders Road Running Club and usually held in early December.

Bahamas Grand Prix. International powerboat race pitting European and U.S. racing drivers in Formula One competition, held annually in Nassau Harbour on New Providence Island. Spectator viewing is excellent along the lake shores, and competition is keen for top prizes in this National Powerboat Association–sanctioned series, usually in mid-December, sometimes earlier in the autumn.

Fox Hill Day. An old-fashioned country fair held in one of the oldest settlements on New Providence Island, about six miles from downtown Nassau. Look for down-home Bahamian cooking, arts-and-crafts stalls, and marvelous gospel singing, as this early slave settlement celebrates Emancipation Day a week later than the rest of the Bahamas. Held annually on the second Tuesday in August. Emancipation Day is a public holiday celebrated on the first Monday of August each year.

Goombay Summer Festival and Discovery Season. The annual summer and autumn festivals feature special social, cultural, and sporting events scheduled every day of the week from June 1 to mid-December. In Nassau, special events include: beach parties, boat cruises, and Bahamian cookouts; golf and tennis tournaments; racquetball, squash, and volleyball competitions; sailing, windsurfing, and diving; native fashion shows, street theater, dance troupes, and art fairs; guided walking tours, Government House tea parties, miniature Junkanoo parades, and goombay music festivals; along with discount coupons for many Nassau attractions including shopping, restaurants, nightclub shows, tours, and sightseeing attractions. Events are held all around the island and all visitors are invited to attend.

International Windsurfing Regatta. Held annually along Cable Beach, with headquarters at the Nassau Beach Hotel. The regatta attracts professional and amateur windsurfers from around the world, competing for cash prizes, and awards. Held in early January.

Junkanoo. A 200-year-old festival based on the dance, music, and mask traditions of African slaves in the New World, Junkanoo was once celebrated throughout the West Indies but survives only in the Bahamas. Two separate Junkanoo Parades are held annually, the first on December 26 (Boxing Day) and the second on New Year's Day. Bay Street in Nassau is the scene of the most colorful and extravagant masquerades, although smaller versions are held on many Bahamian islands at holiday time each year. Tens of thousands of Bahamians and delighted visitors turn out to watch the Junkanoos parade in wildly imaginative and utterly unique fringed-paper costumes, accompanied by the primitive, pulsating beat of goatskin drums, lignum vitae sticks, shak-shak gourds, tin whistles, brass bugles, and clanging cowbells. Hundreds of men, women, and children don costumes and "rush" to the age-old rhythm, and organized groups vie for top prizes awarded to the most ingenious, elaborate, and unusual costumes. Parades begin just before dawn, and prizes are awarded by 9:00 in the morning, although the revelry lasts most of the day.

Southern Ocean Racing Conference. For half a century the last two races of the prestigious international yacht racing annual series have been held in Bahamian waters off Nassau. Held in late February, the Miami-Nassau Race and the Nassau Cup Race are sponsored by the Nassau Yacht Club. Some of the world's most famous yachts and skippers participate, and viewing is excellent along the shoreline of Nassau Harbour and Montagu Bay.

Supreme Court Assizes. Pomp and pageantry in the British colonial tradition mark the formal opening of the quarterly Supreme Court sessions. Ceremonies are held in Parliament Square on the second Wednesday in January and the first Wednesdays in April, July, and October.

Student Getaway Program. Every spring from March through April, Nassau and Paradise Island attract thousands of students on spring break with a series of fun-filled free (or inexpensive) events scheduled daily, such as beach picnics, boat cruises, sports tournaments, fishing and diving trips, and more. To participate students must have an official student I.D. card.

TOURS. A variety of interesting tours is available on the island, with a wide range of activities included. Some of the many possibilities are sightseeing tours of the city and the island; tours to the gardens and nature centers; glass-bottom boat tours to the sea gardens, via motor launch or a Hollywood-style submarine; sailing expeditions to offshore cays for beach-party barbecues; sunset and moonlight cruises with dinner and drinks; and nightlife tours to casino cabaret shows or nightclubs. Tours may be booked at all hotel desks in Nassau, Cable Beach, and Paradise Island, or directly through the following tour operators, all of which offer air-conditioned cars, vans, or buses, knowledgeable guides, and a variety of tour options: *Happy Tours,* tel. 323–5818; *Playtours,* tel. 322–2931; *Majestic Tours,* tel. 322–2606; and *Bahamas Taxi Union,* tel. 323–4555.

Airplanes may be chartered in Nassau for sightseeing tours and visits to the Family Islands. The following carriers offer charter flights from Nassau International Airport: *Pinders Charter Service,* Box N–10456, Nassau, tel. 327–7320 and *Trans Island Airways,* Box N–291, Nassau, tel. 327–8329 or 327–8777.

Guided Walking Tour. Offered June–mid-Dec., tours usually leave from Prince George Wharf and Parliament Square every day except Friday, at 9:30 and 11 A.M., 1:30 and 3 P.M. Information and reservations, 326–9781 or 326–9772.

Horse-Drawn Surrey. Nassau's quaint "carriages" and friendly drivers take you on a tour of the sights along Bay Street and some of the byways in the old city. Cost for two persons is around $8–$10 a half-hour. For an additional person or longer ride, negotiate the charge with the driver ahead of time. Surreys may be hired at Rawson Square or on Frederick Street just off Bay Street. The horses rest 1–3 P.M., May–Oct.; 1–2 P.M., Nov.–April.

Bacardi Distillery. Located off Adelaide Road on the southern shore of New Providence. Guests are welcomed to the "Visitors Bar," where complimentary Bacardi rum and liqueurs, such as the Bahamas' own Nassau Royale, are served. Open weekdays from 10 A.M. to 4 P.M.

HISTORIC SITES AND BUILDINGS. *Blackbeard's Tower.* The ruins of an old stone tower, located on East Bay Street near Fox Hill Road. The ruins command a fine view over Montagu Harbour, Paradise Island, and the offshore cays. The tower is reputed to have been a lookout for the notorious pirate Edward Teach, better known as Blackbeard.

Nassau Public Library. At the south end of Parliament Square, facing Shirley Street, there is an interesting octagonal building that was built as the Nassau Gaol (prison) in 1799. In 1879 it was converted to a library, and since then has served as the main branch of the Bahamas' public library system. The library offers a fine collection of historic documents, prints, and early newspapers.

Water Tower. The highest point on the island of New Providence, located adjacent to Fort Fincastle, at the top of the Queen's Staircase (Elizabeth Ave.). The 126-foot tower rises 216 feet above sea level, and offers a superb panoramic view of the city and the harbor. Observation platform reached by stairs or elevator. Admission charge is 50¢ per person.

Christ Church Cathedral. Located at King and George streets in downtown Nassau. Built in 1837, and since 1861 the seat of the Anglican Bishop.

St. Andrew's. Located at Duke and Frederick streets in downtown Nassau. The Presbyterian *kirk* was built in 1810.

St. Matthew's. Nassau's oldest church, built by Loyalists in 1800. This Anglican church is surrounded by an interesting old cemetery, dating back to the Loyalist era. Located off of East Bay Street, near the Paradise Island Bridge.

St. Francis Xavier. Nassau's oldest Roman Catholic church, built in 1885. The priory (priest's residence) next door is known as Dunmore House, and was built by the Royal Governor in 1787. It served as the residence of governors until Government House was completed in 1803, and from 1829 to 1893 it was the officers' quarters for the West Indian Regiment stationed in Nassau, until it was purchased by the church for use as a priory. Located on Delancey at West Street near downtown Nassau.

St. Augustine's Monastery. Built in 1946 by Father Jerome, famed in Bahamian history as "The Hermit of Cat Island." It is the home of Benedictine monks, an imposing Romanesque structure surrounded by lovely gardens. Located near Fox Hill Road and Bernard Road, off East Bay Street.

Fort Charlotte. Largest of Nassau's forts, built by Lord Dunmore in 1788. The fort, located at Chippingham Road off West Bay Street, overlooks the western end of Nassau Harbour. It offers a moat, ramparts, battlements, ancient cannon, and an intricate system of underground passages and dungeons.

Fort Fincastle. Located high on a hill overlooking Nassau Harbour, the fort was built by Lord Dunmore in 1793. The fort is partially in ruins but offers interesting old guns, a splendid view, and whimsical architecture—it was built in the shape of a ship's prow. It is reached via Elizabeth Avenue or the Queen's Staircase, and is adjacent to the Water Tower.

Fort Montagu. Nassau's oldest and smallest fortification, built in 1741 to guard the eastern approach to Nassau Harbour. In 1776 it was occupied for two weeks by the new American Navy, sent by George Washington to seize His Majesty's cannon and powder in the forts at New Providence.

Government House. The official residence of the governor general. Begun in 1801 and completed in 1803, the mansion is a fine example of British colonial architecture, with strong influence from the southern colonies in America, imported by Loyalists who fled the American Revolution. Splendid tropical gardens, an imposing 12-foot statue of Christopher Columbus, and the Changing of the Guard ceremony at 10 A.M. every other Saturday make Government House a top tourist attraction. A private residence ordinarily closed to the public, it is the site of a "tea party" at 4 P.M. on the last Friday of each month; to participate, see the social hostess at your hotel or call 326–5371. The tropical gardens of Government House are the setting for several summer fetes and fairs.

Gregory Arch. The picturesque arch marking the entrance to Grant's Town, an early slave settlement known as Over the Hill. It is located on the ridge overlooking Nassau at the top of Market Street.

Parliament Square. A cluster of pink, colonnaded government buildings dating from 1803, built by nostalgic Loyalists in the southern colonial style of the Carolinas. For more than 180 years, these buildings have served as the home of the House of Assembly, Law Courts, and Legislative Council. At the center of the square is a famous statue of a young Queen Victoria on her throne, dedicated after her death in 1901. Located in the heart of old Nassau, on Bay Street.

Queen's Staircase. An historic flight of 66 steps carved from the limestone cliff by slaves in 1793, leading to Fort Fincastle at the top of the rise. The brick-paved steps rise 102 feet. The landmark received its current name at the turn of the century upon the death of Queen Victoria—there's one step for each year of her reign. Located off Shirley Street at Elizabeth Avenue, near downtown Nassau.

Historic Homes. Many of Nassau's 18th- and 19th-century historic homes have been well preserved as private residences, such as *Addington House,* the home of the Anglican Bishop; *The Hermitage,* home of the Catholic Bishop; *Dunmore House,* the priory for St. Xavier's Roman Catholic church; and such other landmarks as *Jacaranda* and *Cascadilla,* both privately owned. Two notable Bahamian mansions have been converted to small inns and gourmet restaurants and are open to the public. *Graycliff,* located on West Hill Street, dates back to the mid-1700s and is an exceptionally well-preserved example of Georgian colonial architecture. *Buena Vista,* a 200-year-old colonial estate, is set amid five acres of tropical gardens and ancient trees. Located on Delancey Street near St. Xavier's.

PARKS AND GARDENS. *Ardastra Gardens.* Beautiful tropical gardens on Chippingham Road, off West Bay Street, near Fort Charlotte. The unique parade of brilliant pink flamingos, who march and strut to the commands of a drill master, has amused Nassau visitors for decades. Show times are 11 A.M. and 4 P.M., Mon.–Sat. Gardens hours, Mon.–Sat., 9 A.M.–5:30 P.M. Admission: $7.50 adults, $3.50 children.

Botanic Gardens. A showcase of tropical and semitropical flora located off West Bay Street, near Fort Charlotte. 18 acres of flowers, shrubs, and flowering trees and a playground for children. Visiting hours 10 A.M.–4 P.M. daily. Admission: $1 adults, 50¢ children.

Coral World Marine Park. Tel. 328–1036. A new underwater observatory 20 feet beneath the sea allows you to see a living coral reef and reef life without getting wet. Viewing decks, restaurants, and bar. Located off Bay Street, between Cable Beach and downtown Nassau, at Silver Cay. Admission: $12 adults, $8 children.

Royal Victoria Hotel and Gardens. Nassau's oldest hotel, built in 1861, welcomed guests for more than a century until it was closed in the early 1970s. The grounds and gardens are well maintained and offer over 300 species of tropical and subtropical plants. Located on Shirley Street, opposite the Nassau Public Library. Admission free.

Sea Gardens. Beautiful underwater gardens and living reefs with a great variety of tropical fish life, located in Nassau Harbour. Access is via a fleet of small glass-bottom boats, which depart at frequent intervals all day long from the docks between Rawson Square and Prince George Wharf. The waters are crystal-clear and visibility is excellent, making tours to these unique gardens a favorite of visitors for more than a century. Admission: $7.

Versailles Gardens and French Cloister. Located on Paradise Island. Lovely terraced gardens, full of tropical plants and flowering shrubs, stretching across the island from harborside to oceanside. Dotted here and there throughout the gardens are museum-quality statues garnered from the William Randolph Hearst collection. On a rise overlooking the harbor is a beautiful 14th-century French cloister, once an Augustinian monastery in Montrejau, France. Admission free.

Seafloor Aquarium. Located near Fort Charlotte on West Bay Street and Chippingham Road. The aquarium is a showcase of Bahamian underwater reef and fish life, with huge tanks offering fine viewing of exotic species. On the grounds, there is an interesting little workshop that produces handcrafted jewelry made from the tortoiseshell, conch, and whelk shells. Open 9 A.M.–5:30 P.M., Mon.–Sat. Aquatic shows featuring trained sea lions and porpoises are offered at 10:30 A.M., 12:30, 2:30, and 4:30 P.M. Admission: $7 adults, $3 children.

The Retreat. Village Road between Shirley Street and Bernard Road. Tel. 323–1317 or 323–2848. An 11-acre tropical garden with a fine collection of rare palms; headquarters of the Bahamas National Trust. Open Mon.–Fri., 9 A.M.–5 P.M. Admission free. Guided tours $2 (Tues., Wed., Thurs.).

BEACHES. Most of the great hotels on the island are spread along private beaches, but there are several excellent public beaches around the island, all without admittance charge except the famed Paradise Beach on Paradise Island. Among the best beaches are: *Adelaide Beach,* on the southern shore of the island, near Adelaide Village. *Caves Beach,* on West Bay Street, beyond the Cable Beach hotels and near Blake Road, which leads to Nassau International Airport. Nearby are large cave formations reputed to have been pirates' hideaways. *Fort Montagu Beach,* on East Bay Street near Fort Montagu, a popular gathering spot for Bahamians, especially on Sunday afternoons, when there's a good "rake and scrape" band. There's a good beach bar serving juicy burgers and frosty beers. *Goodman's Bay,* on West Bay Street, just before the Cable Beach hotel strip, popular with Bahamians for picnics and cookouts on weekends and public holidays. *Paradise Beach,* the Bahamas' most famous beach, which stretches for more than a mile on the western end of Paradise Island. Admittance charge is $3, which includes a welcome drink, towels, use of changing rooms and lockers. *Western Esplanade,* also known as Lighthouse Beach, sweeps for several miles along the shore from the Sheraton British Colonial Hotel westward along West Bay Street. There are changing rooms and concession stands.

PARTICIPANT SPORTS. For the resort vacationer in Nassau, Cable Beach, and Paradise Island, there is an almost unlimited selection of sporting activity for beginners through experts. Rates are subject to change.

Boating and Fishing. The following marinas offer deep-sea fishing charters by the day or half-day, and sailboat charters by the day, week, or longer: *East Bay Yacht Basin.* Bare-boat charter sailboats offered at an average charter rate of $150–$200 per day. The marina offers 25 slips. Box SS–6394, Nassau. Tel. 322–3754. *Nassau Harbour Club.* Deep-sea fishing charters arranged, ranging from $175 per half day to $300 per day, with bait, tackle, and crew provided; 66 slips. Box SS–6379, Nassau. Tel. 323–1771. *Nassau Yacht Haven.* Deep-sea charter fishing boats available, complete with bait, tackle, and crew. Rates average $250 per half day and $400 per full day. Dock facilities include 120 slips. Box SS–5693, Nassau. Tel. 322–8173. *Hurricane Hole Marina* on Paradise Island. Deep-sea fishing charters available at varied rates depending on size of boat and length of charter; 46 slips. Box N–1216, Nassau. Tel. 326–3601.

Diving. There are many excellent dive sites offshore on the reefs surrounding the island of New Providence, easily reached on dive excursions for beginners and experts offered by several operators who serve resorts on Cable Beach, in Nassau, and on Paradise Island. The following offer one or more dive trips daily, with rates beginning at about $50 per trip. Many also offer certification and instruction. *Bahama Divers Ltd.* Two dive trips daily, from 9 A.M. to noon and 2 to 5 P.M. Sites include drop-offs, wrecks, coral reefs, coral gardens, ocean blue hole. Located on East Bay Street, Box N–5004, Nassau. Tel. 326–5644 or 322–8431. *Peter Hughes Dive South Ocean* at the Divi Bahamas Beach Resort. Two dive boats. Dive sites include drop-offs, coral gardens, shallow reefs. Three dive trips scheduled daily at 9 A.M., 1 P.M., and 7 P.M. Box N–8191, Nassau. Tel. 326–4391. *Sun Divers.* Daily dive trips scheduled to shallow reefs, deep reefs, and drop-offs. Two dive boats. Headquartered at the Sheraton British Colonial Hotel. Box N–10728, Nassau. Tel. 322–3301. *Coral Harbour Divers.* Daily trips to reefs, caves, and wreck sites off the western end of the island; four dive boats. At Orange Hill Beach Inn, Box SS–5635, Nassau. Tel. 326–4171. *Dive Dive Dive Ltd.* Daily trips to reefs, walls, wreck sites; 2 dive boats. At Smuggler's Rest Resort, Box N–8050, Nassau. Tel. 326–1143. *Underwater Wonderland.* Unique underwater adventure for nonswimmers and nondivers. Walk on the ocean floor amid coral reefs and sea gardens without getting your hair wet! Using sealed diving helmets, linked to an air supply from a boat, Captain Chris Hartley personally conducts twice-daily cruises and "undersea walks" (except Sun.). Tour includes half-day cruise aboard the 57-foot yacht *Pied Piper.* Rates are $28 per person, departures at 9:30 A.M. and 1:30 P.M. At Nassau Yacht Haven, East Bay Street. Tel. 322–8234.

Golf. There are four excellent 18-hole championship golf courses on the island. All are open for play by the general public except the Lyford Cay Golf Club, which is open only to members and their guests. Greens fees average $20–$25 for 18 holes, $10 for 9 holes. Some hotel courses are free to guests. Golf cart rentals are $20–$25; club rentals are $10–$12. *Cable Beach Golf Club.* Located opposite the new Cable Beach Hotel and Casino. Par 72, 18 holes, with a restaurant, pro shop, and clubhouse. Box N–3026, Nassau. Tel. 327–8231. *Paradise Island Golf Club.* Par 72, 18-hole championship, oceanside course at the eastern end of Paradise Island. Restaurant and pro shop. Box N–4777, Nassau. Tel. 326–3925. *Divi Bahamas Beach Golf Club.* Located adjacent to Divi Bahamas Beach Resort, on the southwestern end of New Providence. A USGA-rated, 18-hole, par 72 course. Facilities include a lounge, bars, restaurant, and pro shop. Box N–8191, Nassau. Tel. 326–4391.

Horseback Riding. Available on the southwestern shore near Coral Harbour, at *Happy Trails Stable.* Rate for 1½-hour trail rides is $30, which includes transportation to and from your hotel. Experienced guide accompanies riders. Tel. 326–1820.

Parasailing. Exciting flights over the ocean waters along the shore of Cable Beach and Paradise Island. Parasailors are harnessed to a parachute, then take off from a special raft, towed by a speedboat. The following hotels offer parasailing: *Nassau Beach Hotel* on Cable Beach, $25 per ride, $40 for a double ride. Tel. 327–7711. *Cable Beach Hotel,* $25 for five minutes, $40 for 10 minutes. Tel. 327–7070. *The Grand Hotel* on Paradise Island, $20 for 7–10 minutes. Tel. 326–2011. *Paradise Island Resort & Casino,* $25 for five minutes, $40 for ten minutes. Tel. 326–3000.

Tennis. The following hotels and resorts have tennis courts open to hotel guests and visitors. Rates run $2–$8 per hour; court use may be free to guests.

Cable Beach: *Ambassador Beach Hotel.* Eight asphalt courts, four lighted for night play. Lessons available. Tel. 327–8231. *Cable Beach Hotel and Casino.* Five clay and five all-weather courts lighted for night play, three indoor squash courts, three racquetball courts, and pro shop. Tel. 327–6000. *Cable Beach Inn.* Two hard-surface courts. Lessons available, including group tennis clinics. Tel. 327–7341. *Nassau Beach Hotel.* Nine Flexipave surface courts, six lighted for night play. Lessons available. Tel. 327–7711.

Nassau: *Nassau Squash and Racquet Club.* Located on Independence Drive. Three Har-Tru surface courts, plus squash and racquetball courts. Open seven days a week. Tel. 322–3882. *Royal Bahamian.* 2 Flexipave courts, lighted. Lessons available. Tel. 327–6400. *Sheraton British Colonial Hotel.* Three hard-surface courts, lighted for night play. Lessons available. Tel. 322–3301. *Atlantis Hotel.* Two asphalt-surface courts. Tel. 323–4481. *Divi Bahamas Beach Resort.* Four asphalt-surface courts, two lighted; ball machine. Tel. 326–4391.

Paradise Island: *Britannia Towers.* Nine hard-surface courts. Tel. 326–3000. (Paradise Island Resort and Casino.) *Club Mediterranee.* 20 Har-Tru courts, nine lighted for night play; ball machines, video replay machine; lessons available. Tel. 326–2640. *Holiday Inn.* Four asphalt-surface courts, two lighted for night play (reservations only). Lessons available. Tel. 326–2101. *Loews Harbour Cove.* Two asphalt-surface courts lighted for night play, lessons available. Tel. 326–2561. *Ocean Club.* Nine Har-Tru courts, four lighted for night play; lessons available. Tel. 326–2501. *Paradise Towers.* Three asphalt-surface courts, lighted for night play. (Paradise Island Resort and Casino.) Tel. 326–2000. *Sheraton Grand Hotel.* Four asphalt-surface courts lighted for night play. Tel. 326–2011.

Windsurfing. The following hotels offer windsurfing: *Ambassador Beach,* $11 per hour. Tel. 327–8231. *Cable Beach Hotel,* $12 first hour, $8 per additional hour; lessons $35 per hour. Tel. 327–7070. *Paradise Island Resort & Casino,* $25 per hour; lessons free. Tel. 326–3000.

Boat Cruises. One of the highlights of most Nassau vacations is a boat cruise through the harbor and to some of the lovely offshore cays. Many small, glass-bottom boats are available at oceanfront hotels and from the docks and marinas, usually offering one- to two-hour tours of the sea gardens and reefs that fringe Nassau's shores. Rates average $5–$7 per person. Other longer and more elaborate cruises of the surrounding waters and cays are also available, many including beach parties, picnics, and entertainment. They may be booked through the tour desk at your hotel or directly through the operator. Several examples follow, with approximate rates. All rates quoted are subject to change.

M/V *Calypso.* New 80-foot catamaran offers full-day excursions from Nassau Harbour to beautiful Blue Lagoon Island, a private secluded cay off Paradise Island. The *Calypso* has three decks, native bands for dancing, and snack bars on board. Day excursions are $35 per person. Dinner cruises offered Mon., Wed., and Sat. at $30 per person; moonlight cruises offered on Fri., 8 P.M. to midnight. Tel. 326–3577.

El Galleon. Replica of an 18th-century Spanish galleon offers day cruises ($20 per person) to an island for swimming, snorkeling, and a picnic lunch; dinner cruises ($35 per person) with music and dancing. After

11 P.M. the ship becomes a dockside disco ($15 admission includes two drinks). Departs from a Bay Street dock (behind Victor's Department Store). Tel. 328–7772.

J&M Sports Fishing & Cruises. Fishing and sightseeing cruises by the day or week. Choice of three boats: 50' *Hatteras* sleeps six, with captain, mate, and cook; 33' *Bertram,* sleeps two, with captain and mate; and 27' *Sport Fisherman,* accommodates six, with captain. Rates vary by length of cruises and boat chosen. Deveaux and Bay Street. Tel. 325–2871 or 324–2178.

Keewatin Sailing Cruise. Daily cruises aboard a 56-foot *Alden* schooner, which departs from the British Colonial and Loews Harbour Cove docks around 9:30 A.M., returns around 4 P.M. Cruise includes sailing and a two-hour beach party with picnic lunch at lovely Rose Island off Paradise Island. $30 per person. Tel. 325–1821.

Nautilus Cruise. A unique 97-foot glass-bottom submarine, built originally for the James Bond movie *Thunderball,* cruises Nassau Harbour and nearby sea gardens, reefs, and wrecks. Viewing is superb through individual underwater glass portholes, although the ship does not submerge. Departs John Alfred Wharf at Deveaux Street (next to Captain Nemo's Restaurant) at 9:30 and 11:30 A.M. and 1:30 and 3:30 P.M. Rate is $15 per person. Dinner cruises depart at 6 P.M., cost $25 per person. Moonlight cruises, priced at $20 per person, offer excellent viewing with underwater lights. Tel. 325–2871.

Tropic Bird. One of the largest catamarans on the Atlantic offers daily cruises from Prince George Wharf to a lovely Paradise Island beach. Goombay music and beach picnic. Cost for the three-hour cruise is $15 per person. Departure at 10:15 A.M. Tel. 322–2931.

SPECTATOR SPORTS. Amateur, professional, and semipro teams compete in baseball, basketball, softball, cricket, soccer, rugby, racing regattas, and other sports. The local daily newspapers give the times and locations. Clifford Park near Fort Charlotte on West Bay Street affords good spectator facilities for cricket, soccer, and rugby matches (weekends).

MUSIC, DANCE, AND STAGE. Nassau has a sophisticated international population, and many Bahamians and foreign residents are involved in local musical and theatrical societies that put on amateur and semiprofessional productions. Other organizations promote performances by guest artists from abroad, often as fund-raising events for charitable organizations. Among the active groups on the island are the *Nassau Music Society* and the *Bahamas Music Society,* both of which sponsor guest artists. Amateur theatrical groups include the *Bahamas Drama Circle, Nassau Players,* and the *Bahamas School of Theatre;* amateur dance groups include the *National School of Dance* and the *Nassau Civic Ballet.* Choral groups are also popular in the capital city, as well as gospel singers and choirs. Among these are the *Diocesan Chorale, Lucayan Chorale, Chamber Singers, Nassau Operatic Society,* and the *Renaissance Singers.* In addition, Bahamian dialect comedy has had a successful revival in recent years, with *James Catalyn and Friends,* an excellent professional troupe, offering regularly scheduled performances. All locally produced and guest performances are well publicized on the island through newspapers, flyers, and placards placed at hotel desks. Many performances are held at the 50-year-old, newly renovated *Dundas Centre for the Performing Arts* on Mackey Street in Nassau, tel. 322–2728.

SHOPPING. The prestigious international business magazine *Forbes* recently published an article which claimed that the two cities in the world with the best buys on watches were Hong Kong and Nassau. The article could have mentioned several other items available in Nassau that belong on any world-class "best buys" list—German and Japanese cameras and optics, French perfumes bottled and packaged in France, all the great names and patterns of European china and crystal, Scottish cashmeres, Irish linens, and Colombian emeralds (which, if uncut, unpolished, or unmounted enjoy an unusual duty-free entrance status to the U.S.). There are hundreds of shops throughout New Providence that offer a broad selection of all these items, but most are clustered along an eight-block stretch of Bay Street in old Nassau or spill over onto a few side streets downtown. Some of the most elegant jewelry and clothing stores have branches in the shopping arcades or the large oceanside hotels on Cable Beach and Paradise Island. The shops that follow are all located on Bay Street or within a block or two on the side streets in downtown. Savings on many big-ticket items average 20 to 50 percent over identical purchases in the U.S. and Canada. However, if you plan to make a major purchase, it is always wise to check out the prices back home before you begin your vacation. Store hours are 9 A.M. to 5 P.M. Monday through Saturday, although some shops close at noon one day a week, usually Thursday or Friday. Only the Strawmarket is open seven days a week. Most shops accept major credit cards.

Bay Street

Barry's. British woolens, sweaters, suitings for men and women. Tel. 322–3118.

Bernards. An extensive collection of china and crystal. Agents for such lines as Wedgwood in china; Lalique in crystal. Also carries Ernest Borel and Seiko watches and gift items. Tel. 322–2841.

John Bull. The longest established and largest camera store in the Bahamas, noted for excellent buys on watches. In cameras, Konica, Nikon, Olympus, Hasselblad, Minolta, and Vivitar. In watches, included are Rolex, Concord, Corum, Omega, Pulsar, Longines, and Seiko. There's also an extensive selection of gold and silver jewelry and very good buys on saltwater or freshwater pearls under the name Adeana Creations (manufactured in the Bahamas, and duty-free to the U.S.). Three shops on Bay Street and on Paradise Island. Tel. 322–3329.

Carib Jewelers. Fine china, crystal, and watches. Tel. 322–1239.

Colombian Emeralds. Fine investment-quality gems unmounted or mounted in original settings, an excellent selection of gold and silver jewelry, plus Girard-Perregeaux and Seiko watches. Certified appraisals and a U.S. service office. The shop also has a Royal Doulton boutique. Tel. 322–2201.

Discount Warehouse. Good buys in jewelry set with precious and semi-precious stones, gold and silver jewelry. Best buys are on coral and conch-shell costume jewelry made on the premises. Watches. A money-back guarantee if you can buy identical items in Nassau for less. Tel. 325–1522.

Francis Peek. Fine antiques and collectibles. Outstanding collection of Vista Alegre hand-painted birds and Herend china from Hungary. Tel. 322–2332.

Gold Ltd. Direct importers of fine gold jewelry sold by weight. Prices vary daily with the London gold fixings. Tel. 322–1851.

Gold Mine. Imports gold and silver jewelry items which are sold by weight based on daily quotations. Additional items include gemstones of investment quality and gift items. Tel. 322–4957.

Gold and Silversmiths Ltd. A fine line of handcrafted Caribbean jewelry in gold and silver by Y de Lima of Trinidad. Tel. 322–8651.

Greenfire Emeralds Ltd. Specializes in cut, uncut, polished, and unpolished emeralds, and exquisite handcrafted jewelry designs and settings. Branch stores in the Paradise Towers and Grand Hotel on Paradise Island. Tel. 326–6564.

Island Shop. "Everything Under the Sun," one of Nassau's oldest and best-known shops. Men's, women's, and children's fashions, swimwear, and sportswear, including cashmeres, lambswool, and Shetland sweaters. Also carries a line of cameras and watches. The shop offers the largest selection of books by Bahamians and about the Bahamas found anywhere in the islands. Tel. 322–4183.

Johnson Brothers Ltd. The Bahamas' oldest and finest designers and manufacturers of conch, whelk, tortoiseshell, and coral jewelry. Superb handcrafted items in all price ranges. Sold at their Bay Street shop and in other fine stores throughout the Bahamas. Tel. 322–4098.

Lightbourns Pharmacy. Serving Nassau shoppers since 1889, with the largest selection of imported designer French perfumes in Nassau. Beauty products by Dior, Orlane, and Stendahl; Badedas and Roger & Gallet soaps. Tel. 322–2095.

Little Switzerland. A new arrival to the Bahamas—but a favorite store in many parts of the Caribbean. Several branches on and off Bay Street. Top-quality watches and expensive gift items. Tel. 322–8502.

Mademoiselle. Another Nassau "landmark," offering a fine selection of men's, women's, and children's fashions including an Androsia boutique (handcrafted batiks from the island of Andros). A wide selection of moderate to expensive gift items, jewelry, and watches. Branches on Cable Beach and Paradise Island. Tel. 322–1404.

Nassau Shop. One of Nassau's oldest and largest department stores, with an excellent collection of clothing for men, women, and children. Watch brands include the Piaget Polo, Baume & Mercier, Lanvin, and Concord. Broad range of Irish linens, European leather belts and bags, gold and silver jewelry, plus hundreds of souvenir items in all price ranges. Tel. 322–8405.

Nomad Ltd. A new shop in an old Bahamian home at the eastern end of Bay Street. An all-Bahamian line of hand-printed and painted casuals including T-shirts, beach bags, and accessories. Featuring an expanding collection of the finest Bahamian art and craft work. Tel. 325–3541.

Perfume Bar. All the great names in designer and imported perfumes. One-stop perfume shopping, as prices vary little from store to store. Several branches. Tel. 322–8400.

Pipe of Peace. "World's most complete tobacconist" and one of Nassau's best-known shops for half a century. Also offers a good line of watches, cameras, and stereos. Branches at Paradise Village, Harbour Cove. Tel. 325–2022.

Relax-Sir. For the best-dressed men around town, European designer fashions in shirts, slacks, leisure, swimwear, and shoes. Tel. 322–2422.

Strawmarket. One of the world's largest strawmarkets, and the action spot of old Nassau. Hundreds of straw ladies hawk their wares, amid tens of thousands of brilliantly decorated and magically woven hats and bags, baskets and totes, mats and slippers, wall hangings and dolls, and more. You'll also find queen conch shells, king helmet shells, sea fans, and corals of every shape from the Bahamian sea. Look for necklaces and bracelets strung with pea shells, sharks' teeth, and bright beans, berries, or pods; primitive African print dashikis and shirts, skirts, and the marvelous "Seven-Way Calypso Dress" in matching fabric and prints, all fashioned and sewn by the island women. Or seek out original oils and prints by local artists and fearsome wood carvings, reminders of the Bahamian-African heritage. Bargain with the vendors—all prices are negotiable, and the straw ladies love to bargain. The Strawmarket is open from early morning to early evening, seven days a week, and it is located in Nassau's Market Plaza on Bay Street.

Solomon's Mines. Another classic Nassau shop known for decades to Bay Street shoppers, offering the largest assortment of china, crystal, jewelry, and French perfumes in the Bahamas. Tel. 322–8324.

Treasure Box. A jewelry boutique famous for an exclusive line of exotic elephant-hair and 18-karat rolled-gold rings, bracelets, and earrings. Also offered are a beautiful collection of Chinese cloisonné accessories, cultured pearls, coral, jade, and conch jewelry. Tel. 322–1662.

Treasure Traders. A wonderful collection of crystal, Lladró figurines from Spain, the Studio-Line by Rosenthal, as well as Austrian Swarovski pieces. Tel. 322–8521.

T-Shirts Unlimited. That says it all. Two shops on Bay Street and a third shop on Marlborough Street. Tel. 322–1336.

Vanité. Original Hummel figurines and dolls. Anri Toriart, Schatz clocks, music boxes, children's gifts. Tel. 322–2594.

British Colonial Arcade
(At the west end of Bay Street)

Black Coral and . . . One of Nassau's finest art studios, featuring stunning black-coral sculptures and gold and diamond jewelry by renowned international sculptor Bernard K. Passman. Tel. 325–3364, 325–4538.

Optique Shoppe. Designer eyeglasses and sunglasses. Eye examinations, one-day service on prescription glasses and repairs. Tel. 325–2386.

Trader Vic's. British and Irish woolen sweaters, cashmere scarves and shawls by Dalkeith, Lyle & Scott, Braemar. Tel. 322–1719.

Charbay Plaza
(Near Rawson Square, on harbor side of Bay Street)

Galaxy Shoes. Men's and women's imported European footwear and leather accessories. Tel. 325–2443.

Jade Dolphin. Nassau's newest department store, with an extensive collection of Scottish cashmeres, clan plaids, Irish linen, jewelry, and cameras. A broad selection of watches. Tel. 325–7554, 325–8750.

International Bazaar
(Arcade linking Bay Street and the harbor)

Candy Bar. Finest candies and chocolates from around the world, homemade Bahamian candies and Scottish shortbreads featured. Tel. 322–4466.

Maison Pierre. Men's designer fashions and gift items. Tel. 325–7523.

Patrick's Camera Specialists. 24-hour film processing, camera repairs, and a wide range of cameras and accessories. A branch in the Britannia Beach Hotel. Tel. 325–0851.

Pied Piper. Large selection of gifts and souvenirs, from European chocolates to imported backgammon and chess sets and Citizen watches. Tel. 325–3515.

Off Bay Street

Amanda's, Marlborough Street. Cashmeres by Pringle of Scotland, Ballantyne, and other fine European sweaters, blouses, gloves, stoles, and scarves. In addition, there is a full line of Mary Chess designs. Tel. 322–2707.

Ambrosine, Marlborough Street. One of the most exclusive women's fashion shops in Nassau, with an extensive collection of Italian resort wear. Also on hand are Thai cottons and silks, Bleyle of West Germany pants and jackets, and dozens of gift items. Tel. 322–4205.

Bahamas Fragrances & Cosmetic Factory, Charlotte Street. Made-in-the-Bahamas aloe suntan, after-tan, body lotions, and cosmetics. Tel. 323–8030.

Balmain Antiques, Charlotte Street. One of the world's largest and finest collections of antique prints, maps, and charts of the Bahamas and West Indies. Many of investment quality, and there is no U.S. duty on antiques. Same-day framing by expert craftsmen. Upstairs location, next to Cellar Restaurant. Tel. 323–7421.

Brass and Leather Shop, Charlotte Street. Exclusive agents for prestigious Land luggage, along with other fine leatherware. An extensive collection of English brassware. Two shops on Charlotte Street. Tel. 322–3806.

Caprice, formerly of Nassau and Freeport, now located outside the gates at Lyford Cay. One of Nassau's original and exclusive fashion boutiques catering to some of the world's most elegant women. Tel. 326–4167.

Chez Mizpah, Marlborough Street. Lovely designer boutique featuring women's fashions, sportswear, swimwear, imported lingerie, footwear, makeup, and accessories. Custom fitting and designs available. Tel. 322–8653.

Coin of the Realm, Charlotte Street. A fine collection of investment-grade coins and stamps; mountings for both gold and silver coins, and chains. Exclusive jewelry items. Tel. 322–4862.

Cole's of Nassau, Parliament Street. A favorite fashion shop for Bahamians and visitors alike, with a colorful collection of designer dresses, beachwear, sundresses, and accessories. The shop also offers the famous rattan-handle "Bermuda Bags." Tel. 322–8393.

Harbour View Gifts, Charlotte Street. North on the harbor. A broad range of leather and eelskin goods, tropical resort fashions, porcelain floral arrangements, and many other gift items, including Ravisa watches. Tel. 322–8351.

Impact. Marlborough Street. Contemporary women's fashions by Jeffrey Taylor—some outrageous, some gorgeous—and imports. Tel. 322–3073.

Leather Masters, Bank Lane. Exclusive line of Gucci handbags and leather accessories, plus other fine leather products from Europe. Tel. 322–7697.

The Linen Shop, Parliament Street. Wide selection of Irish linens. The shop also carries Bahama Hand Prints, European silk blouses, Belgian tapestries, hand-embroidered infant's wear, and unique gift items. Tel. 322–4266.

Marlborough Antiques, Marlborough Street. A fine collection of European antiques and Bahamian art. Occasional art exhibitions featuring local artists and an annual exhibition with emphasis on the 500th anniversary in 1992 of Columbus's landing in the Bahamas. Tel. 328–0502.

Mr. Photo. One-hour mechanized film processing. The shop will print your photos on postcards for a unique message to folks back home. Carries a full line of Fuji film. Near the Strawmarket, on the harbor. Tel. 323–7070.

St. Michael Shop, with numerous branches throughout Nassau. These stores sell the merchandise of the London department chain Marks and Spencer.

Scottish Shop, Charlotte Street. Nassau's most complete line of Scottish products including: tartans, clan jewelry, cashmere sweaters, Edinburgh crystal, kilts and skirts, mohair rugs, heraldic plaques. Perthshire paperweights, Peggy Nisbet dolls. Thistle pottery and Kangol hats. Tel. 322–4720.

Sundance Kids, Parliament Street. Imported children's clothing, shoes, accessories. Tel. 322–4136.

Undercover Agents, Frederick and Shirley Streets. Exotic and seductive lingerie from France and Italy. Tel. 323–3755.

Off East Bay Street, Near Paradise Island Bridge

Bahama Hand Prints, Mackey Street. Workshop and showroom for one of the Bahamas' oldest and most famous cottage industries, original silk screen designs on fine cotton blends in fabrics or fashions. Watch the whole process, from design to finished piece, or choose a ready-made item for men, women, or children. There are also many handmade gift items such as tea towels, place mats, tablecloths, pot holders, and more. Located north of Shirley Street, about ¼ mile from the Paradise Island Bridge.

Nassau Glass Art Gallery, Mackey Street. Nassau's largest and most complete art gallery, with works of Bahamian artists on exhibit and for sale, as well as Haitian art and other foreign originals and reproductions in a broad price range. Expert framing, packing, and shipping anywhere in the world. Located on Mackey Street, about ½ mile south of the Paradise Island Bridge. Tel. 322–8165.

RESTAURANTS. Nassau, Cable Beach, and Paradise Island offer a cornucopia of dining pleasures in all price ranges, from down-home Bahamian cooking to haute cuisine, and ambience ranging from candlelight-and-crystal to plastic-and-chrome. There are world-famous dining legends such as *Café Martinique,* a must since James Bond made it famous in *Thunderball,* and Graycliff, where everyone who is anyone wines and dines.

We call $36 and up *Deluxe;* $25–$35 *Expensive;* $15–$24 *Moderate;* and under $15 *Inexpensive* for a three-course meal for one, excluding tip and beverage. Be sure to call ahead for reservations. The following credit card abbreviations are used: AE, American Express; DC, Diners Club; MC, MasterCard; V, Visa.

Cable Beach

Baccarat. *Deluxe.* Tel. 327–6400. The Meridien Royal Bahamian Hotel's superb French restaurant. Expect a name change for the restaurant as the hotel, formerly the Balmoral Beach Hotel, is now operated by Meridien Hotels. Beautiful room, lovely view, lace cloths, and Wedgwood china. Fine wine list, extensive menu of traditional gourmet French dishes. The *mignon de veau saveurs,* a tender cut of veal loin, has a light, slightly sweet sauce with a hint of coconut. Dinner only, jackets suggested. AE, DC, MC, V.

Frilsham House. *Deluxe.* Tel. 327–7711. Nassau Beach Hotel's new gourmet restaurant in an oceanside mansion. Small, intimate dining rooms with Chippendale and Queen Anne furnishings and a terrace overlooking the sea. The fresh fish specials of the day are recommended. Extensive wine list. Jackets requested. AE, DC, MC, V.

Regency Room. *Deluxe.* Tel. 327–6000. Elegance at the lavish new Cable Beach Hotel and Casino, at the top of the four-story atrium lobby. Superb selection of Continental cuisine. Try the crème de papaya soup, mousse of deep-sea scallops in champagne, and entrecôte villette (aged prime steak). Classic wine selection. Dinner only, jackets required. AE, DC, MC, V.

Sol e Mare. *Deluxe.* Tel. 327–6200. Superb Northern Italian specialties in an elegant setting overlooking the sea. Located in the Crystal Palace Casino. Try the veal marsala with fettuccine Alfredo and Italian pastries. Fine Italian and French wines. Dinner only, jackets required. AE, DC, MC, V.

Lobster Pot. *Expensive.* Tel. 327–7711. Fine seafood at the Nassau Beach Hotel. Nautical decor, relaxed setting, indoor or outdoor dining. Specialties include flying fish pie, bouillabaisse carib, and Nassau grouper. Good, reasonable wines. Dinner only. AE, DC, MC, V.

Albrion's. *Moderate.* Tel. 327–7922. At Casuarinas Apartment Hotel, some of the best Bahamian food on Cable Beach. Located across West Bay Street in the new wing, with indoor and outdoor dining, breakfast, lunch, and dinner. Famous dishes include conch creole, pork chops with peas 'n' rice, Eleutheran pineapple, and guava duff. AE, DC, MC, V.

Androsia. *Moderate.* Tel. 327–7801. Bahamian and American dishes in a nautical setting at the Henrea Carlette apartment hotel. Breakfast, lunch, and dinner served daily. Veal Montesquieu, red snapper Vera Cruz, filet mignon Cecelia, and, for dessert, homemade pies and cakes. AE, MC, V.

The Back Stage Deli. *Moderate.* Tel. 327–6200. A New Yorker's delight at the Cable Beach Casino. Thick deli sandwiches of pastrami and corned beef; smoked fish, chopped liver, and other favorites. AE, DC, MC, V.

Pasta Kitchen. *Moderate.* Tel. 327–8231. In the Wyndham Ambassador Beach Hotel. The prettiest casual dining room on Cable Beach; paneled walls, traditional furnishings, small and intimate. Homemade pastas and pizza. Dinner only. Casual dress. AE, MC, V.

Swank Pizza. *Moderate.* Tel. 327–7495. At Cable Beach shopping center; on Woodes Rogers Walk, downtown Nassau; Paradise Island Village; and Oakes Field. Casual atmosphere, friendly service featuring sizzling steaks, seafood, and delicious pizza till the wee hours. (Ever tried conch pizza?) AE, MC.

Traveller's Rest. *Moderate.* Tel. 327–7633. West of Cable Beach, near Gambier Village. Legendary Bahamian cookery, informal indoor-outdoor-oceanside dining. Try the fine turtle steak or conch fritters, and Courage on tap. AE.

Nassau

Buena Vista. *Deluxe.* Tel. 322–2811, 322–4039. Superb nouvelle cuisine in historic old Bahamian house up the hill from Bay Street on Delancey. Creative cookery, attention to detail, and personalized service are hallmarks; rack of lamb, stuffed shrimp, Bahamian lobster, and soft island music are trademarks. Excellent California and European wines. Dine indoors or on the tropical garden terrace. Dinner only, jackets suggested. Closed Sundays.

Graycliff. *Deluxe.* Tel. 322–2796, 325–4832. Magnificent 200-year-old colonial mansion, filled with antiques and English country-house charm. Outstanding Continental and Bahamian menu includes Beluga caviar, French escargots, and foie gras with truffles for starters. Delights are grouper au poivre vert, chateaubriand, and tournedos Rossini, with elegant pastries and flaming coffees for dessert. Wine cellars recognized as the finest in the Caribbean by Relais et Chateaux. Located on the hilltop off Bay Street across from Government House. Open for lunch and dinner. Jackets suggested. AE, DC, MC, V.

Ristorante Da Vinci. *Deluxe.* Tel. 322–2748. Impeccable service with notable Italian and French cuisine. Homemade pastas highlight house specialties of beef, veal, and fresh seafood. Try the veal scallopine or scampi meuniere, topped off with a flambéed dessert and brandied coffee. Soft piano and strings provide background music; candlelight and crystal make for romantic decor. One of the finest wine selections in the Bahamas, priced at $14–$250. Dinner only, jacket required. Located near downtown on West Bay Street. AE, MC, V.

Del Prado. *Expensive.* Tel. 325–0324. Stained-glass windows, a fountain, and international fare prepared to order at the El Greco Hotel on West Bay Street. Gracious service and friendly atmosphere, marked by excellent French and Italian specialties. House favorite is steak Diane flambéed at your table; a variety of Bahamian grouper dishes such as le filet de grouper Normandy, sautéed in a tempting wine sauce. Excellent *carte de vin* with vintage champagnes and French wines. Dinner only, jackets required. AE, DC, MC, V.

La Regata Room. *Expensive.* Tel. 322–8431. Pilot House Hotel at the foot of the Paradise Island Bridge, a traditional gathering spot for yachtsmen and the sport-fishing set (it is just across the street from Nassau Yacht Haven). The atmosphere is casual and friendly, the food excellent. Choose from American or Continental dishes—lobster sautéed in brandy, mushrooms, and shallots is a favorite. Dancing nightly to a goombay beat or an island balladeer, indoors or outdoors amid tropical greenery on the poolside terrace. Lunch and dinner. AE, DC, MC, V.

Liz's. *Expensive.* Tel. 322–4780. In the heart of downtown Nassau, just off Bay Street on Elizabeth Avenue. Delightful island decor, casual and friendly atmosphere. Thick, juicy steaks and seafood—try the grouper royal, with bananas and chutney. Dinner only. AE, MC, V.

Sun And. . . *Expensive.* Tel. 323–1205. Located in the Fort Montagu Beach area, at Lakeview Road off Shirley Street. A fine old Bahamian home amid tropical gardens and a blue lagoon. Known for more than a decade for fine dining. Now owned and operated by Chef Ronny, who formerly presided over the cuisine at Graycliff and at the posh millionaire's hideaway of Cat Cay. Al fresco dining under the palms or amid candlelit elegance indoors, from an international menu that includes such unusual delicacies as veal sweetbreads and duckling paté, along with hearty entrees of roast beef, rack of lamb, and grilled steaks. Dinner only, jackets suggested. AE, DC, MC, V.

Bayside Buffet. *Moderate.* Tel. 322–3301. 1 Bay St., in the Sheraton British Colonial Hotel, with the best harborside view in all of Nassau. Super salad bar, fresh seafood, steaks and ribs. All-you-can-eat buffet at lunch and dinner. AE, DC, MC, V.

Blackbeard's Forge. *Moderate.* Tel. 322–3301. In the Sheraton British Colonial. Nautical decor and tabletop grills for your steak, lobster, shrimp, or chicken. Entrée price includes soup, salad, vegetable, dessert, and coffee. Modest wine list. Casual dress. Lunch and dinner. AE, DC, MC, V.

Captain Nemo's. *Moderate.* Tel. 323–8394. Right on the water overlooking busy Nassau Harbour and Paradise Island. Bahamian dishes are featured—try the cracked conch or chicken with peas 'n' rice. Dining indoors or on the terrace. Easy nautical decor and ambience. About four blocks east of Rawson Square, at John Alfred Wharf, Deveaux Street. Lunch and dinner. No credit cards.

Charley-Charley's. *Moderate.* Tel. 322–2425. Delancey and Augusta Streets. Sauerbraten, wienerschnitzel, apple schnapps; snapper, conch chowder, and rum punch. Open until 3 A.M. Closed Sun. AE, DC, MC, V.

Green Shutters. *Moderate.* Tel. 325–5702. A classic English pub in a classic old Bahamian house just off Rawson Square on Parliament Street. Good hearty pub fare like steak-and-kidney pie, roast beef and Yorkshire pudding, with five imported beers on draught. Casual and friendly atmosphere. Lunch and dinner.

Mai Tai. *Moderate.* Tel. 326–5088, 323–3106. One of the prettiest settings in old Nassau, at Waterloo Lodge. Located on East Bay Street near Fort Montagu. Excellent Chinese and Polynesian food presented with flair; tall tropical drinks, flaming appetizers, and everything from pork fried rice to sizzling *War Bah* and sweet-and-sour ribs. Lunch and dinner daily to midnight. AE, DC, MC, V.

The Poop Deck. *Moderate.* Tel. 322–8175. Join the local folk and sailors overlooking the boats at the Nassau Yacht Haven. Fine local dishes or the good old American hamburger. Lunch and dinner. AE, MC, V.

Pronto Ristorante. *Moderate.* Tel. 323–3771. New Italian dining spot overlooking the harbor and marina at Nassau Harbour Club, presided over by Pino Garofanelli, doyen of Nassau's best Italian cookery for more than 20 years. Extensive menu, relaxed atmosphere, and spectacular view from second-floor vantage point—eat indoors or outdoors under a covered terrace. East Bay Street near the Paradise Bridge. Lunch and dinner. AE, MC.

Roselawn Café. *Moderate.* Tel. 325–1018. Delightful atmosphere indoors or outdoors in an old Bahamian house just off Parliament Square on Bank Lane downtown. Count on fresh homemade pastas, lasagna, fettuccine, spaghetti al dente; or try the Spanish paella—delicious. Lunch and dinner except Sunday, live entertainment. AE, MC, V.

The Terrace. *Moderate.* Tel. 322–2836. At the Parliament Hotel just off Bay Street at Rawson Square. Attractive, tropical outdoor setting. Succulent Bahamian dishes such as conch curry and sousse chicken, plus steaks and chops. Superb native buffet Tues. and Fri. Live music nightly. Lunch and dinner.

Tony Roma's. *Moderate.* Tel. 325–2020. "The Place for Ribs" branch of the Florida/California/New York minichain, which draws crowds everywhere. Succulent barbecued baby back ribs are the house specialty, along with delicious "loaves" of French onion rings. Located on West Bay Street between downtown Nassau and Cable Beach. Live entertainment nightly. Lunch and dinner. AE, MC, V.

Larry's Pub II. *Inexpensive to Moderate.* Tel. 322–3800. On the cross-island airport road at Thompson Boulevard and John F. Kennedy Drive, on the way to Nassau International. A friendly, casual pub atmosphere. Steaks and burgers offered, but notable for cracked conch, native steamed turtle, and broiled Bahamian lobster. Open daily till 2 A.M. AE, MC, V.

The Shoal. *Inexpensive to Moderate.* Tel. 323–4400. Also located on the airport road, closer to downtown, at Nassau Street. Fresh seafood and Bahamian dishes are excellent—try the "Fisherman's Special," with steamed conch, fried grouper, and sweet plantains, plus the best johnnycake in Nassau. Lunch and dinner. No credit cards.

Bahamian Kitchen. *Inexpensive.* Tel. 325–0702. One block off Bay Street at Market Street and Trinity Place. Authentic Bahamian cooking, turtle steak, okra soup, stew fish, steamed mutton, and local desserts like guava duff, rum cake, and coconut pie. Lunch and dinner. No credit cards.

Charley's Place. *Inexpensive.* Tel. 322–3882. Located in the Nassau Stadium on Fowler Street. Exquisite Bahamian cuisine. Open daily from 7 A.M. to midnight. No credit cards.

Choosy Foods & Bakery. *Inexpensive.* Tel. 326–5232. Market Street near the Strawmarket. Clean, simple cafe offering natural foods, health foods, baked goods. Thick sandwiches, homemade soups, fresh fruit juices, herbal teas. Try the vegetable pie in a whole wheat crust. Lunch and dinner except Sunday. No credit cards.

Europe. *Inexpensive.* Tel. 322–8032. Near downtown, in the Ocean Spray Hotel opposite Lighthouse Beach. Simple, quiet dining room with hearty German dishes, Bahamian and American specialties. Breakfast, lunch, and dinner, plus late snacks. AE, MC, V.

Grand Central. *Inexpensive.* Tel. 322–8356. A landmark for Greek cooking since the 1930s, right downtown on Charlotte Street just off Bay Street. Very simple, counter and booths, but notable Greek salads, shish-kebobs, and pastries, plus Bahamian specialties like boiled fish and johnny-cake, conch chowder, green turtle steak. Breakfast, lunch, and dinner. AE, DC, MC, V.

Harbour Moon Chinese Restaurant. *Inexpensive.* Tel. 322–1599. At Bay and Deveaux Streets. Original Chinese dishes. Cantonese and Szechuan. Open to midnight, daily. Takeout, too. AE, MC.

Marietta's. *Inexpensive.* Tel. 322–8395, 325–1809. On Okra Hill off East Bay Street near the Paradise Island Bridge. Neat 40-room family-owned hotel with a very popular native restaurant. Great island dishes—try the Andros crab stew. (Many Bahamians say it's the best home cooking in town.) Breakfast, lunch, and dinner. AE, V.

Palm Restaurant. *Inexpensive.* Tel. 323–7444. Bay Street downtown opposite the John Bull shop. Food is plentiful, wholesome, and delicious. Soups, salads, pastas, and hot or cold sandwiches for lunch or late afternoon snacks; 16 flavors of Ho-Jo ice cream and homemade pies at *Scoops* next door. Breakfast and lunch. AE, MC, V.

Nola's Bake Crabs. *Inexpensive.* Tel. 328–3437. Fish cakes and baked crabs to take out. Open daily to 4 or 5 P.M. No seating, no credit cards.

Paradise Island

Café Martinique. *Deluxe.* Tel. 326–3000. Fin de siècle decor and elegant Parisian flair. Continental dining indoors and dancing on a moonlit terrace overlooking the Paradise Lagoon. A full French à la carte menu—try the turtle soup and shrimp de jong or escargots and beef Wellington, topped off with a piping hot Grand Marnier soufflé and flaming coffee. Superb wine list. Dinner daily and elegant Sunday brunch, jackets required. (Next to Britannia Towers.) AE, DC, MC, V.

The Courtyard Terrace. *Deluxe.* Tel. 326–2501. Perhaps the most romantic setting in the Bahamas, with some of the finest international cuisine. Al fresco dining under the stars in the Ocean Club's lovely inner courtyard amid tropical greenery, tinkling fountains, and soft music. The chateaubriand is classic and the curried shrimp memorable. Excellent choice of French and European wines. Dinner only, jackets required. AE, DC, MC, V.

Bahamian Club. *Expensive.* Tel. 326–3000. A stately setting of brass, leather, and gleaming oak paneling showcases prime beef carved at your table, succulent steaks, and an unmatched Caesar salad. Music and dancing nightly. Located in the Britannia Towers. Dinner only, jackets required. AE, DC, MC, V.

Blue Lagoon. *Expensive.* Tel. 326–2400. The fine dining spot on Paradise, at Club Land 'Or (across the water from Café Martinique). A spectacular view from the third-floor vantage point, warm and welcoming service, attractive decor. Seafood stars include crawfish cocktail, and consommé de poisson, followed by broiled grouper amandine or lobster thermidor; for beef lovers, there's steak au poivre vert or chateaubriand. Island combo and dancing on the terrace at poolside. Dinner only. AE, DC, MC, V.

Boat House. *Expensive.* Tel. 326–3000. Casual dining amid nautical decor. Excellent service, personalized at your table, where your waiter cooks your dinner to order at your own grill. Succulent prime steaks and seafood delicacies are featured; hearty portions. Located on the Paradise Lagoon across from Britannia Towers. Dinner only, jackets suggested. AE, DC, MC, V.

Coyaba Room. *Expensive.* Tel. 326–3000. Authentic Cantonese cuisine in a romantic South Sea island setting. The specialties are rich sweet-and-sour ribs, Polynesian-style chicken, and lobster Cantonese. Located in the Britannia Towers. Dinner only, jackets suggested. AE, DC, MC, V.

Grill Room. *Expensive.* Tel. 326–2000. The Paradise Towers' newest restaurant, with a bird-of-paradise motif, classically elegant decor. Steaks and seafood sizzling from the grill; duckling a l'orange or escallope of veal with avocado and crabmeat rate high. The appetizers are succulent—try fresh oysters, salmon paté, or gin-and-tomato soup. Wind up with French pastry or fruit flambé. Rare wines and attentive service. Dinner only, jackets suggested. AE, DC, MC, V.

Gulfstream. *Expensive.* Tel. 326–2000. Fresh Bahamian and imported seafood dominate the menu at Paradise Towers' attractive dining spot, with everything from Alaskan king crab to Bahamian crawfish. Excellent service, relaxed atmosphere, contemporary decor. Dinner only, jackets suggested. AE, DC, MC, V.

Villa d'Este. *Expensive.* Tel. 326–3000. The most notable Italian cuisine in the Bahamas, served with elegance and flair in a tasteful old-world setting at the Britannia Towers. The fettuccine in a rich creamy cheese sauce and the veal marsala are memorable. Choose anything from the devastatingly delicious Italian pastries. Dinner only; jackets suggested. AE, DC, MC, V.

Captain's Table. *Moderate.* Tel. 326–2561. Harbour Cove Hotel offers excellent, informal dining in a nicely nautical atmosphere with a superb view of old Nassau Harbour. American, Bahamian, and Continental cuisine served up by "hands" in seamen's kit. Try the sirloin steak with green peppercorns, or turtle steak. Guitar-music background. Dinner only. AE, DC, MC, V.

Neptune's Table. *Moderate.* Tel. 326–2101. At the Holiday Inn on Pirate's Cove. A very attractive room with a ship's motif. Hearty seafood plus thick steaks and prime ribs. Or try the poolside deck, with island barbecues and theme parties nearly every night of the week, accented by calypso entertainment and dancing indoors and outdoors. Dinner only. Jackets suggested. AE, DC, MC, V.

Café Casino. *Inexpensive.* Tel. 326–3000. New York–style delicatessen in the Paradise Island Casino, serving everything from hot pastrami and corned beef sandwiches to a complete meal. Open daily from noon till the wee hours. Relaxing and informal. AE, DC, MC, V.

Paradise Beach Pavilion. *Inexpensive.* Tel. 326–2541. Indoor and outdoor dining for breakfast, lunch, and dinner, with live entertainment in the evenings, a good native buffet and show on Wed. Hearty food from burgers and sandwiches to full meals. Located on Paradise Beach at the Paradise-Paradise resort. AE, DC, MC, V.

Spices. *Inexpensive.* Tel. 326–3000. A tropical lobby restaurant at the Britannia Towers, serving breakfast, lunch, and dinner daily—try the eggs Benedict or chef's salad for lunch while you people watch amid island greenery in the great bustling hotel-and-casino complex. AE, DC, MC, V.

Swank Club Pizzeria. *Inexpensive.* Tel. 327–7495. Twenty different varieties of pizza served in a relaxed, casual setting at the Paradise Island Village shopping center. Excellent Italian spaghetti or lasagna, spicy Bahamian chowders. Beer and wine. Plus a dozen flavors of Howard Johnson's ice cream. AE, MC.

Note: On both Cable Beach and Paradise Island, vacationers can take advantage of unique Dine-Around plans, which permit sampling of many different restaurants and cuisines at special package rates or discounts. Listed below are typical programs. Rates and specifics may vary with the season; for details check with your travel agent or ask about Dine-Around options when making reservations.

Cable Beach: Guests from any of the following hotels may take advantage of the Cable Beach Dine-Around plan: *Crystal Palace Hotel and Casino, Ambassador Beach Hotel, Nassau Beach Hotel,* and the *Meridien Royal Bahamian.* To participate, guests must be registered under the Modified American Plan or under a package arrangement that includes breakfast and dinner as part of the daily rate. Inform the front desk at your own hotel that you want to dine in one of the other hotels or the casino and you will receive a credit coupon for up to $25 (depending on your hotel).

After dining at the restaurant of your choice, present the coupon, and the value will be deducted from your check. You pay only the difference.

Paradise Island: The Gourmet Dine-Around Plan offered for guests of the *Paradise Island Resort and Casino* is even simpler. For a flat rate of $50–$55 (depending on the season) per person per day, you may enjoy breakfast and dinner anywhere in the resort complex, plus the dinner and show at the casino's Le Cabaret theater. Unlimited menu selection is included at all of the top gourmet restaurants—Café Martinique, the Ocean Club's Courtyard Terrace, Coyaba, Boat House, Gulfstream, Grill Room, Villa d'Este, Bahamian Club, and more. (Wines, alcoholic beverages, and 15 percent gratuity not included.)

NIGHTLIFE. There is nonstop entertainment nightly in Nassau, along Cable Beach and on Paradise Island. All of the larger hotels offer lounges with island combos for listening or dancing, restaurants with soft guitar or piano background music, or dancing under the stars. Many offer weekly "theme nights" at poolside, accompanied by a barbecue or native buffet and a goombay-calypso band. Many private restaurants around the island offer entertainment along with dining or a local combo for dancing after dinner. Both casinos, at Cable Beach and Paradise Island, offer a variety of entertainment. There are half a dozen lights-and-action discos, and another half-dozen native nightclubs with music, singers, and goombay-calypso-Junkanoo acts. Acts change, combos move from club to club, discos switch to slow dance music, headliners appear from North America or Europe, now and then an old favorite closes and a new one opens. The nightlife and entertainment scene, here as everywhere, changes constantly—but here are some old and new "standbys" that shouldn't be missed when you're vacationing in Nassau:

Casino Theaters. *Bahama Rhythms Theatre,* a supper club and disco in the Crystal Palace Casino, offers a fast-paced, French-flavored, Las Vegas–type spectacular. The revue features a corps of long-legged showgirls, spectacular costumes, and a musical tribute to Broadway and Hollywood, as well as a space odyssey complete with spaceship and laser lights. Theater-style seating for 1,000; 12 performances each week, twice-nightly Tues.–Sun. Tickets are priced around $14, for the show. Reservations: 327–6200. *Le Cabaret Theatre,* in the Paradise Island Casino, offers a Las Vegas–style revue. The multimillion-dollar showgirl extravaganza features elaborate feathered and jeweled costuming, laser lighting, magicians and acrobats, live jungle animals, and a comedian. Viewers sit at stageside tables where drinks and dinner are served. Thirteen performances weekly; per-person cost is approximately $23 with two drinks and $38 with dinner. Reservations: 326–3000.

Discos. *Waterloo Discotheque,* at Waterloo Lodge, an old mansion on East Bay Street next to the Mai Tai restaurant. One of Nassau's newest swinging nightspots, till the wee hours. Tel. 326–5088. *Le Paeon.* The Peacock, at the Sheraton Grand Hotel on Paradise Island, offers four sound zones and an ocean view. Open nightly. Tel. 326–2011. *Pastiche,* at the Paradise Island Casino, with dazzling decor, sound, light, and plenty of action. Open nightly. Tel. 326–3000. *City Limits.* Independence Drive. Disco and rock to 4 A.M. nightly except Mon. Tel. 323–4706 or 323–4077. *Confettis.* At Captain Nemo's, Deveaux and Bay Sts. Patio bar, live entertainment, disco to 4 A.M. nightly except Mon. Tel. 323–8426.

Hotels, Restaurants, and Lounges. *Bayside Lounge.* Sheraton British Colonial arcade. Dining and dancing nightly from 9:30 P.M. to 2:30 A.M. to live and disco music. Tel. 322–3301. *Blue Lagoon.* Club Land 'Or resort on Paradise Island. Dining with piano music in the background; dancing to an island combo on the terrace overlooking the Paradise Island Lagoon. Open nightly except Sunday. Tel. 326–2400. *Captain's Lounge.* Dancing nightly to the music of a live calypso/goombay band. At the Pilot House Hotel on the Nassau side of the Paradise Island Bridge. Tel. 322–8431. Cover/minimum. *The Palace.* A very popular local island combo, Al Collie and the VIP's, operate a nightclub-style disco with live music and entertainment, two dance floors. Off Bay Street on Elizabeth Avenue. Tel. 325–7733. Cover/minimum. *Junkanoo Lounge.* Crystal Palace Hotel and Casino. Live music and entertainment nightly with calypso rhythms and dancing. Tel. 322–7070. Cover/minimum. *La Marina Restaurant and Bar.* Live music and dancing on the terrace nightly at the Nassau Harbour Club overlooking the marina. Tel. 323–1771. *Out Island Bar.* In the Nassau Beach Hotel on Cable Beach. Lively atmosphere, live and loud music from an island combo nightly. Tel. 327–7711. Cover/minimum. *Pirate's Cove.* At the Holiday Inn on Paradise Island; live indoor and outdoor entertainment nightly, with "theme nights," native shows, and staff shows weekly. Tel. 325–6451. *The Terrace.* At the Parliament Hotel on Parliament Street. Outdoor dining and dancing in the gardens on a roofed terrace. Live entertainment nightly. Tel. 322–2836. *Rendezvous Lounge.* Top island entertainment, nonstop dancing till the early hours nightly. In the Britannia Towers at the Paradise Island Resort and Casino. Local and international groups. Tel. 326–3000. Cover/minimum. *Trade Winds Lounge.* More top island entertainment and nonstop dancing till the early hours nightly. In the Paradise Towers at the Paradise Island Resort and Casino. Tel. 326–2000. Cover/minimum.

Native Nightclubs. *Peanuts Taylor's Drumbeat Club.* The Bahamas' most famous entertainer for 25 years, Peanuts Taylor, master bongo drummer, stars in his own all-star native review nightly. Adding to the fun is Bahamian songstress Portia Butterfield, a goombay/calypso band, a group of fire dancers, and a true limbo artist. Nightly at 10:30 P.M. West Bay Street, just west of the Sheraton British Colonial Hotel. Tel. 322–4233. Admission charge.

CASINOS. The three casinos on New Providence Island open early in the day and remain active into the wee hours of the morning and offer Continental gambling. Visitors must be 18 to enter a casino, 21 years of age or over to gamble; Bahamians or Bahamas residents are not permitted to gamble. Dress code is more formal at night.

Crystal Palace Casino. The former Cable Beach Casino, with soaring ceilings and a balcony lounge, state-of-the-art slot machines (5¢ to $1), 51 blackjack tables, 9 roulette wheels, 7 craps tables, and other games, is open daily, 9 A.M.–4 A.M. Complimentary gaming lessons every afternoon. Other amenities include a casino bar with big-screen satellite TV, a New York–style delicatessen, and a gourmet restaurant, Sol e Mare. Tel. 327–6200.

Paradise Island Casino. More formal, elegant atmosphere, with English and Continental dealers and croupiers. Long known as one of the most glittering gaming palaces in the Caribbean, it is linked to the Britannia Towers and the Paradise Towers. The casino features 41 tables of blackjack with a $5 minimum bet, 7 craps tables, 8 roulette tables, 2 Big Six tables, and a private room—a casino within the casino—for high rollers. There are 500 slot machines, from 25¢ to $1 and multiples. Slot machines are open 24 hours, gaming tables open 10 A.M. until dawn, and gaming lessons are offered free in the afternoon, with a complimentary cocktail. Amenities include several casino bars; a New York–style delicatessen; several gourmet restaurants adjacent; Pastiche, a sound-and-lights disco; and the Cabaret Theatre, with table seating for about 800, fine dining, and an elaborate revue. Tel. 326–3000.

Divi Bahamas Casino. Newest of the Bahamas gambling spots, the casino is scheduled to open early in 1990.

GRAND BAHAMA ISLAND

Freeport, Lucaya, and West End

Over the last three decades, Grand Bahama Island has emerged as a major international resort destination, attracting 1.3 million visitors a year and rivaling the most popular destinations in the Caribbean.

One of the largest islands in the archipelago, Grand Bahama forms the northern border of the Bahamas, with its western tip lying less than 60 miles off Florida's Palm Beach coast. Its 530-square-mile interior is heavily forested with palmetto, casuarina, and Caribbean pines. The 96-mile southern coastline is pocketed by sheltered harbors, bordered by miles of unspoiled white-sand beaches, and fringed with a nearly unbroken line of spectacular reefs. Virtually unknown and largely unpopulated two generations ago, Grand Bahama was developed in the early 1960s by a visionary group of American, European, and Bahamian entrepreneurs. Today, Grand Bahama boasts 53,000 residents, a major industrial complex, a deep-water cruise-ship port, a modern international airport, and one of the most glittering residential, resort, and country club centers in the Bahamas.

Centerpiece of Grand Bahama's development is the attractive, well-planned "garden city" of Freeport, where broad boulevards and sophisticated shops are linked by a palm-lined road to the suburb of Lucaya, set among thousands of acres of lush tropical greenery and sprawling along miles of canals and ocean beach. Scattered here and there are large and small hotels, a world-famous International Bazaar, six superb golf courses, a pair of enormous casinos, and the new festival marketplace, Port Lucaya.

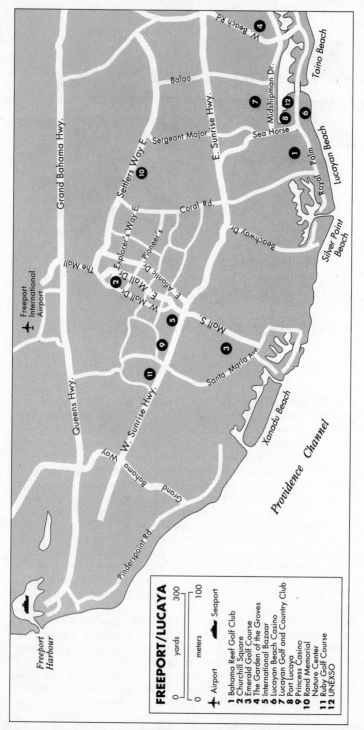

FREEPORT/LUCAYA

yards   0   300
meters   0   100

✈ Airport   ⚓ Seaport

1 Bahama Reef Golf Club
2 Churchill Square
3 Emerald Golf Course
4 The Garden of the Groves
5 International Bazaar
6 Lucayan Beach Casino
7 Lucayan Golf and Country Club
8 Port Lucaya
9 Princess Casino
10 Rand Memorial Nature Center
11 Ruby Golf Course
12 UNEXSO

Exploring Freeport/Lucaya

There are no historic sites or crumbling forts to explore around Freeport/Lucaya, but there are several interesting sights that should not be missed, and many sporting adventures well worth trying. Best bet for an overview of the city and suburban attractions is a two-hour bus tour that stops by most hotels. The tour moves through downtown Freeport and the lovely residential areas and exclusive suburbs, along oceanside beaches and seaside resorts, and around the cruise-ship harbor and industrial park, with stops at the colorful International Bazaar and the lively town center. A bus tour of Grand Bahama Island, from Freeport to West End, lasting most of a day, is also available. Or you can rent a car or scooter and explore the island on your own.

The best place to begin your tour is at the Ministry of Tourism Information Center at the International Bazaar on West Sunrise Highway. Pick up maps and brochures on local attractions. While there you may want to sign up for the unusual "People to People" program. Available only in Nassau and Freeport, this volunteer program matches up visitors with Bahamians of similar interests and hobbies for a genuine personal and cultural exchange. All expenses are taken care of by the Bahamian volunteers—there are more than 1,000 in Freeport/Lucaya. It can be a vacation experience you'll treasure for years. You can enroll at the Information Center or through the social hostess at your hotel. Details from the People to People coordinator, tel. 325-8044.

You will enjoy driving or riding around Freeport/Lucaya. Broad, landscaped dual carriageways (the Grand Bahamian name for a divided highway) and treelined streets wind through parks, past lovely homes, and along lush green fairways. All are complete with well-marked lanes, traffic lights, and traffic circles. Always keep in mind that all traffic is on the left, British style, even bikes and scooters.

International Bazaar and Strawmarket

The colorful International Bazaar on West Sunrise Highway next door to the Princess Casino is within easy walking distance of downtown Freeport hotels and adjacent to the Princess resort complex. If you are staying at one of the oceanside resorts, hop on the bus or take a taxi. If you drive, park near the casino; you won't be able to ride or bike through the narrow lanes. And bring along your walking shoes, because you'll probably want to spend hours sampling the bazaar's delights.

You'll enter the International Bazaar through the 35-foot red-lacquered Torii Gate, traditional symbol of welcome in Japan. Within the bazaar, you'll find street markets and exotic shops, with bargain wares from around the world (most at prices 20 to 40 percent lower than in the United States and Canada). Along the narrow winding lanes and byways, there's a bit of London, Paris, and Rome; something of Istanbul and Tangiers, Acapulco and Hong Kong; with Latin American touches from Colombia and Brazil; and Asian style from Japan, India, and Thailand. English pubs and French cafés, a Japanese steak house and a Chinese tearoom, Polynesian, Italian, and health-food dining spots suit any taste or budget. Nearly a dozen different countries are authentically represented in the 10-acre bazaar, and there are nearly a hundred different shops. If all this suggests a vast Hollywood movie set, that's all right—it was created by one of the film world's leading set designers.

Before beginning your shopping and sightseeing tour of the labyrinthine bazaar, drop by the picturesque native Strawmarket located just to the right of the entrance. Bargain with the straw ladies for a colorful woven hat and a roomy handcrafted tote bag in which to carry home your bargains. Here you'll find thousands of delightful souvenirs and practical gift items woven by hand from straw, raffia, and palm fronds. The straw ladies will even personalize your souvenir with your own name or most anything you choose. You'll find handcrafted jewelry made from conch along with wood carvings and sculptures of native pine, lignum vitae, or mahogany. All prices are negotiable, and the straw ladies love to bargain—but don't expect to bargain with the shopkeepers in the elegant stores and jewelry salons in the bazaar. The savings in these stores are substantial on imported watches and cameras, gold and silver, cashmere and linens, crystal and china, colognes and perfumes, and the prices are fixed.

Travel eastward by car to the first traffic circle and turn left onto the Mall. This will take you to Churchill Square and the Freeport town center, where residents do their shopping, away from the tourist attractions.

Churchill Square, the busy heart of downtown Freeport, can be reached from the East Mall Drive. Here are banks, the post office, the police station, and dozens of shops arranged around the square and on the side streets. The Pantry Pride supermarket is useful for stocking up on necessities, and behind the store you'll find a wonderful open-air produce market where you can pick out mangoes, papaws, and other fruit for snacking as you walk. If you're even hungrier, Mum's Coffee Shop and Bakery, at 7 Yellow Pine Street, has delicious homemade bread and pastry, hot soups, and thick sandwiches.

Rand Memorial Nature Center

Heading north on the Mall to Settler's Way East, then turning right and following the treelined highway, will take you to the Rand Memorial Nature Center. The hundred-acre park, composed of natural Grand Bahama woodland, preserves more than 400 varieties of subtropical plants, trees, flowers, and foliage indigenous to the Bahamas. It is also a sanctuary for thousands of native and migratory birds. Look carefully for two rare and lovely native hummingbirds. One is the Cuban emerald, independent, fearless, and bright emerald green, usually found sipping the nectar of a bright hibiscus blossom. The other is the tiny Bahama woodstar, shy and easily missed (it is little bigger than a flying insect) but brilliantly hued, with a bright reddish-violet forehead and throat. It is found only in the Bahamas.

Within the park, a mile of well-marked nature trails leads to a sparkling 30-foot waterfall tumbling to a lovely blue lagoon. Here you can photograph the brilliant pink flamingos (national bird of the Bahamas) that live and nest along its shores. Those who want to learn all about the flora and avian life in the park may take one of the walks conducted by resident naturalists. They'll tell you all about where the "straw" comes from that is woven into hats and bags at the Bahamian markets, and even show you how bubble gum "grows." They'll point out hundreds of varieties of plants, including wild vanilla orchids, devil's potato, straw lily, five fingers, and love vine. They may even introduce you to the native raccoons and "curly-tailed" lizards, or the world's smallest snake.

Garden of the Groves

Leaving the nature center, continue east on Settler's Way to Balao Road or West Beach Road, then turn south to Midshipman Road, which fringes Lucayan Harbour on the north. If it's time for lunch, and pub fare with an English flair appeals to you, make your way to the Britannia Pub on King's Road overlooking Bell Channel. After lunch, head back to Midshipman Road and continue east to another wondrous natureland, the Garden of the Groves.

These prize-winning botanical gardens were named for Wallace and Georgette Groves, the developers of Freeport/Lucaya. The park, which covers more than a dozen acres, features some 5,000 varieties of rare and familiar subtropical and tropical trees, shrubs, plants, and flowers. Entrance is through a lovely "hanging garden," a canopied arbor of lush, green tropical vines. Centerpiece of the gardens is a series of cool waterfalls, fountains, winding streams, and tranquil lagoons. Well-marked pathways lead past clearly identified plant species, the verdant fern gully and grotto, and a tiny native-stone interdenominational chapel (a replica of the earliest church on Grand Bahama). There is also an interesting small museum where you can learn about the history of Grand Bahama Island over the last four centuries and the modern development of Freeport/Lucaya. There are many quiet shady benches throughout the gardens for resting and relaxing or sharing a picnic lunch.

On leaving the Garden of the Groves, head for the sea—some of Grand Bahama's most beautiful beaches and interesting harbors are in the Lucayan area, off Midshipman Road. Travel west, then turn south on West Beach Road to Jolly Roger Drive, which runs along the ocean. Drop by Taino Beach, the island's prettiest public beach, and plan drinks or dinner at the Stoned Crab, a rustic, romantic seaside restaurant with a dining terrace overlooking the water.

UNEXSO and the Dolphin Experience

If you'd like to learn to dive on your vacation, or if you are a trained diver interested in reef, wreck, cave, or blue-hole dives, you will want to investigate the Underwater Explorers Society (UNEXSO). It's a comprehensive scuba-diving school with an international reputation that attracts divers from around the world. For beginners there's an 18-foot-deep dive training tank; the society also offers a certification course, advanced training for instructors, and a diving medicine course for physicians. UNEXSO is close by the Lucayan Beach Hotel, off Royal Palm Way. There you can pick up brochures and rate sheets, talk to the instructors, and mingle with the divers. The crowd is casual, relaxed, full of wondrous tales of the underwater world, and there's a nearly nonstop showing of underwater films and slides to pique your interest in exploring beneath the sea.

UNEXSO's new neighbor, the Dolphin Experience, is one experience you won't want to miss. In 1987 five wild bottlenose dolphins were brought to Lucaya, placed in a huge open-water pen, and trained to interact with people. As the dolphins cavort in their pool, swimmers and snorkelers dive in with them, and the dolphins seem to love it; they greet the swimmers enthusiastically, nuzzle them gently, swim alongside them, and offer rides to swimmers who cling to their dorsal fin. The training has now reached the stage where the dolphins are released from their pens to swim freely with their trainers—and tourists—in the adjoining canal. The next phase will be to take them offshore to Lucaya's ocean coral reef. The trainers emphasize that their work is scientific. The dolphins are not taught any tricks and there is no show.

Those who want to enjoy the Dolphin Experience can sign up for the assistant trainer program at $95 a day, a swim with the dolphins for $45 an hour, or a dolphin seminar at the side of the pool for $5—ideal for people who don't want to get wet. There are no age limits for the seminars and swims, and you may bring along whatever equipment you like—or rent your equipment at UNEXSO.

Port Lucaya

Port Lucaya is the new festival marketplace on the waterfront, adjacent to UNEXSO and the Lucayan Beach Resort and Casino, just ten minutes from downtown Freeport. Some 85 shops, boutiques, restaurants, and lounges are housed in attractive low-rise tropical-colonial style buildings, painted in pastels and featuring such Bahamian architectural details as louvered Bahama shutters, covered verandas, and ceiling fans. The complex overlooks Lucayan Harbour, with a 50-slip marina for yachts, fishing boats, day cruisers, glass-bottom boats, and *El Galleon,* a replica of a 16th-century Spanish galleon that offers day and dinner cruises before turning into a disco at night. The entertainment at Port Lucaya is nonstop, with strolling minstrels, steel bands, mimes, and more. Restaurant fare ranges from conch cuisine to gourmet, and the shops stock bargains in crystal and china, linens and lingerie, jeweled watches, Bahamian handicrafts, European fashions, imported perfumes, and cameras. Port Lucaya is a three-minute stroll from the Lucayan Beach Resort and Casino, the Holiday Inn–Lucaya Beach, and the Atlantik Beach Hotel and Country Club.

Exploring Grand Bahama Island

East of Freeport/Lucaya

To explore Grand Bahama Island east of Freeport/Lucaya, and to visit the island's newest ecological wonderland, return to Midshipman Drive and travel east. Beyond the Garden of the Groves, take the left branch, which becomes East Sunrise Highway curving north. At the next branch in the road, a right turn will take you to Casuarina Bridge, which spans the Grand Lucayan Waterway. This broad canal meanders across the island from north to south, providing protected passage for yachts cruising the northern Bahamas and effectively cutting the island in two.

Beyond the bridge, you come to a stop sign. The road to the left dead ends in two miles. The road to the right is Casuarina Drive, a straight line for miles through untamed pine forests. Finally the road curves south toward the sea, and the next bend in the road will take you eastward again. The turnoff for Old Free Town leads to an abandoned village whose set-

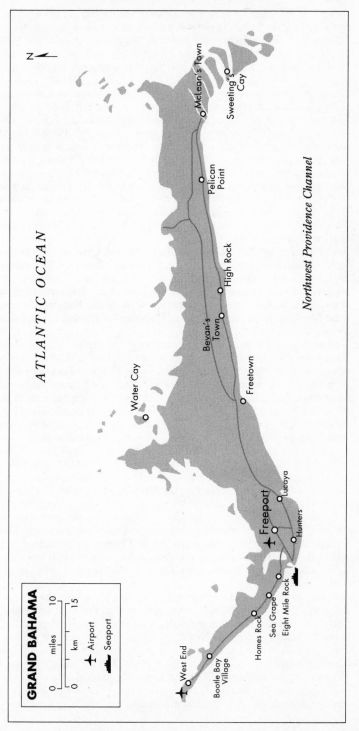

tlers were "relocated" to New Free Town, a small village to the east. The ruins of Old Free Town are not much to see, but the area is noted for its "blue holes," vast surface openings to underwater cave systems. The Mermaid's Lair and Owl Hole are two blue holes located just off the road; UNEXSO brings teams of divers here for cave diving specialty certification.

Continuing eastward along the main road, watch for the Lucayan National Park and Caverns sign. The entrance, on your left, is twelve miles from the stop sign mentioned earlier. The Bahamas National Trust is presently improving facilities here to attract more visitors. By 1990 it is hoped to have guides at the park. In the meantime, there is a large map of the area showing the various features. This stop is a must for ecologists, scientists, naturalists, and cave aficionados, an experience for all who enjoy nature and wild, untrammeled stretches of ocean beach. Here is the "largest explored underwater cave system in the world," more than seven miles long. The park's extensive pathway system takes you up to a spectacular lookout point above a natural hammock and down stairways into a pair of massive caves.

The caverns are Ben's Cave and Burial Mound Cave, both sinkholes where the collapse of the cavern roof has opened up the caves. Inside there are harmless bats, and access to the caverns is restricted during their mating season. Burial Mound Cave has been the site of the discovery of Indian artifacts and human bones, now on exhibit at the Grand Bahama Museum (near the Garden of the Groves at Midshipman Road and Magellan Drive).

Continue on the boardwalk pathway over the bridge crossing Gold Rock Creek, to Gold Rock Beach—a brisk 10-minute walk or a leisurely 20-minute stroll. Signs identify the island's ecological zones as you proceed from pine forests through a rocky area with abundant century plants and Ming trees, over a mangrove swamp, and over the high dunes to Gold Rock Beach, one of the most beautiful and remote stretches of sand on the island. This is a perfect place for beachcombing, lying in the sun, reef snorkeling, or swimming and lunching (if you've brought your picnic with you; there are no concession stands here!). The small island just offshore is Gold Rock Cay. No guided tours are currently offered at the park, but serious naturalists and cave divers can make arrangements for a professionally guided tour by contacting the Ministry of Tourism in Freeport (352–8044).

Leaving Lucayan National Park and Caverns, you can head west on the main road, then north again, and west to Casuarina Bridge and East Sunrise Highway, which will return you to Freeport (approximately 25 miles). Or you can continue eastward through a series of small native villages along the shore to McLean's Town, the easternmost point on the island accessible by road.

If you go eastward, you will pass through a U.S. military base, Gold Rock Missile Tracking Station, important once as the first down-range station for tracking launches from Cape Canaveral, Florida. Just beyond is the "relocated" village of New Free Town, and beyond that is Bevin Town, with the Three Sisters restaurant, the Star Club bar, a gasoline station, and a repair shop, the only one on this end of the island. The next village along the seashore is High Rock, prettily situated on a bluff overlooking the sea. The unimposing Oceanview restaurant is a good place to stop for a snack or a hearty Bahamian meal; you can carry your lunch across the street to a palm-thatched shelter and enjoy a splendid ocean view with the waves crashing against the rocks below. The road deteriorates to the east through Pelican Point (located on a beautiful broad beach) before linking up with a new paved road that takes you into McLean's Town, where the road (and the island) ends. If you want to venture farther east, there is a ferry that runs from McLean's Town to the tiny settlement of Sweeting's Cay.

West of Freeport/Lucaya

Traveling the Queen's Highway westward from Freeport/Lucaya takes you through a series of small villages, many more than 100 years old. Some were thriving towns back in the Roaring Twenties, when rum-runners made Grand Bahama their headquarters and fast speedboats and seaplanes plied the Florida Channel nightly, bringing illicit loads of liquor to Prohibition-weary U.S. mainlanders. Just west of town is Hawksbill Creek, which has a colorful harborside fish market. Continuing westward, the road loops around the busy commercial harbor areas, where you might see huge oil tankers and sleek white cruise ships, great oil refineries and sprawling factories. Back on the main road to West End, you will pass through the village of Eight Mile Rock, a long, narrow hamlet that sprawls for eight miles along both sides of the road. Drive down one or two of the side streets for a look at some of the small, attractive older homes, then drop into St. Stephen's Church, built on the seashore in 1851. Also near the beach is Fragrance of the Bahamas, a small native perfume factory housed in a former Baptist church. Distilled from local flowers and plants such as hibiscus and frangipani, the scents are delightful—try "Island Promises" for a unique Bahamian souvenir. Just down the road a quaint little village called Seagrape has a tiny bakery offering some of the best bread on Grand Bahama. The next village is Holmes Rock, where Harry's American Bar promises a good Bahamian lunch, a frosty drink, and a splendid view overlooking the sea and Deadman's Reef. Be warned: the bar is normally closed from Labor Day to Christmas and only serves lunch. Almost next door is the more expensive Buccaneer Club, open only for dinner. Continuing on, you'll pass Bottle Bay and West End Point, where there are fine views of the offshore cays of Indian Cay, Wood Cay, and Memory Rock Light.

West End

The road (and the island) ends, appropriately enough, at West End, a seaside village with a couple of churches and a dozen bars. Stop for a cool drink at the Star, a weathered old building that was a hotel in the 1940s. Nearby Austin's Calypso Bar, with its local music and dancing most nights, is a favorite with locals and visitors from the huge Jack Tar Village resort just down the road. Jack Tar is an all-inclusive, Club Med–style resort where visitors are welcome at a PGA-rated 27-hole golf course and 16 tennis courts; details available at the clubhouse.

As you head back for Freeport/Lucaya, you may want to stop at the Buccaneer Club, whose German-Swiss owners offer Bahamian-American cuisine with a Continental flair. If your timing is right, you'll enjoy a fantastic view of the sunset from the patio.

PRACTICAL INFORMATION FOR
GRAND BAHAMA ISLAND

HOW TO GET THERE. By air. Freeport's International Airport is well served. *TWA* has service from Boston and Chicago. *Eastern* has a through flight from Columbus, OH. *Delta* and *Aero-Coach* have direct service from Fort Lauderdale, and *Turks and Caicos Airlines* has flights from Grand Turk and Provencales. Delta and Eastern, with the aid of commuter airlines, offer service from Key West, FL. Three airlines, *Bahamasair,* Eastern, and *Pan American,* fly in from Miami. *Air Canada* has a direct flight from Montreal. New York visitors can fly on Bahamasair, out of Newark, or on Pan American or TWA, from the JFK airport. Delta has service from Orlando and Eastern has a flight from Pittsburgh. TWA offers two flights a day from St. Louis, and *Piedmont* has service from Tampa and West Palm Beach. *ComAir* is the newest service providing flights from several cities.

By sea. *SeaEscape* offers 13 one-day cruises to Freeport/Lucaya out of Miami and Fort Lauderdale. The ships depart Florida at 8:30 A.M. and return by 11 P.M. SeaEscape Ltd., 1080 Port Blvd., Miami, FL 33132. Tel. 305–379–0000; 800–327–7400 in the U.S.; 800–432–0900 in FL; 800–327–2005 in Canada. Crown Cruise Line's *Viking Princess* sails to Freeport every Mon., Tues., Thurs., and Sat. from the Port of Palm Beach, departing at 9.30 A.M., returning at midnight. Crown Cruise Line, P.O. Box 10265, Riviera Beach, FL 33419. Tel. 407–845–7447; 800–841–7447. The largest of the ships making daily trips is the 1,100-passenger *Discovery 1,* which makes the journey four times weekly and takes about five hours. The cruise line and the Freeport Harbour Company officially opened a new terminal for the ship in Freeport at the end of 1988. Discovery Cruises, 8751 W. Broward Blvd., Suite 300, Plantation, FL 33324. Tel. 305–525–7800. The *Dolphin, Emerald Seas, Carnivale,* and *Sunward II* sail weekly from Miami or Fort Lauderdale on four-day combination cruises to Nassau and Freeport.

TELEPHONES AND EMERGENCY NUMBERS. Area code for Grand Bahama Island is 809. Ambulance: 352–2689 or 352–6735; fire department: 352–8888; police: 911; Air Sea Rescue: 352–2628.

HOTELS. There is an excellent range of accommodations on Grand Bahama Island, from luxurious full-service resorts in town and along the beaches to small in-town motel-style hotels and attractive self-catering apartment complexes. The rates for hotel rooms and apartments on Grand Bahama are in most cases significantly lower than comparable accommodations on New Providence Island. All hotels offer MAP (Modified American Plan), which includes breakfast and dinner daily. Packages are available at all Grand Bahama resorts. We have indicated whom to contact for reservations, and in many cases, you'll note that they may be made through the Bahamas Reservation Service, tel. 800–327–0787 in the U.S. and Canada, abbreviated as BRS.

Hotel price categories, based on high-season, double occupancy on Grand Bahama, are $145 and up, *Expensive;* $90–$144, *Moderate;* and $89 *Expensive; Moderate;* and and below, *Inexpensive.* Low season rates tend to run 10 to 20 percent lower than winter season rates, and package rates run from 20 to 40 percent lower.

Freeport

Bahamas Princess Resort and Casino. *Expensive.* Reservations for either Princess property: Box F-2623, Freeport, Grand Bahama Island. Tel. 352–6721 (Country Club) or 352–9661 (Tower); toll-free in the U.S.: 800–223–1818, in New York 800–442–8418; or Princess Casino Vacations, 800–545–1300. Located 3½ miles from Freeport International Airport. 15 percent service charge added. The international chain operates two fine resorts in Freeport: the Princess Tower and the Princess Country Club, with a total of 965 rooms. Princess also runs the Princess Casino and two championship 18-hole golf courses, the Emerald and Ruby. Both hotels are located on West Sunrise Highway, next to the casino and International Bazaar. As neither resort is on the beach, Princess provides complimentary bus service to its private beach club at Xanadu Beach.

Princess Towers. Dramatic, Moorish-style architecture, a dazzling octagonal lobby and a colonnade of Arabesque arches. There are 400 rooms in a ten-story tower. All are spacious, attractively decorated, air-conditioned, and have private telephones and cable TV. There are several excellent restaurants, coffee shop and poolside dining; varied entertainment nightly in notable lounges, and the *Sultan's Tent Disco.* A large freshwater pool, six tennis courts for day and night play, and a landscaped waterfall and Jacuzzi.

Princess Country Club. A sprawling, low-rise resort with a two-story main building housing the lobby, restaurants, and bars. There are 565 guest rooms in nine two- and three-story wings radiating from a central pool and patio area. Landscaping is lush and tropical, and the pool is an extravaganza of tumbling waterfalls, islands, greenery, and a Jacuzzi. Rooms are large, well furnished, air-conditioned, and equipped with private telephones and cable TV. There are six fine restaurants, some offering poolside dining; several bars and lounges provide entertainment almost every night. Six tennis courts for day and night play, and a well-equipped fitness center with exercise room, health club, and dance theater. Here, too, are the most extensive meeting and convention facilities on the island. Note: Several wings of this resort have been converted to time-share kitchen apartments under the name Princess Vacation Club International.

Xanadu Beach Hotel. *Expensive.* Box F-2438, Freeport, Grand Bahama; tel. 352–6782. Located five miles from International Airport. A luxurious oceanside resort with 184 rooms, two three-bedroom villas and one two-bedroom villa. Located on a mile-long ocean beach, with a full-service marina. Three tennis courts lighted for night play, boats and fishing charters for hire, and a large freshwater pool. Dining possibilities include *Escoffier* (a gourmet restaurant) and the *Persian Room,* where the decor is Persian tapestries from the Howard Hughes collection. A casual bar with entertainment, a disco, and—Monday nights—barbecue on the beach with a calypso band and goombay music. The two top floors, formerly the residence of the reclusive Howard Hughes, have been divided into four luxury corner suites, very grand and very expensive.

Silver Sands. *Moderate.* Box F-2385, Freeport, Grand Bahama; tel. 373–5700 or through BRS. A comfortable apartment hotel with 164 studio and 1-bedroom units, each with balcony, full kitchen, and bar. 2 swimming pools, 2 tennis courts, and water sports. 2 bars with frequent live entertainment, an Italian restaurant, and beachside snack bar. 7 miles from the airport.

Castaways Resort. *Inexpensive.* Box F-2629, Freeport, Grand Bahama; tel. 352–6682, or through BRS. One hundred thirty unpretentiously furnished motel-style rooms, air-conditioned, with TV and telephones. There is a restaurant, bar, lounge, and the popular *Yellowbird Nightclub.* Amenities include an indoor/outdoor patio, pool, and gardens. 15 percent service charge added. Located three miles from the airport, adjacent to the Princess Casino and International Bazaar.

Lucaya

Atlantik Beach Hotel. *Expensive.* Box F-531, Lucaya, Grand Bahama; tel. 305–592–5757, 800–622–6770, or through BRS. A Swiss International Hotel favored by Europeans with a mix of Canadians and Americans. 123 rooms, 52 one-, two-, and three-bedroom apartments with kitchens, all attractively furnished. Corona Classic Club offers luxury amenities and VIP treatment. Set along a beautiful beach, offering a range of water sports, beach club, pool, and windsurfing school. Several attractive dining rooms and a lounge with entertainment. The hotel operates the Lucayan Golf & Country Club, an 18-hole championship course nearby. 6 miles from the airport.

Genting's Lucayan Beach Resort & Casino. *Expensive.* Box F-336, Lucaya, Grand Bahama; tel. 800–772–1227, 800–331–2538, or through BRS. Once Grand Bahama's premiere resort, now fully restored to its former glory. Set along 1½ miles of ocean beach, with 248 well-appointed rooms. *Les Oursins,* a gourmet dining room, is one of five restaurants, and there are five bars and lounges. The glittering *Lucayan Beach Casino* offers all games of chance and a lavish theater revue. Lanai Wing features Club Lucaya, with VIP amenities. Full sports program includes windsurfing, parasailing, UNEXSO scuba, 2 swimming pools, 4 tennis courts, and golf nearby. 6 miles from the airport.

Holiday Inn. *Expensive.* Box F-760, Lucaya, Grand Bahama; tel. 373–1333, 800–465–4329, or through BRS. Typical Holiday Inn comforts, in a tropical resort setting. 500 attractive rooms, set along a mile of ocean beach. Day and night activity, health club, pool, 4 tennis courts, water sports, and a children's playground. 3 dining rooms, 3 lounges with entertainment, and the *Panache* nightclub. The three-year renovation now under way has been planned in phases to prevent the disruption of guests. 6 miles from the airport.

Lucayan Marina Hotel. *Moderate.* Box F-336, Lucaya, Grand Bahama; tel. 800–772–1227, 800–331–2538, or through BRS. Formerly Lucayan Harbour Inn, refurbished, now operated by Genting's Lucayan Beach Resort. There are 143 modest but comfortable rooms; a delightful restaurant, *Hemingways,* with indoor-outdoor dining, and a full service 150-slip marina. A favorite with the yachting set and the young dive crowd from UNEXSO. A ferry plies back and forth to the beach and casino, and guests enjoy the privileges and amenities of the *Lucayan Beach Resort and Casino.*

West End

Jack Tar Village. *Moderate.* 403 South Akard, Dallas, TX 75202; tel. 800–527–9299. Self-contained all-inclusive resort at western end of Grand

Bahama Island, 32 miles from Freeport. Air charters arrive at the resort's international airport at West End. There are 537 rooms, neatly furnished. Amenities include a huge swimming pool, 27 holes of golf, a full-service marina with charter boats for fishing, a full scuba program and 16 tennis courts. Also features several dining rooms, bars, and a full schedule of group entertainment.

APARTMENT RENTALS. In addition to the apartment hotels and resorts offering housekeeping facilities listed above, the following offer apartment rentals for vacationers:

Coral Beach. Box F-2468, Freeport, Grand Bahama. Tel. 373–2468/9. Five efficiency apartments and six rooms in a landscaped condo setting along a nice private beach. Amenities include balcony or terrace, attractive furnishings, roof solarium, pool, central dining room, and bar.

Channel House Resort Club. Box F-1337, Freeport, Grand Bahama; tel. 373–5405. 18 studio and one-bedroom apartments located across from the Holiday Inn and Lucaya Beach. Attractive setting with a pool and tennis courts. Club membership plans available.

TIME SHARING. There is a growing number of time-sharing resorts and condominium properties on Grand Bahama Island. A sampling follows:

Bahama Reef. Box F-2695, Freeport, Grand Bahama; tel. 373–5580. Eleven one-bedroom units and one three-bedroom penthouse for time sharing and rental. Located 3½ blocks from the beach and near the Bahama Reef Country Club. Rental boats available.

Dundee Bay Villas. One World Development Ltd., Box F-2690, Freeport, Grand Bahama; tel. 352–4222. One-, two-, and three-bedroom units located on the beach next to the Xanadu Beach Hotel. Time sharing and rentals.

Freeport Resort & Club. Box F-2514, Freeport, Grand Bahama; tel. 352–5371. Located on wooded acreage near Princess Casino, International Bazaar, and golf courses. Choice of apartment sizes and styles.

Lakeview Manor Club. Box F-2699, Freeport, Grand Bahama; tel. 352–2283. Located on the fairway of the fifth hole of the Ruby Golf Course. Time sharing and rental. One- and two-bedroom apartments.

Mayfield Beach & Tennis Club. Box F-458, Freeport, Grand Bahama; tel. 352–9776. Located on Port of Call Drive at Bahama Terrace, on the ocean. Pool, sundeck, tennis court, various sizes of apartments.

North Star Resorts. Box F-2997, Freeport, Grand Bahama; tel. 373–4250 or 373–4636. Located along the Grand Lucayan Waterway. 72 apartments with two bedrooms attractively furnished, two baths, and full kitchen. Tennis courts and dockage.

Ocean Reef Resort and Yacht Club. Box F-898, Freeport, Grand Bahama; tel. 373–4661. Three-bedroom, three-bath luxury apartments with a complete marina and swimming pool. Located near the Casino, Bazaar, and golf courses.

Princess Vacation Club. Box F-207, Freeport, Grand Bahama; tel. 352–6721. Part of the Bahamas Princess Resort & Casino complex in Freeport, adjacent to the Casino and Bazaar. Apartments are located in the Princess Country Club Hotel and owners have access to all of the resort's amenities, pools, golf courses, tennis courts, and beach club.

Woodbourne Estates. Box F-1098, Freeport, Grand Bahama; tel. 352–4069. Located on Hawksbill Street, Bahama Terrace, near the International Bazaar and Casino. Two-bedroom apartments, with full kitchen.

For additional rental apartments, homes, condominiums, and time-sharing vacations contact the following realtors: *Timesales (Bahamas) Ltd.,* Box F-2656, Freeport, Grand Bahama; tel. 352–7039. *Caribbean International Realty,* Box F-2489, Freeport, Grand Bahama; tel. 352–8795/6. *Charlow Realty Ltd.,* Box F-3814, Freeport, Grand Bahama; tel. 373–5443.

HOW TO GET AROUND. Metered taxis meet all in-coming flights at Freeport International Airport and at the cruise-ship port. There is no bus service or other public transportation to or from the airport and cruise-ship port. However, visitors booked on package tours through a travel agent, hotel, or the Bahamas Reservation Service (which specifically include airport transfers) are transported free of charge to their hotel. Within Freeport/Lucaya, scheduled bus routes cover most of the area, including some outlying villages. Check with your hotel desk for bus schedules and sightseeing tour schedules. Motor scooters and bicycles are available for rent at several resorts on the island. Rates for bicycles average $15 per day with a $40 deposit required; average rates for motor scooters are $28 per day (plus $50 deposit) for a single seater, $40 per day (plus $100 deposit) for a two-seater. Full day is 9 A.M.–5 P.M., and crash helmets are mandatory. Rates are subject to change.

Car rentals are offered by the following agencies: *Avis,* with locations at the International Airport, 352–7666; the International Bazaar, 352–7675; and in Lucaya opposite the Atlantik Beach Hotel, 373–1102. *Budget* is located at the International Airport, 352–8844; and at the Atlantik Beach Hotel, 373–4938. *Dollar,* at the International Airport, 352–3714; and Bahamas Princess Country Club. *Sears Rent-a-Car,* at the International Airport, 352–3165. *National* has three locations, at the International Airport, 352–9308; at the Holiday Inn; and at the Xanadu Beach Hotel. *Hertz* is at the International Airport, 352–9250; and at the International Bazaar, 352–4226. Average daily rates range $49–$79, depending on the model; weekly rates, $260–$340. Unlimited mileage with these rates, and the car must be returned with a full tank. Insurance is recommended, and is available through all agencies. A significant deposit is required on all rental vehicles, unless payment is made with a major credit card.

TOURIST INFORMATION SERVICES. The *Bahamas Ministry of Tourism* operates information booths at the Freeport International Airport, the Freeport Harbour Cruiseship Port, and the International Bazaar. The main office is at the Sir Charles Hayward Library on East Mall Drive; Box F-251, Freeport, Grand Bahama; tel. 352–8044. The *Grand Bahama Island Promotion Board* operates an office in the International Bazaar; tel. 352–7848 or 352–8356. Both tourism organizations offer a full range of colorful brochures, maps, rate sheets covering all hotels on the island for both winter and summer seasons, and information on what to do and sights to see on Grand Bahama Island.

SPECIAL EVENTS. Grand Bahama is internationally famous as the "Country Club Island," and year-round there are scheduled golf tournaments that attract amateurs and professionals alike. For dates, entry fees, and regulations, contact the organizations listed in "Tourist Information Services" above, or call the Bahamas Sports Hotline in the United States 800–32SPORT.

In December, between Christmas and New Year's, Grand Bahama offers a week-long celebration of *Junkanoo*. (For a complete description of Bahamian Junkanoo and its historic African roots, see Junkanoo under "Seasonal Events" in the *Facts at Your Fingertips* section.)

Vintage Car Grand Prix made its debut on Grand Bahama in 1986 and was a "roaring" success. It is held annually in December. Headquarters is the Bahamas Princess Resort and Casino in Freeport, and about 200 vintage cars, representing half a dozen different countries, participate. Grand Prix planners schedule 15 races, gala parties, golf, tennis, and fishing tournaments, and a native Bahamian music festival as part of the celebrations. All events are open to the public. Contact the Sports Hotline (800–32 SPORT), BRS, or your travel agent for details and package information.

Student Getaway Programs. Every spring from March through April, the island attracts thousands of vacationing students with a series of fun-filled free (or inexpensive) events such as beach picnics, barbecues, moonlight cruises, sailing and fishing trips, and golf and tennis tournaments.

Conch-Cracking Contest. A real out-island-style native celebration held each Discovery Day, Oct. 12 (Columbus Day) at McLean's Town at the far eastern end of the island. Beach picnics, native food, and goombay music are all part of this free-for-all, fun-filled ritual. Locals sit cleaning mounds of fresh conch by hammering and cracking them. Current record is 25 conch in just over six minutes. Even visitors are invited to join in, but be sure you know how to pronounce the name correctly—"konk"—or you are automatically disqualified.

Princess 10K Road Race. Sponsored annually in January by Bahamas Princess Resort and Casino on their 10K course. Attracts amateurs and professionals from many countries.

Goombay Summer Festival. June–Aug. Bargain packages for airlines and hotels and a full program of daily events in Freeport and Lucaya. Tours, beach parties, fashion shows, horseback riding, beer fests, outdoor concerts, weekly Junkanoo festivals with masquerade costumes, native show acts, and food displays are offered free or at discount prices.

Michelin Long Driving Championship. Some of the world's hardest-hitting golfers take part in the PGA-sanctioned event held in November. It is the culmination of a series of regional contests throughout the U.S. and the Bahamas to establish a champion at driving a golf ball the longest distance. Over $50,000 in prizes are awarded.

Conchman Triathlon. This event, held in November, features cycling, running, and swimming. It started as a local competition but in 1988 was opened up to visitors. The event attracted over 500 entrants from half a dozen countries.

Lucayan Beach TWA Grand Bahama Pro-Am. The 1990 golf tournament—the fourth of its kind—is scheduled to take place in November at the Lucayan Golf and Country Club. Over 100 golfers are expected to participate.

Discovery Season. Sept.–mid-Dec. This fall festival looks forward to the 500th anniversary of Columbus's landfall in 1992. Grand Bahama provides more bargains during this time than the other islands. There are special prices to attract visitors and special prices and events all over the island. On Fridays the shops and restaurants at Port Lucaya marketplace stay open late and provide free entertainment. On the same night, at West End, there is dancing, native food vendors, and junkanoo parades. On Saturdays the Lucayan Beach Resort hosts the Grand Lucayan Festival, featuring a Bahamian buffet, a native show, a junkanoo parade, and an impressive fireworks display. On Sundays the Underwater Explorers Society offers snorkeling trips at half price and two learn-to-dive courses for the price of one. On the same day, the Xanadu Beach offers reduced prices on water sports. On Mondays both casinos conduct free gaming lessons—with free drinks.

TOURS. A variety of guided bus tours is available on Grand Bahama Island. Hourly rates for a taxi/tour with driver range from $20–$25, and for long trips rates can generally be negotiated. Always settle in advance exactly what the charge will be. You can even hop aboard a sightseeing airplane to visit nearby islands or make a day-long expedition to Nassau. Most tours may be booked through the tour desk in your hotel lobby, through information booths at the airport or cruise-ship port, or directly by calling the following ground tour operators and airlines: *Bahamas Travel Agency Ltd.,* Box F-3778, Freeport, Grand Bahama; tel. 352–3141. *Executive Tours,* Box F-2509; tel. 352–8858. *Grand Bahama Tours Ltd.,* Box F-453; tel. 352–7234/7347. *Greenline Tours,* Box F-2631; tel. 352–3465. *International Travel Tours Ltd.,* Box F-850; tel. 352–9311. *Sun Island Tours,* Box F-2585; tel. 352–4811. *Reef Tours Ltd.,* Box 7-2609; tel. 373–5880.

Two airlines that provide sightseeing flights around Grand Bahama, to near-by Family Islands, and to Nassau are: *Helda Air Holdings Ltd.,* Box F-3335, Freeport; tel. 352–8832; and *Taino Air,* Box 7-4006, Freeport; tel. 352–8885.

Glass-Bottom Boat Tours. *Reef Tours Ltd.,* operating from Port Lucaya, offers daily offshore tours to spectacular reefs and sea gardens aboard the *Mermaid Kitty* ("World's largest glass-bottom boat"), at 10:30 A.M., 12:30 P.M., and 2:30 P.M., $20 adults, $10 children. Also offered are daily Tri-Wind Cruises (two hours) and Moonlight Cruises (two hours). Rates are approximately $16 for adults, $8 for children. For information call (373–5880/5891/5892).

Sailing Cruises. Also offered by *Reef Tours Ltd.* Hop aboard a 55-foot Trimaran, as follows: "Snorkeling and Sailing Cruise" daily at 9:30 A.M., $12 adults, $8 children; "Snorkeling/Sailing/Beach Party Cruises" 12 noon, $20 adults, $10 children, including picnic lunch and rum punch; evening "Wine and Cheese Cruise" daily at 6 P.M., weather permitting, $18 per person.

Deep-Sea Fishing. Four-hour trips, 8:30 A.M.–1 P.M., $300 for the yacht with up to six persons, plus $50 each fisherman, $25 each spectator.

Daily cruises depart from St. Tropez Marina aboard the 65-foot pleasure yacht *Shangri La.* "Snorkeling, Swim and Sail Cruise" at 11:30 A.M. "Wine and Cheese Cruise" at 3 P.M.; "Sunset Booze Cruise" at 6 P.M. For rates and reservations call 352–4222.

PARKS AND GARDENS. *Rand Memorial Nature Center.* Settler's Way East. One-hundred-acre park and preserve for more than 400 varieties of native subtropical plants, trees, flowers, and foliage, plus sanctuary for thousands of native and migratory birds. Within the park are well-marked nature trails. Guided walks offered by resident naturalists. Open daily with a nominal charge for admission. Guided tours at 10:30 A.M., 2 P.M., 3 P.M. Closed Saturday. For information call 352–5438.

Garden of the Groves. Prize-winning botanical gardens covering more than a dozen acres. Some 5,000 varieties of rare and familiar subtropical and tropical trees, shrubs, plants, and flowers. Well-marked pathways with identifying markers for plant species; tiny native-stone chapel. Small museum traces four centuries of Bahamian history and displays Lucayan Indian artifacts. $2 admission. Open 10 A.M.–5 P.M. The gardens are open daily except Wednesday. For information call 373-2422.

PARTICIPANT SPORTS. Grand Bahama offers five tournament-quality championship 18-hole golf courses, among the best in the Caribbean. The island is bordered by 60 miles of ocean beach and fringed by living reefs offering some of the most thrilling diving anywhere. UNEXSO, a world-class scuba school, is located here. There are 50 hard-surface and clay tennis courts, most lit for night play, and six full-service marinas for boat charters, fishing, snorkeling, and sightseeing adventures and many other sports facilities.

Fishing and Boating. Small-boat rentals are available through your hotel or at beach concessions in oceanside resorts. Fishing is excellent around Grand Bahama. Snapper, yellowtail, hogfish, grunts, kingfish, and jacks may be caught on nearby reefs; in deep-water channels there are marlin, wahoo, and sailfish; bonefish are caught in the marshy flats. Boats can be chartered at several marinas, and rates begin at $35 an hour for self-drive runabouts; $30 per person for four hours of drift fishing; and $50 per person for half a day of deep-sea fishing (party of six). Recommended marinas are:

Lucayan Harbour Marina. Tel. 373–1639. Charter boats, fishing excursions, dockage, and taxidermist agency.

Running Mon Marina. Tel. 352–6834/5. Complete marina service, dockage, taxidermist agency, six sport-fishing charter yachts, and fishing trips.

West End–Jack Tar Village. Tel. 346–6211. Full-service marina, with deep-sea fishing, drift fishing, and bonefishing expeditions arranged.

Xanadu Beach Hotel Marina. Tel. 352–6780. Bahamas Air Sea Rescue base, dockage, and 28- and 46-foot sport-fishing boats on charter for deep-sea fishing.

Golf. Green fees range $14–$20 for 18 holes, $9–$11 for 9 holes. Electric carts are $20–$24 for 18 holes, $12–$14 for 9 holes. The higher rates apply in winter season.

Bahamas Princess Golf Courses. The Emerald and the Ruby, both 18-hole championship layouts, PGA rates at par 72. Each course has its own clubhouse, restaurant, and pro shop. Golf carts are mandatory on both courses. Golf packages available through the Bahamas Princess Resort and Casino. Both located in Freeport, tel. 352–6721.

Bahama Reef Golf & Country Club. Within easy walking distance of hotels in the Lucaya beach resort area; 18-hole championship course, par 72. Driving range, pro shop, lessons available on request. Electric carts mandatory in the morning, pull carts permitted after 1 P.M. Tel. 373–1055.

Lucayan Golf & Country Club. Naturally hilly setting overlooking picturesque Bell Channel in Lucaya; 18-hole championship course, par 72. Practice range, putting green, pro shop; clubhouse serves lunch and dinner. Electric carts mandatory. Tel. 373–1066.

Golf–West End. Jack Tar Village offers three nine-hole courses, which can be played in various combinations for 9, 18, or 27 holes. All are championship rated, par 36. Electric carts mandatory. Tel. 346–6211.

Horseback Riding. *Pinetree Stables,* located on Beachway Drive, Freeport, offers guided riding trips three times daily through island trails and along the beach. Dressage and jumping lessons by appointment. Tel. 373–3600.

Parasailing. Soar high over the water harnessed to a parachute and towed by a speed boat. You don't even get wet—launch and landing are from a moored raft. Expensive, but enthusiasts say it is worth every penny. Available at the *Atlantik Beach Hotel, Holiday Inn, Lucayan Beach Hotel,* and *Xanadu Beach Hotel.* About $20 for a six-minute flight.

Scuba-Diving. One of the most famous scuba schools and NAUI centers in the world is UNEXSO, the Underwater Explorers Society, adjacent to the Lucayan Beach Resort. Beginners can learn to dive on their vacation for $59, which includes all equipment, three hours of professional instruction in the club's training pools, and a shallow reef dive. For experienced divers, there are four dive trips daily, night dives, inland blue hole dives, and multi-dive discounts. Certification, instructor training, dive medicine courses for physicians, and cave-diving training are all available. The club has equipment for rent and for sale, nine professional instructors, four dive boats, a unique 18-foot training tank, and a decompression chamber. Additional amenities are a small Underwater Museum and a good little dive shop with equipment, sportswear, T-shirts, and a wide selection of books on shells, reefs, fish, and coral—some for reading underwater. The Tides Inn snack bar and lounge serves liberal libations and super sandwiches, with good conversation and nonstop underwater films. Tel. 373–1244 or write UNEXSO, Box F-2433, Freeport, Grand Bahama. UNEXSO serves most hotels in Freeport/Lucaya.

Tennis. *Bahamas Princess Country Club* has six Laykold courts, two lighted. *Bahamas Princess Towers* has six courts, three Laykold, three clay, all lighted. Both hotels charge $5 per hour daytime, $10 per hour at night. *Holiday Inn* has four hard-surface courts, none lighted. $5 per half-hour, $10 per hour. *Lucayan Beach Hotel* has 4 hard-surface courts, guests free, visitors pay a fee, pro instruction available. *Silver Sands Hotel* has two hard-surface courts, guests free, visitors $3 per hour. *Xanadu Beach Hotel* has four hard-surface courts, two lighted, $5 per hour. *West End–Jack Tar Village* has 16 courts, ten cushions, six clay, all lighted, guests only unless special arrangements are made with the front desk.

Windsurfing. Several hotels offer rentals at beach concessions, and the *Atlantik Beach Hotel* offers a complete windsurfing school, with instruction, simulation, variety of boards, and certification. For courses, rates, and dates call 373–1444 or write Atlantik Beach Hotel, Box F-531, Freeport, Grand Bahama.

MUSIC, DANCE, AND STAGE.
Freeport and Lucaya have a sophisticated population of Bahamian professionals and foreign entrepreneurs, as well as a growing community of American, Canadian, and European visitors who spend several months a year on the island. Many have become active in promoting the performing arts. One group, *Friends of the Arts,* sponsors plays, musical groups, and guest artists from abroad, with tickets available to the general public. A local amateur group, *The Grand Bahama Players,* presents several Bahamian dialect comedies each year, and the *Freeport Players Guild* puts on ambitious productions of popular Broadway dramas, musicals, and comedies at the 400-seat *Regency Theatre* in Freeport (tel. 352–5533). Performances by local groups and guest artists

are well-publicized in the daily newspaper, on local radio and TV; posters and flyers are generally available at tourism information centers and at most hotel desks.

SHOPPING. There are hundreds of stores, shops, and boutiques throughout the Freeport/Lucaya area, in hotels and resorts, shopping centers, and in the downtown center. However, the best bargains on fine imported goods such as perfumes, cameras, crystal, china, watches, cashmeres, linens, and European fashions are to be found in the International Bazaar or at the new Port Lucaya Market Place, where savings can be as much as 20 to 40 percent over U.S. and Canadian prices. (And remember there is no sales tax anywhere in the Bahamas.) Shop carefully and compare prices before making any major purchase—and "know before you go." Take a tip from experienced travelers—if you are in the market for an expensive foreign camera, watch, china, crystal, or silver patterns, check prices before you leave home by phoning your local department and discount stores—then you'll be sure that you are getting a real Bahamian bargain. The shops listed below are open 10 A.M. to 6 P.M. and are located in the *International Bazaar,* Freeport.

Anata-O. Large collection of Italian gold and silver jewelry and precious stones in interesting settings. Chains, bracelets, and money clips.

Bahama Coins & Stamps. Excellent selection of collectible international stamps and coins. Coin jewelry and Bahamas Coin Collections.

Bahama Mama. Delightful "Bahamas Hand Print," silk-screened patterns on fine cotton and washable blends sold by the yard or made into fashions. Designs are handcrafted with delightful Bahamian patterns. Large selection of souvenirs and T-shirts.

Beachcomber. One stop for an excellent variety of Bahamian handicrafts and souvenirs, including sharks' teeth mounted and unmounted; coconut-shell jewelry; driftwood and shell items and souvenirs.

Bombay Bazaar. Exotic Indian brassware; jewelry in coral, jade, and tigereye; colorful clothing for men, women, and children.

Casa Miro. An excellent collection of fine Spanish porcelain including Nao and Lladró, along with small gift items from Spain such as tooled leather purses and wallets, colorful fans, Majorca pearls, 14- and 18-carat gold jewelry.

Casablanca. Wide selection of imported French perfumes and a variety of Lancôme cosmetics and skin-care products.

Charm Chest. This haven for charm collectors sells unique Bahamian designs and zodiac signs fashioned in 14- and 18-carat gold and sterling silver. Also offers fine fashion jewelry and watches.

Colombian Emeralds Ltd. Largest and finest jewelry store in the Bahamas, offering substantial savings as well as certified appraisals, unconditional guarantees, and a U.S.-based service office. Magnificent collection of set and unset emeralds; outstanding diamond, sapphire, ruby, pearl, gold, and silver jewelry. You can watch exquisite jewelry being made by local craftsmen. Note: No U.S. duty is charged on unmounted emeralds.

Discount Bazaar. Specializing in brand-name watches and gold and silver jewelry at discount prices. Check this shop and compare prices before making a major watch purchase elsewhere in the Bazaar.

El Galleon. Attractive Spanish antiques and gift items, a large selection of watches, imported jewelry.

Gemini II. Fashion swimwear, European sportswear; exclusive agents on the island for Esprit.

Ginza. Full line of imported cameras. Fine gold and silver jewelry, including Mikimoto pearls.

Glass Blower Shop. Watch the glass-blowers make ships and figurines.

Hong Kong Tailors. Custom-made, Hong Kong–tailored suits from a wide selection of wool and lightweight fabrics. Ten days to two weeks delivery time.

India House. Exotic brassware, lacquerware, wood carvings, and jewelry.

Kon Tiki. Exquisite shells from Bahamas and Philippines. Jewelry and souvenirs.

La Sandale. European designer footwear; watches by Michel Herbelin and Courréges.

Leather & Things. Imported luggage, handbags, briefcases, and accessories.

London Pacesetter Boutique. British and European sportswear. Excellent selection of Gottex swimwear, Pringle and Braemar cashmeres.

Midnight Sun. Grand Bahama's finest collection of crystal and porcelain figurines. Two shops in the International Bazaar—second shop offers imported gourmet cookware, cutlery, dinnerware. Both feature unique Lapponia jewelry designed by Bjorn Weckstrom and fashioned from Lapland gold.

One World. Fine imported clothing and designer accessories from the Far East; silk blouses, kimonos, lambswool sweaters, unusual handbags.

Perfume Bar. Outstanding collection of French perfumes at discount prices.

Pipe of Peace. Superb collection of pipes, tobaccos, cigars, lighters from around the world. Good selection of watches.

The Plaka. A good collection of Greek handicrafts, jewelry in gold and silver, and an interesting selection of Grecian clothing for men, women, and children.

Strawmarket. Just to the right of the International Bazaar—this is not to be missed. Thousands of souvenirs and practical gift items woven by hand from straw, raffia, and palm fronds. Other handcrafted items made from shell, wood, berries, etc. All prices are negotiable, so be sure to bargain with the straw ladies.

The new *Port Lucaya Market Place* has a total of 85 shops, boutiques, and restaurants in an attractive harborside setting. The stores stay open later here and there is always some free entertainment—strolling minstrels, local musicians, and a bandstand—to give you a break from shopping.

RESTAURANTS. There is a nearly endless list of restaurants, dining rooms, country clubs, bars, lounges, and oceanside or poolside snack shops in the Freeport/Lucaya area and in the International Bazaar. The choice of cuisines and atmospheres is nearly as varied, with everything from gourmet dining Continental or American style to native specialties like cracked conch, boil fish, or peas 'n' rice with grouper; from exotic Indian curries and Japanese Kobe steak to the familiar American fast-food franchises.

We call $36 and up *Deluxe;* $25–$35 *Expensive;* $15–$24 *Moderate;* and under $15 *Inexpensive* for a three-course meal for one, excluding tip and beverage. Be sure to call ahead for reservations, particularly at Expensive to Deluxe restaurants. It is wise to call ahead to verify a restaurant's policy regarding credit cards. The following credit card abbreviations are used: AE, American Express; DC, Diners Club; MC, MasterCard; V, Visa.

Freeport

The Crown. *Deluxe.* At the Princess Casino. Tel. 352–7811. An international gourmet dining room. Jackets required. Lunch and dinner daily. AE, DC, V.

Escoffier. *Deluxe.* Newly re-opened in Xanadu Beach Hotel. Tel. 352–6782. Elegant decor. If it lives up to its former reputation for superb French cuisine and elaborate Sunday brunch, it will be one of the best on the island. Dinner only. Jackets required. AE, BA, DC, M, V.

Rib Room. *Deluxe.* At the Bahamas Princess Country Club. Tel. 352–6721. English hunting-lodge motif. A gourmet steak house whose specialty is beef. Try the steak Diane or fine prime rib—both are outstanding. Dinner only, jackets required. AE, DC, V.

Ruby Swiss Restaurant. *Deluxe.* Gourmet dining room on West Sunrise Highway, next to the Princess Towers. Tel. 352–8507. Grand Bahama's largest selection of true gourmet fare, overseen by a noted Swiss chef. Breakfast buffet and menu selection for early golfers; fine luncheon menu includes Swiss sausages, quiche Lorraine, smoked salmon, fresh seafood. Superb dinner offerings include veal Cordon Bleu, fondue Bourguignonne, beef Wellington. Escoffier desserts and fine Swiss pastries. Superb wines to $150, cognacs and liqueurs. Dancing and entertainment in the evenings. Lunch and dinner daily. AE, MC, V.

La Trattoria. *Deluxe.* In the Princess Towers. Tel. 352–9611. Elegant restaurant, with the finest international Italian cuisine. Dinner only. Jackets required. AE, DC, V.

Morgan's Bluff. *Expensive to Deluxe.* Small, casual dining room at the Princess Towers. Tel. 352–9611. Nautical decor and superb fish, shrimp, and lobster in light nouvelle sauces. Dinner only. AE, DC, V.

Guanahani's. *Expensive.* Tel. 356–6721. Very attractive Bahamian architecture and island decor, located poolside at the Princess Country Club hotel. Informal dining on such specialties as Chinese smoked ribs, pan-fried grouper, and lobster pot. Prix-fixe dinner menu includes everything from salad to the chocolate fondue specialty dessert. Dinner only. AE, MC, V.

Island Lobster House. *Expensive.* On the Mall in Freeport. Tel. 352–9429. Live music and dancing to calypso music, exotic tropical drinks. Menu includes a good salad bar, filet of grouper, steak, and the specialty: whole Bahamian lobster stuffed with crabmeat. Lunch and dinner daily. AE, MC, V.

Sir Winston Churchill Pub. *Moderate.* On the Mall in Freeport. Tel. 352–8866. Serves lunch (moderate) and dinner (expensive) daily. The Chartwell Room for dinner features English roast beef with Yorkshire pudding. Lively pub atmosphere with dart games, British brews, and authentic pub decor. AE, V.

Mai Tai. *Moderate.* Overlooks the Princess Emerald Golf Course. Tel. 352–7637. A classic Chinese menu, graceful atmosphere, exotic tropical drinks. Try one of their famous Polynesian or Szechuan specialty entrees. Lunch, dinner, and late snacks. AE, MC, V.

Churchill Square Restaurant. *Inexpensive.* Downtown Freeport. Tel. 352–2296. Good native specialties such as boil fish, stew fish, curry mutton, conch omelet with johnny cake, and guava duff. Indoor and outdoor seating, bar. Breakfast, lunch daily. Most major credit cards.

Mum's Coffee Shop and Bakery. *Inexpensive.* In Freeport's downtown shopping center. Tel. 352–3416. Super sandwiches on fresh Bahamas bread, hot soups including conch chowder, and a delicious selection of pastries. Daily for breakfast and lunch. No credit cards.

Pancake House. *Inexpensive.* In Freeport on Sunrise Highway. Tel. 373–3200. All sorts of pancakes served until 10 P.M.; a good selection of lunch and dinner specialties including steak and seafood. No credit cards.

Freeport/International Bazaar

Japanese Steak House. *Expensive.* In the Oriental section. Tel. 352–9521. Hibachi tables, kimono-clad staff, and Japanese decor. Experts prepare traditional Kobe steaks, shrimp, fish, and chicken. Dinner only. AE, MC, V.

Café Michel. *Moderate.* French section. Tel. 352–2191. Indoor/outdoor dining in a delightful French sidewalk-café setting. Excellent omelettes and crêpes, plus pizza. Breakfast, lunch, and dinner except Sun. AE, MC, V.

China Palace. *Moderate.* In the Great Oriental Pagoda. Tel. 352–5610. Very good Chinese food at very reasonable prices. Cantonese cuisine and some Polynesian and American offerings served in an exotic setting. The Pagoda Bar offers a fine variety of tropical drinks. Lunch and dinner Mon.–Sat., Sun. dinner and late snacks only. AE, DC, MC, V.

The Pub on the Mall. *Moderate.* At Ranfurly Circus in Freeport, opposite International Bazaar. Tel. 352–5110. A splendid English pub with authentic decor and atmosphere. Two dining rooms: The Prince of Wales Lounge serves such pub fare as fish and chips and steak and kidney pie; Bass ale is on tap. Baron's Hall, with elegant banner-hung medieval splendor, serves superb dinners at night—try the coquille St. Jacques, Cornish game hen, or roast beef and Yorkshire pudding. AE, MC, V.

Le Rendezvous. *Inexpensive.* In the French section. Tel. 352–9610. A sidewalk café in the French manner, with striped umbrellas on the terrace. Open 24 hours, indoors and outdoors, serving all kinds of snacks—ice cream, sandwiches, pancakes—or full meals, including pizza. The closest thing to French food here is le hamburger. Calypso band plays frequently. MC, V.

Lucaya

Lucayan Country Club. *Deluxe.* Tel. 373–1066. A beautiful room with splendid views across the golf course. Lunch features chef's salad, eggs Benedict, omelettes, cold stone crab. For dinner: oysters Rockefeller and fine Continental cuisine including rack of lamb, scampi, chateaubriand, and roast pheasant, flaming desserts. Good wine selection. AE, MC, V.

Les Oursins. *Deluxe.* Tel. 373–7777. Elegant gourmet dining room in the Lucayan Beach Hotel. Continental cuisine with a French accent. Outstanding veal dishes, rack of lamb, and a memorable Caesar salad. Sophisticated atmosphere, attentive service, fine wines. Dinner only. Jackets required. All major credit cards.

Bahama Reef Club. *Expensive.* Tel. 373–1056. Fine dining room at Bahama Reef Country Club, overlooking the golf course. Specializes in seafood, rack of lamb, and steak. Open for dinner and late-night suppers. Major credit cards.

Captain's Charthouse. *Expensive.* On East Sunrise Highway at Beachway Drive, Lucaya. Tel. 373–3900. Treetop-level dining in an attractive setting. Menu features prime rib, steaks, Bahamian lobster, and a fine salad bar. Live calypso music and dancing. Happy hour nightly 5–7 P.M. AE, V.

Britannia Pub. *Moderate.* On the water overlooking Lucaya Harbour. Tel. 373–5919. English Tudor pub decor; British pub fare for lunch and dinner, plus Bahamian specialties and a delicious Greek shishkebab. Informal, comfortable, with an open fireplace and Courage beer on tap. Darts and electronic games. Free happy hour fish and chips. AE, MC, V.

Lucayan Lobster & Steak House. *Moderate.* Tel. 373–5101. Large, sprawling restaurant with attractive decor, located on Midshipman Road in Lucaya. Casual, informal atmosphere with good cracked conch, lobster tail, and New York strip steak entrees. Dinner only. AE, MC, V.

The Stoned Crab. *Moderate.* A delightful, romantic oceanfront restaurant on Grand Bahama's most beautiful public beach—Taino Beach in Lucaya. Tel. 373–1442. Informal atmosphere indoors and on a terrace overlooking the sea. Frosty island drinks and fresh seafood or char-broiled steaks. Specialties of the house are stone-crab claws and Bahamian lobster. Good wine selections. Dinner only; open 4 P.M. to midnight. AE, MC, V.

The Surf Sider. *Inexpensive to Moderate.* Taino Beach. Tel. 373–1814. Friendly, homey service and delicious Bahamian dishes: curried mutton, chicken sousse, turtle steak. The bar serves the usual blend of tropical drinks and several "bush medicine" brews for the adventurous. No credit cards.

The new **Port Lucaya Market Place** has 13 different restaurants ranging from gourmet *(Luciano's)* to fast food *(Pizza Hut).* There are also snack and specialty outlets for everything from ice cream to chocolates and pastries.

Outside Freeport

Buccaneer Club. *Expensive.* Located at Deadman's Reef, Eight Mile Rock. Tel. 348–3794. Lovely grounds, oceanside patio, indoor or outdoor dining in a rustic wooden chalet. Excellent native and Continental meals featuring steak, lobster, veal, chicken, or seafood. Dinner only. Open Nov. through April. No credit cards.

Pier I. *Expensive.* Tel. 352–6674. Attractive stilt-house restaurant overlooking the cruise-ship port. Good hearty Bahamian and seafood specialties; a lovely view. Calypso entertainment, lunch and dinner daily except Sunday. AE, MC, V.

Harry's American Bar. *Moderate.* At Deadman's Reef. Tel. 348–6263. Casual dining indoors or out on the oceanside patio. Conch chowder, fish and chips, chicken and burgers. Lunch only. Closed Labor Day to mid-Dec. No credit cards.

Freddie's. *Inexpensive.* Tiny but terrific. At Hunters, just outside of Freeport. Tel. 352–3250. Hearty Bahamian cooking—souse pigfeet or boil fish, steamed conch, and curried mutton, all served up with peas 'n' rice and johnnycake. Or choose steak and lobster. No credit cards.

Scorpio's. *Inexpensive.* West Atlantic at Explorer's Way, Freeport. Tel. 352–6969. True Bahamian meals, including boil fish and stew fish at breakfast (a favorite throughout the Bahamas), and conch—served chowdered, fractured, steamed and scorched, or chopped up raw in a hot sauce and served as salad. Peas 'n' rice, chicken, grouper, and lobster along with steaks and burgers. Bar with TV, pool room, and video games. No credit cards.

Star Restaurant. *Inexpensive.* Tel. 346–6207. Open practically around the clock, in a weathered old hotel at West End, which claims to be the oldest hotel on the island, built by Austin Grant in the 1940s. The hotel hasn't let rooms for years, but Austin Jr. operates it as a bar and restaurant. Try the cracked conch or grouper fingers, with a cold beer. Rustic. No credit cards.

NIGHTLIFE AND ENTERTAINMENT. Both are plentiful on Grand Bahama Island, particularly in the Freeport/Lucaya area. Top attractions on the island are the lively French revue at the Princess hotel's *Casino Royale Theatre;* the Las Vegas–style extravaganza at the Lucayan Beach Hotel and Casino's *Flamingo Showcase Theatre;* the native nightclub shows featuring calypso bands and steel drums, limbo dancers, fire-eaters, and Bahamian balladeers; and half-a-dozen late-night discos that mix recorded music with live musicians. Also popular with visitors are the Caribbean luaus, goombay and Junkanoo festivals regularly scheduled at poolside or oceanside by the major hotels. A sampling of nightlife offerings:

Atlantik Beach Hotel. Yellow Elder Lounge has dancing to a live band Fri. and Sat. from 9:30 P.M. Tel. 373–1444.

Austin's Calypso Bar. Next to the Star Restaurant, near Jack Tar Village at the West End settlement. Local island combo, dancing, and merriment most evenings attract a good mix of locals and "change of pace" vacationers seeking a respite from the wholesome and predictable entertainment at the resort compound. Tel. 346–6207.

Bahamas Princess Country Club Hotel. In the Palm Pavilion, a goombay Festival, with live calypso band and buffet dinner. Sat. from 6:30 P.M. Tel. 352–6721.

Bahamas Princess Towers Hotel. The Sultan's Tent Disco provides action under the lights nightly. Cover charge. Tel. 352–9661.

Casino Royale Theatre. Adjacent to the Princess Casino. *Soirée,* an elaborate, high-stepping French-style showgirl revue, is on twice nightly except Mon. Show times 8:30 and 10:30 P.M., price around $20 with two drinks included. Reservations necessary. Tel. 352–7811.

Flamingo Showcase Theatre. Adjacent to the Lucayan Beach Casino at the Lucayan Beach Hotel. An elaborate Continental-style revue with variety and comedy acts. Two shows nightly, dinner optional. Price for the show, two drinks, tax, and gratuities is $20 per hour. Tel. 373–7777.

Freeport Inn. In Freeport, at the East Mall and Explorer's Way. A live native show daily from 10 P.M., except Mon. and Wed., featuring fire dancers, limbo artists, and steel drums. Calypso band every evening, Tue.–Sun. Tel. 352–6648 or 352–2805.

Holiday Inn. On the beach in Lucaya. The hotel features poolside theme nights daily and a weekly Construction Party in honor of the ongoing hotel renovation: Guests wear hard hats and receive miniature construction souvenirs. The Bahamian Showcase, a native revue with goombay band, singers, dancers, and an illusionist, Mon., Wed., and Sat. nights, is packaged with a sit-down dinner from 7:30 P.M., all for $25. Soft island music nightly 5 P.M.–1 A.M. *Panache Nightclub* offers dancing nightly 9 P.M.–3 A.M., to an excellent local reggae-calypso band. Cover charge. Tel. 373–1333.

Studio 69. In Lucaya. Newest and swingingest disco on the island attracts an enthusiastic crowd of locals and visitors. Disc jockey and recorded music. Throbs nightly to the wee hours. Cover charge. Tel. 373–2158.

Yellow Bird Show Club. At Castaways Resort in Freeport. One of the best native shows on the island, featuring top Bahamian artists in a colorful revue with calypso, limbo, fire dancers, balladeers, and steel drums. Nightly except Tues. from 8 P.M. Cover charge. Tel. 352–6682.

CASINOS. *Princess Casino.* At the Bahamas Princess Resort and Casino. A captivating, much-photographed Moorish-style extravangaza. The interior matches the exterior in opulence. The 20,000-square-foot casino is one of the largest in the Bahamas or Caribbean. Games include 450 slot machines (the latest models are computerized, with link-progressive jackpots paying off as high as $100,000—and they can be played on credit!), 40 blackjack tables, eight dice tables, eight roulette wheels, two money wheels, and 24 assorted video games. The casino also offers a fine gourmet restaurant, the *Crown Room;* a delightful coffee shop, the *Garden Cafe;* the elevated *King's Court* casino bar, where you can watch all the action below, plus the *Casino Royale Theatre.* (See "Nightlife and Entertainment" above.) Tel. 352–7811. For information call 653–3794 in Miami, 800–432–2294 in Florida, and 800–422–7466 in the United States; or call Princess Casino Vacations, 800–545–1300 in the United States.

Lucayan Beach Casino. At the Lucayan Beach Hotel and Casino. Attractive decor, Continental gaming including blackjack, money wheels, dice tables, baccarat, and state-of-the-art slot machines with big money payouts. Includes the *Flamingo Showcase Theatre* and supper club, and several dining options from casual to gourmet. Tel. 373–1224. In the United States call 800–331–2538 or 800–772–1227 for casino package tours.

THE FAMILY ISLANDS

Abacos, Andros, Bimini, Cat Island, Chub Cay,
Crooked Island, Eleuthera, Exumas, Great Inagua,
Long Island, Rum Cay, and San Salvador

The Family Islands have been known to generations of visitors as the Out Islands, situated "out" and away from the glitter of Nassau and Freeport. They are beautiful, peaceful, and secluded, where endless, nearly empty beaches are a trademark, water sports a way of life. There are no all-night discos or casinos, no international bazaars, and few gourmet restaurants. Entertainment is local: a village combo on Saturday night, a piano bar in the clubhouse, a guitar on a moonlit terrace. Betting on the size of the next fish, the depth of the next dive, or the length of the next drive replaces the roll of dice or the turn of a card. There are no cities and few settlements that can even be described as small towns. Sightseeing tends to be a quiet stroll through a picturesque village, island-hopping in a small boat between sheltered harbors, or a picnic excursion to a nearby cay.

Getting to the Family Islands can be slightly more complicated than getting to Nassau or Grand Bahama, even though most of the islands have direct, scheduled service from Nassau by the national flag carrier Bahamasair. Some islands, such as the Abacos, Bimini, Eleuthera, and the Exumas, are served directly by scheduled commuter airlines based on the Florida mainland. Others, particularly in the more remote regions, are served by licensed air charters operating from Florida gateways.

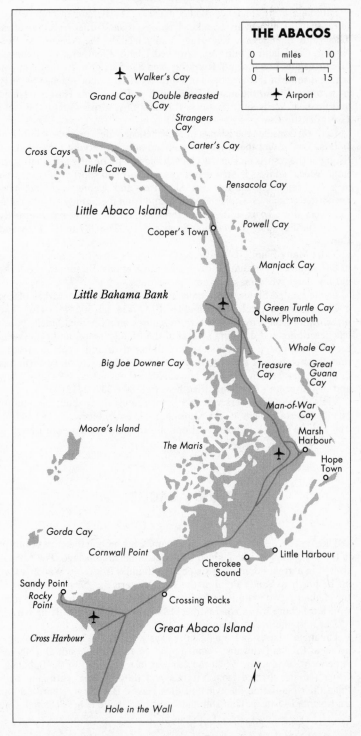

THE ABACOS

0 miles 10

0 km 15

✈ Airport

Walker's Cay

Grand Cay

Double Breasted Cay

Strangers Cay

Carter's Cay

Cross Cays

Little Cave

Pensacola Cay

Little Abaco Island

Powell Cay

Cooper's Town

Manjack Cay

Little Bahama Bank

Green Turtle Cay
New Plymouth

Whale Cay

Big Joe Downer Cay

Treasure Cay

Great Guana Cay

Man-of-War Cay

Moore's Island

Marsh Harbour

The Maris

Hope Town

Gorda Cay

Cornwall Point

Little Harbour

Cherokee Sound

Sandy Point
Rocky Point

Crossing Rocks

Great Abaco Island

Cross Harbour

N

Hole in the Wall

Although more than 700 islands make up the Bahamian archipelago, fewer than 30 of them are populated and less than 20 offer resort facilities. This guide includes the following Family Islands: the Abacos, Andros, Bimini, Cat Island, Chub Cay, Crooked Island, Eleuthera, the Exumas, Great Inagua, Long Island, Rum Cay, and San Salvador. In addition, you will find some of the developed offshore cays that can be reached by ferry or water taxi from the main islands, such as Eleuthera's Harbour Island and Spanish Wells and the Abacos' Elbow Cay, Great Guana Cay, and Green Turtle Cay.

Here we consider the islands in alphabetical order, providing information on how to get there, the carriers and airports serving each island, a listing of the resorts and sports on each island, and other general information. A local address is provided for each resort and sport facility, as well as a local telephone number; a U.S. address and telephone contact have been listed whenever available. Mail to and from the Family Islands tends to be very slow. To expedite your reservation, telephone the resort directly or call the Bahamas Reservation Service, 800–327–0787 in the USA and Canada.

Note: Many Family Island resorts and hotels close for a month or two in late summer or autumn for repairs and vacations. Be sure to check the closing dates when making your reservations.

In the United States, the Family Islands Promotion Board has offices at 255 Alhambra Circle, Coral Gables, FL 33134, tel. 305–446–4111. The organization can provide you with brochures on individual hotels, booklets describing and detailing several of the islands, maps, and rate sheets for both summer and winter seasons of all Family Island hotels and resorts that are members of the promotion board. The Ministry of Tourism has information offices in Nicholl's Town, North Andros (tel. 809–329–2167), and in Governor's Harbour, Eleuthera (tel. 809–332–2412).

VHR Worldwide offers vacation home rentals throughout the Family Islands. Contact them at 235 Kensington Avenue, Norwood, NJ 07648. Tel. 201–767–9393. Other rental options are listed under each island.

THE ABACOS

The Abacos, in the northeastern Bahamas, are among the most beautiful of the out-island chains making up the Bahamian archipelago. The Abacos stretch in a great boomerang shape for 140 miles from tiny Walker's Cay in the north to Sandy Point at the southwestern tip. Near the center of the chain are two main islands, Great and Little Abaco, fringed on their windward shore by an emerald necklace of cays forming a living barrier reef against the broad Atlantic.

The main islands and the offshore cays were settled two centuries ago by New England Loyalists who fought on the British side during the American Revolution. When the war was lost, they fled to the Bahamas. Other families arrived from Virginia and the Carolinas, bringing with them their plantation lifestyle and their slaves. But life was hard for the transplanted settlers. Thin soil and coral rock made it nearly impossible to wrest a living from the land. Many turned to the sea for sustenance, some to the dark art of "wrecking."

Charts of these waters had never been drawn, and there were no lighthouses in all of the Bahamas until 1836. The piratical wreckers worked by night, showing false lights to lure ships onto rocks and shoals to destruction—then harvesting the ships' cargo. Not all of the wrecks were caused by unscrupulous islanders, of course—many ships were lost in storms and foundered on hidden reefs as they passed through the Bahamas between the Atlantic Ocean and the Caribbean Sea. But by fair means or foul, "wrecking" was a thriving industry in the Abacos until the middle of the 1800s.

The days of loyalist plantations and the dark deeds of the wreckers have long ago faded into history and legend. Today, some 7,000 descendants of the early settlers and their slaves live in harmony together on the Abaco islands. Friendly and hard working, many still are seafarers, and earn their living as boat builders and boat repairmen, fishermen or fishing guides. And increasing numbers earn their living in the thriving tourist industry, since the Abacos are linked to the rest of the world by modern airports at Marsh Harbour and Treasure Cay.

There is a broad variety of vacation lifestyles for visitors to the Abacos. Most of the tourist accommodations are near the busy little town of Marsh Harbour and the nearby offshore village of Hope Town on Elbow Cay. Others are located at the vast Treasure Cay complex 50 miles to the north, and in the small island villages of Green Turtle Cay, just off its shore.

The calm, turquoise waters that lie between the main islands and the offshore cays are known to Bahamians and international yachtsmen as "The Sea of Abaco." The nearly 1,000 square miles of sheltered cruising grounds are arguably the best in the entire Bahamas or Caribbean. Two major bare-boat charter operators headquartered in the Abacos allow you to take advantage of this natural playground for sailors.

Marsh Harbour and Treasure Cay

Marsh Harbour, on Great Abaco Island, is an attractive, busy little town, the commercial center of the Abacos. The whole town and colorful harbor can easily be explored on foot or bicycle. A variety of stores and shops line the main road through town—which boasts the island's single traffic light. A favorite stop for tourists is the Loyalist Shoppe, which offers a good selection of imported gift items such as crystal, china, watches, and jewelry; a selection of newspapers, magazines, and books on the Bahamas; and handcrafted souvenirs. On a hilltop overlooking the town and the sea is an eccentric miniature "castle." It is the creation of Dr. Evans Cottman, an American scientist who lived on the island for many years, author of *Out Island Doctor,* a fascinating book on his Bahamian experiences.

In Marsh Harbour, there are several good inexpensive restaurants for lunch or dinner. Cynthia's Kitchen serves up native dishes such as curried goat in a friendly, frill-less atmosphere; Keys Bakery features the best baked goods on the island plus a range of meals from burgers to full-course Bahamian dinners. Just outside of Marsh Harbour, in the settlement of Dundas Town, is a "must stop" for locals and tourists alike: Mother Merele's Fishnet Restaurant (open for dinner only, after 6:30), where Bahamian cookery reigns supreme. You'll find baked turtle pie and conch fritters, hot johnnycake, homemade coconut ice cream, and deep-dish pineapple and key-lime pies. Mother Merle herself presides over the rustic out-island setting. For more elegant yet casual dining, try the delightful Jib Room at Marsh Harbour Marina. An outdoor veranda and nautical dining room overlook the busy harbor, and the menu includes char-broiled steaks and fish, brandied seafood, and many island favorites. Atmosphere is rustic but charming, and prices are moderate.

For a driving tour of the main island, a fair road winds northward to Treasure Cay, through vast Abaco pine forests where wild horses and boar are known to roam. Sights along the way include two colorful native villages, Dundas Town and Murphy's Town; and a sprawling tropical nursery, Bahamas Plants Ltd., which ships 100,000 ornamental plants to the U.S. market each week.

At Treasure Cay, you'll find a beautiful residential-resort community, a multimillion-dollar complex set on 1,400 acres of tropical greenery, along a stunning four-mile-long strip of broad, white-sand beach. Treasure Cay is not an island, but a large peninsula, connected to the mainland of Abaco by a narrow spit of land. There are a few small settlements in the area, clustered near the resort, and a good native eatery called A Touch of Class, where locals and tourists gather for fine Bahamian cooking and friendly service, music, and dancing. In the surrounding countryside, there is a huge 3,000-acre truck farm, which grows winter vegetables, avocados, and citrus fruit for shipment to the Florida market.

But the main attraction in this part of Abaco is the Treasure Cay Beach Hotel and Villas, one of the most complete residential resorts in all of the islands. It offers dozens of gracious oceanside homes, privately owned by Americans, Canadians, and Europeans; several outstanding apartment-villa complexes overlooking the sea, the harbor, or the golf course and available for purchase or vacation rental; and an attractive small hotel that operates on an all-inclusive package program. Amenities include a full-service marina for yachts to 200 feet; an 18-hole championship golf course designed by Dick Wilson; ten tennis courts; five freshwater pools; and a full scuba training facility. A 450-acre water sports and recreational center called Treasure Island, on nearby Great Guana Cay, is reached by a 550-passenger cruise boat. Just offshore is the charming island village of Green Turtle Cay, easily reached by regular ferry service.

A rugged road winds south from Marsh Harbour for more than 50 miles to Sandy Point, a rustic fishing village at the southwestern tip of the Abacos. There are miles of beautiful ocean beach on the point, offering some of the finest shelling in the Bahamas. There is excellent fishing nearby, and boats can be rented for angling or shelling expeditions to Rocky Point and Gorda Cay offshore where, collectors claim, the shelling is even better. The dense woodlands in this area are a nature preserve set aside by the Bahamas National Trust as a sanctuary for the endangered Bahamian parrot. More than a hundred other species have been counted by avid bird watchers.

The Offshore Cays

No trip to the Abacos would be complete without at least a day or two to explore the quaint island villages on the offshore cays. They are easily accessible by modern water taxis that cross the few miles of sheltered waters to the cays on a regular daily schedule.

Elbow Cay and Hope Town

The village of Hope Town on Elbow Cay overlooks a sheltered harbor dominated by a great 120-foot-tall peppermint-striped lighthouse— perhaps the most photographed landmark in all the Bahamas. When the Imperial Lighthouse Service put up the great light in 1838, the Hope Town villagers nearly sabotaged the entire project. They had counted on at least one wreck a month on their shores and feared that the light would end their prosperity. Yet in 1860 the settlers were still living off wrecks despite their new lighthouse. Today the lighthouse keeper at Hope Town welcomes visitors (Mon.–Fri., 10 A.M.–4 P.M.) hearty enough to climb the steep winding stairs to the top for an unsurpassed view of the turquoise waters and emerald cays that make up the great fringe reef off Abaco's shores. The great light is one of the last hand-powered kerosene-fueled beacons in the Bahamas.

Two narrow lanes circle the village and the harbor, one called Up Along, the other Down Along. Follow either for an interesting walking or biking tour of the delightful village, whose saltbox cottages, white picket fences, and flowering gardens will remind you of New England—but with the grays and browns of northern climes replaced by the pretty pastels of the tropics. The best example of Loyalist architecture in the village is the Wyannie Malone Historical Museum, filled with memorabilia and artifacts of Hope Town and the Widow Malone, who settled on the island with her children in 1875. Many of her descendants still live in Hope Town. Look for the Ebb Tide Gift Shop on Up Along, which offers a variety of hand prints, coral and shell gifts; or Jeff's Native Touches with some unusual handcrafted souvenirs. Drop by Lorraine's Bakery for fresh, hot Abaco bread and donuts, or plan lunch at the Village Inn on Down Along, overlooking the harbor—inexpensive, with the accent on fresh seafood and conch chowder.

Great Guana Cay

A startlingly beautiful island, Great Guana Cay's principal attraction is a seven-mile-long beach on the ocean side fringed by sheltered waters within an unbroken line of offshore reefs. There's excellent snorkeling among colorful sea gardens and schools of tropical fish and fine shelling (especially after a "norther"). The tiny village has less than a hundred people and no roads. Flowered lanes and pathways wind amid tall coconut palms and island greenery. The spectacular reef attracts divers and underwater photographers, fishermen, and yachtsmen. Drop in to the Guana Beach Resort for a frosty "Guana Grabber" or hearty Bahamian lunch.

Little Harbour

Southernmost stop on the ferry line (by special arrangement only), Little Harbour is the private island paradise of the Johnston family, artists and sculptors with an international following. Margot and Randolph and their three sons sailed to the island back in 1951 and decided to make it their home. They've told the story of their Swiss Family Robinson–style experiences in a book, *Artist on His Island*. The Johnstons have built a foundry for casting his superb bronze sculptures and a ceramic studio where she creates charming porcelain figurines of Bahamian fishermen, birds, fish, and boats. (Visitors are welcome at the studios from 10–11 A.M.,

2–3 P.M., or by appointment.) Nearby, their son Peter and his wife, Debbie, both noted sculptors, have a studio and bar called Pete's Pub and Gallery, offering cool drinks and good company along with an excellent variety of family art at a broad range of prices.

Man-of-War Cay

Nearly everyone who lives on Man-of-War Cay is named Albury, and most people are descendants of the early Loyalist settlers, proud of their heritage and their religion. The Alburys still build sturdy handcrafted Bahamian workboats at their boatyard on the harbor, much as their forefathers did 200 years ago. There is no crime on Man-of-War Cay, no jail, no cars, few television sets, fewer telephones, and absolutely no liquor is sold or consumed. But the islanders are warm, friendly, and openly hospitable, willing to chat, direct you to some of their favorite fishing, crabbing, or picnicking spots, and show you where to rent a bicycle or golf cart (the only mechanized transport on the island) for exploring the tiny cay and its long, beautiful beaches. (No scanty bikinis or short shorts please; the islanders disapprove.)

Some of the most delightful, creative craft shops in the Bahamas are on Man-of-War Cay. Look for Joe Albury's shop near the boatyard at harborside, where you will find hand-carved boat half-hulls, wooden furniture, and nautical accessories; or drop into Uncle Norman Albury's Sail Shop in the center of town, where the women of the family turn out handsome canvas or nylon duffle bags, sailing shirts and jackets, hats, and totes—each handmade, hand-signed, and (optionally) emblazoned with a chic Man-of-War Cay embroidered patch. Nearby you'll find Sally's Sea Side Shop, offering handmade shirts, blouses, sundresses, and skirts of fine denim or batiked and silk-screened island fabrics, as well as handcrafted straw hats and bags. All come at moderate to expensive prices. After your sightseeing stroll and shopping spree, drop by Albury's Dock 'n' Dine restaurant at the harborside for crispy conch fritters, hearty conch chowder, fresh fish, or perhaps just a tall frosty milk shake. And don't miss the devastatingly delicious homemade candy sold at the Bite Site, which is also a good spot for collectible bumper stickers, decals, banners, and posters with the unique Man-of-War Cay messages.

Green Turtle Cay and New Plymouth

Green Turtle Cay is a sprawling, two-mile-by-four-mile island with many deep bays, sounds, and a nearly continuous strip of fine ocean beach. Located just two miles off the shore of Treasure Cay, it boasts three main harbors: White Sound (dominated by Bluff House and the Green Turtle Cay Club on opposite shores), Black Sound, and Settlement Creek, location of picturesque New Plymouth village, whose roots go deep in to Abacos' Loyalist past. The Green Turtle Ferry Service from Treasure Cay makes stops at each of the harbors, and also calls at Coco Bay on the northern tip of the island. The easiest way to explore the entire island is by small outboard dinghy or Boston Whaler, which can be rented by the hour or the day at most resorts and marinas.

The town pier is located at New Plymouth. The village perches on a gentle hillside overlooking the busy harbor, and narrow flowered lanes wind between rows of neat little clapboard cottages painted in white and bright colorful gingerbread trim, or in pink, yellow, turquoise, aqua, and green. The most visited attraction is the Albert Lowe Museum, housed in a 150-year-old white clapboard two-story house. It overlooks a sculpture garden with fine bronze busts and a life-size sculpture of two island women, one black and one white, representing the island's earliest settlers, the Loyalists and their slaves. The museum and garden are the creation of Alton Roland Lowe, who named the museum for his father, a famous carver of wooden ship models. Both the father's and the son's works are on display in the museum, along with a priceless collection of memorabilia of Green Turtle Cay, dating back to the Loyalists' arrival in 1783–1785. The opening of the sculpture garden in 1983 marked the beginning of a two-year Loyalist Bicentennial Celebration, commemorated with a series of attractive postage stamps reproducing Lowe's oil paintings of the Loyalists' era. Look for the old Loyalist cemetery near the harbor, where weathered headstones date back to the 1780s.

After your stroll through the village, you might stop for an informal lunch or snack at Miss Betty MacIntosh's Sea View Restaurant and Bar (inexpensive Bahamian specialties), or for a cool drink and local gossip at Miss Emily's Blue Bee Bar—both are favorites of locals and visitors. Or linger over an elegant lunch or dinner at New Plymouth Inn, a historic 150-year-old house operated as a small inn and fine restaurant. Try the turtle steak or lobster salad with a vintage wine or a frosty stein.

PRACTICAL INFORMATION FOR THE ABACOS

HOW TO GET THERE. By air. Two international airports are located at Marsh Harbour and Treasure Cay. More than 50 miles and a rugged road separate the two, so visitors to the island must be certain they are routed to the proper airport. Both Marsh Harbour and Treasure Cay are served daily by *Bahamasair* from Nassau. They are served also by licensed, scheduled commuter airlines operating from Florida gateways, such as *Aero Coach, Caribbean Express, Eastern Express,* and *Piedmont Shuttle.* In addition, there are occasional charters that operate to the Abacos from U.S. cities in the Northeast and from Toronto and Montreal (check with your travel agent for details). At Walker's Cay, northernmost island in the Abaco chain, there is a private airstrip served by *Walker's Cay Airlines,* which offers daily scheduled service from Fort Lauderdale.

By mail boat. The mail boat M/V *Deborah K II* sails every Wed. from Potter's Cay Dock in Nassau and calls at Cherokee Sound, Cooper's Town, Green Turtle Cay, Hope Town, and Marsh Harbour, returning to Nassau each Mon. The M/V *Champion II* departs Potter's Cay Dock each Thurs., calling at Sandy Point, More's Island, and Bullock's Harbour, returning to Nassau each Sat. Call the Dock Master at Potter's Cay Dock in Nassau for details, tel. 323–1064. One-way fares are $20–$30.

TELEPHONES AND EMERGENCY NUMBERS. Area code for the Abacos is 809, although not all areas may be reached by direct distance dialing (DDD). As most resorts in the Abacos offer telephone service only at the main desk, all emergencies should be reported immediately to the hotel management. There are clinics at Cooper's Town, Fox Town, Marsh

Harbour (main clinic and health center, two resident nurses, and two private doctors), More's Island, Sandy Point, and Treasure Cay (private clinic with resident dentist and doctor). In Marsh Harbour: police, 919; clinic, 367–2510.

HOTELS AND RESTAURANTS. Hotels and hotel restaurants listed here are grouped according to the nearest airport, then by the island or town in which they are located. The telephone numbers given are reservations numbers; in many cases reservations may also be made through the Bahamas Reservation Service (BRS), tel. 800–327–0787.

Hotel price categories, based on double occupancy in high season, are: $150 and up, *Super Deluxe;* $125–$149, *Deluxe;* $100–$124, *Expensive;* $75–$99, *Moderate;* under $75, *Inexpensive.* The following credit card abbreviations are used: AE, American Express; DC, Diners Club; MC, MasterCard; V, Visa.

Marsh Harbour Airport

MARSH HARBOUR. Abaco Towns-by-the-Sea. *Deluxe.* Reserve direct: Box 486, Marsh Harbour, Abaco; tel. 367–2221, or through BRS. There are 54 modern, elegant townhouse villas, completely furnished with an island flair. Each features living room, kitchen, dining area, master bedroom, two baths, guest bedroom, and private patio. Well-landscaped gardens, a sparkling pool, and two tennis courts, all overlooking the sea. Available for purchase, time share, or vacation rental. Each villa accommodates up to six. AE, MC, V.

Great Abaco Beach Hotel. *Expensive.* Box 419, Marsh Harbour, Abaco; tel. 367–2158; or through BRS. On a hillside overlooking the sea, 30 attractive, oversized, air-conditioned rooms (each with a telephone) and five housekeeping villas. Spacious grounds include a freshwater pool, two tennis courts, and a sheltered strip of beach. There's fine dining in the 200-seat restaurant, which attracts visitors and locals from around the island. The house specialty is fresh-caught seafood (moderate). Also popular is the attractive bar/lounge, which features native singers and combos. The resort arranges all types of fishing charters, scuba trips, boat rentals, and sightseeing tours. Bicycles, mopeds, and cars are available for rental; bus service is provided to Treasure Cay's 18-hole championship golf course. Four miles from the airport. AE, MC, V.

Conch Inn. *Moderate.* Box 434, Marsh Harbour, Abaco; tel. 367–2800/2233. A comfortably casual yachtsman's haven with 14 tasteful, air-conditioned rooms overlooking the harbor and 40-slip full-service marina. The inn is one of the most popular gathering spots on the island for cruising yachtsmen, private fliers, and guests of other resorts. They are drawn by excellent native food (like conch burgers) at the *Conch Crawl* snack shop at the marina, the congenial *Conch Out* bar with island entertainment, and the delightfully tropical *Conch Inn Restaurant,* which serves some of the finest food in the Abacos (moderate to expensive). Other amenities include a large swimming pool, a well-stocked boutique, and a lovely ocean beach a brief stroll away. A two-bedroom housekeeping cottage and two efficiency apartments are also available. 6 percent service charge added. Located three miles from the airport. AE, MC, V.

Ambassador Inn Motel. *Inexpensive.* Box 484, Marsh Harbour, Abaco; tel. 367–2022. All six rooms are air-conditioned, and the motel has a dining room and a bar. No credit cards.

HOPE TOWN, ELBOW CAY. Accessible by ferry from docks near Marsh Harbour Airport. Boats meet incoming and outgoing flights.

Abaco Inn. *Expensive.* Abaco Inn, Hope Town, Abaco; tel. 367–2666; or through BRS. A friendly, relaxing hideaway that sprawls along three lovely beaches at White Sound, Elbow Cay. There are three two-bedroom oceanfront cottages and six double rooms at harborside, all simple but nicely furnished and air-conditioned. Shelling is fine along the broad beaches; there is a nice swimming pool and a thatched solarium for au natural sunbathing. All water sports and water-taxi tours are easily arranged at the resort; rental bicycles are available. An excellent restaurant offers dining indoors or outdoors and features creative cookery, including vegetarian fare and macrobiotic specialties (moderate to expensive). There is local entertainment in a congenial bar/lounge. MC, V.

Hope Town Harbour Lodge. *Moderate.* Hope Town, Abaco; tel. 367–2277; toll free in the U.S., 800–626–5690; or through BRS. A charming old inn on a hilltop overlooking both the harbor and the Atlantic. There are 13 clean and cozy rooms in the main lodge and eight comfortable cottage rooms on the ocean side, clustered around a nice pool. Two attractive dining rooms serve a good international and Bahamian menu, and the traditional Sunday Champagne Brunch draws enthusiasts from all over the island and the mainland. Scuba, boating, water-skiing, fishing, and windsurfing are available at the resort's harborside marina. MC, V.

GREAT GUANA CAY. Guana Beach Resort. *Inexpensive.* Box 474, Marsh Harbour, Abaco; tel. 367–2207, or through BRS. A small, cozy resort with 19 rooms on one of the most strikingly beautiful islands in the Abaco chain. Rooms are neat and simply furnished; some are air-conditioned. There is a dining room serving good, hearty Bahamian dishes, and a congenial bar where cruising yachtsmen gather. At harborside, there's a small marina and dock, and at oceanside a spectacular seven-mile-long beach. MC, V.

Treasure Cay Airport

TREASURE CAY. Treasure Cay Beach Hotel and Villas. *Expensive to Deluxe.* All-inclusive package programs only. Reserve direct: Treasure Cay Beach Hotel and Villas, 2301 S. Federal Hwy. Fort Lauderdale, FL 33316; tel. 305–525–7711; 800–327–1584 in the U.S.; 800–432–8257 in Florida. All of the sophistication of a major international resort with the charm and style of an island village. There is an intimate hotel of 35 rooms, centered amid 1,400 lushly green tropical acres overlooking four miles of broad white-sand beach. Through the gardens and along the seashore are nearly 200 additional accommodations located in beautiful villas and townhouses, rustic cottages and double-deck apartments overlooking the harbor and the sea (available for time share or purchase). All are fully air-conditioned, attractively furnished, and offer full kitchens, large living rooms, terraces, or patios. Units have one, two, or three bedrooms. Sporting amenities include an 18-hole championship, Dick Wilson–designed golf course with clubhouse and pro shop; ten hard-surface tennis courts (four lighted for night play); five freshwater pools; a 150-slip, full-service marina; and a complete scuba-dive operation. There are boat trips to the offshore island of Guana Cay and the resort's new recreational center, Treasure Island; sightseeing trips to Elbow Cay, Man-of-War Cay, and Green Turtle Cay; and drift fishing expeditions. Boat rentals can be made at the marina, scooter and car rentals can be arranged at the hotel. The two good restaurants are the *Abaco Room* in the hotel and the lovely *Spinnaker Restaurant,* with entertainment every evening (expensive), and quiet drinks with a great view at the *Tipsy Seagull Bar* overlooking the marina. The resort also offers a complete shopping center, including doctors' and dentists' offices, bank, and post office. Located 7½ miles from the airport. AE, MC, V.

GREEN TURTLE CAY. Accessible by water taxi from the docks near Treasure Cay Airport. Boats meet all incoming and outgoing flights.

Green Turtle Club. *Expensive.* Green Turtle Cay, Abaco; tel. 367–2572; in the U.S., 305–833–9580; or through BRS. An elegant but informal yachtsman's rendezvous, this private-membership yacht club has ties to the British Royal Yachting Association and the Palm Beach Yacht Club in Florida. Guests are welcomed, however. Thirty-one luxurious, beautifully appointed rooms are available as doubles or in villas and cottages tucked amid tropical greenery on a hillside overlooking the harbor. They contain one to three bedrooms and one to three bathrooms, full kitchens, dining and living rooms, and private terraces. The harborside clubhouse houses a unique nautical bar. The attractive dining room here serves excellent food ranging from gourmet to traditional American fare and authentic Bahamian cuisine, with the accent on fresh seafood. The service is impeccable, and guests enjoy dressing with casual elegance for dinner and dancing on the terrace (expensive). Amenities include a small private beach, a pool, one tennis court, a 22-slip full service marina, boating, and fishing and scuba expeditions. AE, MC, V.

Bluff House. *Moderate.* Green Turtle Cay, Abaco; tel. 809–367–2786 or through BRS. A cozy, comfortable, well-run resort with its clubhouse set atop a high bluff with panoramic views of the sheltered harbor and ocean reefs. The small ocean beach has a beach club for lunch and drinks. Tree houses are scattered on wooded hillside acres; villas with one, two, and three bedrooms are on the beach. Split-level townhouse suites and hotel rooms with water views make up this resort. All rooms are airconditioned, some with kitchen facilities. All have private bathrooms. In the main clubhouse, there is a candlelit dining room where complimentary wine is poured freely and excellent meals feature American, Continental, and Bahamian cuisine. It is a favorite dining-out experience for cruising yachtsmen and guests of nearby resorts (moderate to expensive). The resort has a pool, a tennis court, and two restaurants. Arrangements are easily made at the resort's harborside marina for boating, water-skiing, deepsea and bonefishing expeditions, and water-taxi tours around the island and to the village of New Plymouth. MC, V.

New Plymouth Inn. *Moderate.* Reserve direct: New Plymouth Inn, Green Turtle Cay, Abaco; tel. 367–5211; in the U.S., 305–665–5309. An elegant little historic inn overlooking a tropical garden and sparkling pool. There are just eight carefully restored rooms in the charming antique two-story house. The inn is a fine example of Bahamian colonial architecture. All rooms have private bath and shower. The inn's attractive dining room next door dishes up notable Bahamian specialties such as turtle steaks, fresh native lobster, and conch, as well as roasts, steaks, and chops—all served with vintage wines or imported beers (moderate to expensive). The *Galleon* lounge/bar is a favorite stop of island sightseers. Nearby ocean beach; 15 percent service charge. No credit cards.

Rental Apartments and Cottages: There are many rental units available on Green Turtle Cay. Rates at the following recommended establishments range from inexpensive to moderate:

Linton's Beach Cottages. Green Turtle Cay, Abaco; ask operator for Green Turtle Cay. Four two-bedroom cottages along a lovely private beach, each with living/dining room, full kitchen, and private bath.

Sea Star Beach Cottages. Box 282, Gilam Bay, Green Turtle Cay, Abaco; tel. Green Turtle Cay 5444. Four attractive kitchenette cottages located on 19 oceanside acres along a lovely private beach.

Walker's Cay Airport

Walker's Cay Club. *Expensive to Deluxe.* Reserve direct: Walker's Cay Club, 700 S.W. 34th St., Fort Lauderdale, FL 33315; tel. 305–523–4300; toll-free in the U.S. 800–327–3714; toll-free in Florida 800–432–2092. Served by private scheduled air service from Fort Lauderdale and Chalk's seaplanes from West Palm Beach. A completely self-contained resort on the northernmost island in all of the Bahamas. A favorite of private-plane fliers and international divers, the island is best known for spectacular sport fishing. The club hosts several major tournaments each year, including a leg of the prestigious Bahamas Billfish Championship and the famed Bertram-Hatteras Shootout. There are 62 luxurious hotel rooms, attractively furnished and air-conditioned, and four exclusive villas. The quaint dining room overlooks the sea and serves up Bahamian and American specialties—especially fresh-caught fish—complemented by a superb wine list. The patio bar and lounge are favorite gathering spots for swapping fish tales and watching the weigh-ins at the docks. Sports amenities include a 75-slip full-service marina with a fleet of charter boats and rental skiffs available for both deep-sea and light-tackle fishing expeditions; two hard-surface tennis courts; two swimming pools (one saltwater, one freshwater); and a full scuba program. AE, MC, V.

HOW TO GET AROUND. There is direct **taxi** service to all resorts on Great Abaco Island served by Marsh Harbour Airport, or to the docks for water taxi service to resorts at Hope Town on Elbow Cay, Man-of-War Cay, and Great Guana Cay. From Treasure Cay Airport there is direct taxi service to Treasure Cay Beach Hotel and Villas and to the docks for ferry service to Green Turtle Cay resorts.

Taxi tours of Great Abaco Island may be negotiated at the airports or arranged through your resort. Rental cars are available in Marsh Harbour through *H & L Rentals,* Box 490, Marsh Harbour, Abaco, tel. 367–2840; or *V & R Rentals,* tel. 367–2001.

For **sightseeing** expeditions to the offshore cays from main island resorts, water taxi or ferry service is available from the docks serving both Marsh Harbour and Treasure Cay airports. Services generally coincide with incoming and outgoing flights. Visitors should check at their resorts for exact schedules or contact the following: Marsh Harbour—*Albury's Ferry Service,* at the dock near the Great Abaco Beach Hotel, tel. 367–2306. The firm offers regular service to Hope Town, or Elbow Cay, Man-of-War Cay, and Great Guana Cay; organizes charters on longer trips (for up to eight passengers) to Treasure Cay and Green Turtle Cay. From docks near the Treasure Cay Airport, the *Green Turtle Cay Ferry Service* operates frequently to several points on Green Turtle Cay. There is no phone service, but the ferry stands by on CB channel 11 and may be contacted by radio from the Treasure Cay Beach Hotel and Villas or the airport. In the island villages of the offshore cays, there are few cars. Sightseeing is on foot or by rental bicycle, available at most of the resorts and through small shops in the villages or at marinas along the harbors. Your ferryboat captain or water-taxi driver is a good source of information on where to rent bikes or scooters and how much they should cost.

SPECIAL EVENTS. *Abaco Week,* a "roots" festival held each November, attracts hundreds of visitors from the Bahamas, Key West, Nova Scotia, and the West Indies, where other Loyalists found new homes during the great refugee migrations that began during the American Revolutionary War and peaked after the British were defeated. There are arts-and-crafts fairs, choral groups, Junkanoo masqueraders, plus golf, tennis, and fishing tournaments throughout the Abacos. For details, write the Abaco Chamber of Commerce, Box 509, Marsh Harbour, Abaco; tel. 367–2663.

Bahamas Billfish Championship Tournament. Two legs of the prestigious tournament series are held in the Abacos: *Walker's Cay Billfish Tournament,* held in April, and the *Treasure Cay Billfish Tournament,* held in June. Both resorts host several other major fishing events.

Annual Green Turtle Cay Fishing Tournament. Held in May at the Green Turtle Yacht Club, a fun-filled week for less serious fishermen and families.

Regatta Time in Abaco and the *Green Turtle Cay Regatta* are held in June and July with a fun-filled, three-week-long series of races and regattas throughout the Abacos. Most resorts, marinas, and yacht clubs participate—from Marsh Harbour to Treasure Cay on the main island and the offshore cays of Hope Town, Man-of-War Cay, and Green Turtle Cay. The parties and picnics ashore match the rivalry and revelry at sea, with something for everyone, visitors and locals alike. You don't even need a boat to join in the fun. Traditionally, the race weeks begin the last week of June and encompass both U.S. Independence Day on July 4 and Bahamas Independence Day on July 10, with appropriate celebrations and fireworks marking both occasions. For details contact the Bahamas' sports hotline, 800–327–7678.

SPORTS. Bareboat Charters. Large fleets of modern sailboats and powerboats are headquartered at the marinas in Marsh Harbour and at Hope Town Harbor on Elbow Cay. The yachts may be chartered by the week or longer, with or without crew, and with or without full provisioning. Rates vary by season and size of yacht, and are subject to change:

Abaco Bahamas Charters. Weekly charter rates begin at $900, with full or partial provisions optional. Summer rates are lower, and two-for-one specials offered (two weeks for price of one) from mid-July to mid-Dec. Reserve direct: Abaco Bahamas Charters, Hope Town, Abaco. In the U.S., 800–626–5690.

Bahamas Yachting Services. Rates range from $1,050 to $2,295 per week, with full or partial provisions optional. Skippers available at extra charge. "Instructional Charters" offered in summer, and two-for-one (two weeks for the price of one) from mid-July to end Nov. Reserve direct: Bahamas Yachting Service, Marsh Harbour, Abaco. In the U.S., 305–484–5246.

Fishing and Boating. The Abacos are noted for fine fishing of all types: deep sea, reef, bonefishing, and spearfishing. Small boats for harbor-hopping and sightseeing or light-tackle fishing are available through most resorts. A sampling of the facilities and approximate rates on the mainland and offshore cays:

Great Guana Cay. Deep-sea fishing in 25-foot Bertram, $275 full day; $175 half day. Sailboat rentals, 25- to 26-foot, $350 wk. Reserve direct: Pinder's, tel. 367–2207.

Green Turtle Cay. Two 25-foot sport-fishing boats for deep-sea fishing, $200 full day; $100 half day. 14-foot Boston Whalers also available. Reserve direct: Green Turtle Cay Club, Green Turtle Cay, Abaco; tel. 367–2572.

Hope Town, Elbow Cay. Small boats available for reef fishing and bone-fishing at $60 per half day. Reserve direct: Elbow Cay Club, Hope Town, Abaco; tel. 367–2748.

Treasure Cay. Bonefishing boats with guide, $140 full day; $100 half day. Reef fishing with guide, $35 per person. A 22-foot sport-fishing boat with captain, $250 full day; $200 half day. Reserve direct: Treasure Cay Beach Hotel and Villas, Box TC 4183, Treasure Cay, Abaco; tel. 367–2570.

Walker's Cay. Boston Whalers with guide, $115 full day; $70 half day; without guide, $70 full day, $40 half day. Reef fishing on 23-foot Mako, full day $160, half day $110; 26-foot Mako, full day $300, half day $175 (both with captain). Trolling on 23-foot Mako, full day $200, half day $135; 26-foot Mako, $325 full day, $200 half day. Reserve: Sea Lion Marina, 700 S.W. 34th St., Fort Lauderdale, FL 33315; tel. 305–522–1469.

Golf. *Treasure Cay Golf Club.* 18-hole championship course par 72 designed by Dick Wilson. Clubhouse, resident pro, pro shop, and driving range. No greens fees for guests. Golf carts are mandatory. For advance reservations: Box TC-4183, Treasure Cay, Abaco; tel. 367–2570.

Scuba. Dive trips may be arranged through your resort, or directly through the following operators in the Abacos. Each offers instruction, a full line of equipment for rent or sale, and daily dive trips.

Brendal's Dive Shop. Green Turtle Cay, Abaco. Tel. 367–2572.

Dave Gale's Island Marine. In Hope Town at the Abaco Inn. Reserve direct: Dave Gale's Island Marine, Hope Town, Abaco; tel. 367–2822.

Dive Abaco. In Marsh Harbour, Box 555, Abaco; tel. 367–2014.

Elbow Cay Beach Inn. Offers a scuba program. Contact the resort at 367–2748.

Great Abaco Dive and Photo Center. Boat Harbour Marina, Box 511, Marsh Harbour, Abaco. In the U.S., 305–763–5665.

Treasure Cay Dive Center. Located at Treasure Cay Marina. Reserve direct: Treasure Cay Dive Center, Treasure Cay, Abaco; tel. 367–2570.

Walker's Cay Dive Shop. At Walker's Cay Marina. Resort course and PADI certification available. Reserve direct: Walker's Cay Dive Shop, 700 S.W. 34th St., Fort Lauderdale, FL 33315; tel. 305–522–1469, 800–327–3714.

Windsurfing. *Abaco Inn.* $30 day, $15 half day; tel. 367–2666.

Elbow Cay Club. $25 day, $12 half day; tel. 367–2748.

Green Turtle Cay Club. Free to guests; tel. 367–2572.

Hope Town Harbour Lodge. $20 day; tel. 367–2277.

Treasure Cay Beach Hotel. Free to guests; tel. 367–2847.

Walker's Cay Hotel. $60 day, $15 hour; tel. 305–522–1469.

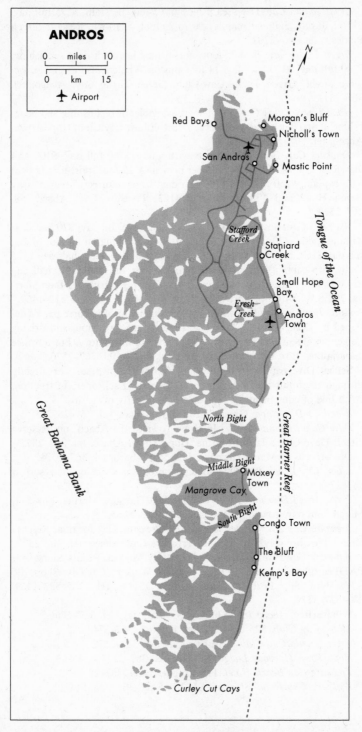

ANDROS

0   miles   10

0   km   15

✈ Airport

Red Bays

Morgan's Bluff

Nicholl's Town

San Andros

Mastic Point

Stafford Creek

Staniard Creek

Small Hope Bay

Fresh Creek

Andros Town

North Bight

Middle Bight

Moxey Town

Mangrove Cay

South Bight

Congo Town

The Bluff

Kemp's Bay

Curley Cut Cays

Tongue of the Ocean

Great Barrier Reef

Great Bahama Bank

N

ANDROS

Vast Andros, largest island in the Bahamian archipelago, lies just 35 miles southwest of Nassau, yet it remains mysterious, mostly unsettled, virtually unexplored. Over 100 miles long and 40 miles wide, the sprawling island is intersected at its midpoint by meandering creeks known as "bights," and its lush green interior is covered with dense forests of pine and mahogany, fringed along the western shore by miles of mangrove swamp. Most of the island's few small settlements and secluded resorts are found along the eastern shore—offering miles of unspoiled beach to roam, great harbor-hopping in small runabouts, and extraordinary bone-fishing and reef fishing. Nevertheless, the island is best known for its spectacular diving. Running the length of its eastern shore is the Andros Barrier Reef, second in size only to Australia's Great Barrier Reef. But unlike the massive reef down under, which lies up to 200 miles offshore and is accessible only by oceangoing vessels, the Andros reef is just minutes away from the beaches, less than a mile offshore. Sheltered waters within the reef average six to 12 feet deep, but "over the wall" lies the fathomless depths of the Tongue of the Ocean. This vast canyon is used by the U.S. and British navies operating under the acronym of AUTEC—Atlantic Underwater Test and Evaluation Center—for testing submarines and underwater weapons systems. The large base, with nearly 1,000 personnel, is located near Andros Town.

Northern Andros can be explored by adventurous travelers with a taxi/tour guide or rental vehicle, which can be arranged through most resorts. However, roads are rugged, fuel and repair stops infrequent, and settlements few and far between. Villages near the airports are easily explored by bicycle or scooter from nearby resorts or by hiking along the beaches, as nearly all of the Andros settlements overlook the sea.

Androsia is a cottage industry, near Small Hope Bay Lodge at Andros Town, that produces attractive, original batik fabric and island fashions in brilliant tropical colors and bold tropical designs. Visitors are invited to see the entire batik process from painting the designs in hot wax, dyeing, and drying, to cutting and sewing the final fashions—and are even invited to create their own designs, a truly unique Bahamian souvenir. The pride of Andros, Androsia fashions for men and women are shipped to hotel shops and boutiques on the other islands, in the Carribbean, and in the United States and Europe—but nowhere are they found in more variety, color, and style (and at lower prices) than in the small shop where they are created. Androsia, operated by Rosi Birch, employs more than 75 local artisans.

The Blue Holes of Andros are vast inland ocean holes that rise up through the coral and are often more than 200 feet deep. Found here and there throughout Andros, they were made famous by Jacques Cousteau. Ask your resort hosts or taxi/tour guide to direct you to local sites.

You may never actually see a *chickcharnie,* but according to Androsians they are everywhere in the pine forests and silk-cotton trees of Andros. Legendary, mischievous creatures, these Bahamian "elves" are said to have three fingers, three toes, fearsome red eyes, green feathers and beards, and hang upside down by their tails. They bring good luck to friendly visitors and enjoy playing tricks—but Androsians will warn you that it's not wise to irritate a chickcharnie. Should a human not believe in them or scoff at them, he may just find that suddenly his head is turned backward on his shoulders.

Great headlands circle a crescent beach at *Morgan's Bluff,* and legend has it that the eighteenth-century pirate Sir Henry Morgan buried his treasure nearby. Located north of the settlement at San Andros and Nicholl's Town, the small village is relatively easy to reach from resort centers in the area.

Red Bays Village was settled in the 1840s by refugee Seminole Indians and blacks escaping Spanish slavery on the Florida mainland. Until very recently, their descendants have lived isolated and virtually unknown in a small island community off the northwestern shore of Andros. Today, Red Bays is connected to the main island by a short causeway and visitors are welcomed, but the people maintain a tribal society unchanged for more than a century in which the leader is acknowledged as chief. Accessible by road from San Andros and Nicholl's Town in the north.

PRACTICAL INFORMATION FOR ANDROS

HOW TO GET THERE. By air. Three airports are ports of entry on Andros: *San Andros* in the north; *Andros Town* in the central area; and *South Andros* at Congo Town in the south. There is an airstrip at *Mangrove Cay.* (Visitors should be certain that they are routed to the proper airport, because on Andros the old adage "you can't get there from here" has meaning.) *Bahamasair* offers a total of 36 flights a week to the airports on Andros from Nassau, and *Small Hope Bay Lodge* and *Andros Beach Hotel* offer private charter flights from Fort Lauderdale, Fla.

By mail boat. The following sail to Andros from Potter's Cay Dock in Nassau: *M/V Lisa J II* sails from Nassau Wed., calling at northern Andros villages of Mastic Point, Morgan's Bluff, and Nicholl's Town, returning to Nassau on Tues. The *M/V Central Andros Express* sails from Nassau Sun., calling at Fresh Creek near Andros Town and Behring Point, returning to Nassau on Wed. *M/V Mangrove Cay Express* sails to Mangrove Cay from Nassau on Fri., returning to Nassau on Wed. Contact dock master at Potter's Cay in Nassau, tel. 323–1064. One-way fare is $16.

TELEPHONES AND EMERGENCY NUMBERS. The area code for Andros is 809. As most Andros hotels offer telephone service only at the front desk, all emergencies should be reported directly to the hotel management. There is a resident doctor in San Andros and health clinics in Mastic Point, Nicholl's Town, and Lowe Sound in north Andros. In central Andros, there is a clinic at Fresh Creek and one at Mangrove Cay. In south Andros, there is a clinic at Kemps Bay. In north Andros: police, 919; clinic, 329–2121 or 329–2291. In central Andros: police, 368–2626; clinic, 368–2038. In south Andros: police, 329–4733; clinic, 329–4620.

HOTELS AND RESTAURANTS. Hotels and restaurants are grouped here according to the nearest airport. The telephone numbers given are reservations numbers; in many cases reservations may also be made through the Bahamas Reservation Service (BRS), tel. 800–327–0787.

Hotel price categories, based on double occupancy in high season, are: over $100, *Expensive;* under $75, *Inexpensive.*

Andros Town Airport

Small Hope Bay Lodge. *Expensive.* Box N-1131, Nassau; tel. 368–2014; 305–463–4191 in FL; in the U.S. 800–223–6961; or through BRS. Sophisticated ambience and rustic comfort in a South Sea–island setting. Just 20 rooms in cottages strung along a white-sand beach amid a grove of coconut palms. All are colorfully decorated in original batiks and have showers and ceiling fans, and a few have waterbeds. A comfortable lodge houses the dining room with a great fireplace, game room, extensive library, and *The Panacea,* an old dory rigged out as a bar (honor system only). The oldest dive resort in the islands, featuring some of the finest diving in the Bahamas, was built by Canadian Dick Birch 25 years ago and is still owned and managed by the Birch family. Nearly everyone samples the snorkeling, and even novices are trained in a few hours and don mask and scuba gear to explore the shallow reefs. For trained divers, there are twice-daily dive trips to the great Andros Barrier Reef just offshore, and for après dive there's a redwood hot tub on the beach. Other sports include "crabbing" expeditions, reef fishing, biking, small-boat sailing, and windsurfing. All rates are AP (American Plan), and all-inclusive packages—with transportation via the resort's private plane from Fort Lauderdale—are featured. Four miles from Andros Town Airport. AE, MC, V.

Chickcharnie Hotel. *Inexpensive.* Reserve direct: Chickcharnie Hotel, Fresh Creek, Andros; tel. 368–2025. Just eight neat, air-conditioned rooms (some with private bath) in a small inn at Fresh Creek. A favorite of avid fishermen. A popular bar and restaurant attracts locals and anglers with good basic food and cool drinks on an attractive patio. Fishing boats and guides for hire; bicycles available. There is a grocery and dry-goods store on the premises. No credit cards.

Nottages Cottages Resort and Fishing Camp. *Inexpensive.* Reserve direct: 809–329–4293. Eighteen cottages, all air-conditioned, with beach privileges nearby. Bar and restaurant. No credit cards.

San Andros Airport

Andros Beach Hotel and Scuba Club. *Inexpensive.* Nicholl's Town, Andros; tel. 329–2582; or contact Neal Watson's Underseas Adventures, Box 21766, Fort Lauderdale, FL 33335; tel. 305–763–2188; 800–327–8150; or through BRS. Twenty-four neat, air-conditioned rooms, attractive grounds, overlooking three miles of pristine beach. Nearby are the Tradewind Villas, 16 cottages with kitchen facilities set in a pretty community, which are operated in conjunction with the hotel and share amenities. There is a main dining room with lounge and bar offering frequent local entertainment, an attractive swimming pool, and a tennis court. A complete diving program including instruction and rental equipment has recently been inaugurated by new management, Neal Watson's Underseas Adventures. Daily dive trips to the nearby Andros Barrier Reef are offered. Fishing and boating excursions can be arranged, and there are rental cars, scooters, and bicycles available. Eight miles from San Andros Airport. AE, MC.

South Andros Airport

Las Palmas Beach Hotel. *Inexpensive.* The Bluff, Andros; tel. 329–4661. A quiet, isolated, Bahamian-owned ranch-style resort; 20 modestly decorated, air-conditioned rooms cluster around a palm-like shaded patio overlooking five miles of unspoiled ocean beach. The dining room serves local and American specialties. Two miles from South Andros Airport at Congo Town. No credit cards.

Royal Palm Lodge. *Inexpensive.* Kemp's Bay, Andros; tel. 329–4543. Small, tidy guest house on the waterfront at Johnson Bay. A one-story stone building with nine air-conditioned, neatly furnished, carpeted bedrooms with private baths. Sandy beach nearby; boating, snorkeling, and diving arrangements can be made. No credit cards.

Mangrove Cay Airport

Bannister's Cottages. *Inexpensive.* Mangrove Cay, Andros. Tel. 329–4188. This economy complex has seven rooms, a restaurant, and a bar. Boating is available and there is a beach close by. MAP only. No credit cards.

Cool Breeze Cottages. *Inexpensive.* Mangrove Cay, Andros. Tel. 329–4465. Thirty-five cottages and four rooms make up this boating and fishing camp. There is a restaurant, a bar, and a beach. No credit cards.

Longley's Guest House. *Inexpensive.* Lisbon Creek, Andros. Tel. Mangrove Cay operator. This is a popular spot for local fisherman and boaters. There are five guest rooms, a bar, and a restaurant. AP only. No credit cards.

Moxey's Guest House. *Inexpensive.* Lisbon Creek, Andros. Tel. Mangrove Cay operator. With its own private beach, this guest house has six bedrooms, a bar, and a restaurant. No credit cards.

White Sands Beach Hotel. *Inexpensive.* Mangrove Cay, Andros. Tel. 329–4159. This economy guest house has 16 rooms and its own private beach. No credit cards.

HOW TO GET AROUND. Fair to poor roads link settlements on Andros, and rental autos, scooters, and bicycles may be booked through most resorts on the island.

SPORTS. Fishing and Boating. The following marinas offer fishing expeditions with boat, tackle, and guides, listed by proximity to nearest airport on Andros. Rates are approximate and are subject to change.

Andros Town Airport Area: *Charlie's Haven,* South of Andros Town at Behring Point. Bonefishing boats with guides, $80 for full day; tarpon-fishing boats with guides, $120 full day. Deep-sea fishing charters can be arranged. Tel. 329–5261. *Chickcharnie Hotel,* at Fresh Creek near Andros Town. Fishing boats with tackle and guides available. Deep-sea fishing, $150 full day, $85 half day; bonefishing, $60 full day, $40 half day; Boston Whalers, $60 per day with guide; Abaco boat, $40 per day with guide, $12 fuel surcharge. Tel. 328–2025.

San Andros Airport Area: *Andros Beach Hotel.* Eighteen-foot Boston Whalers, Sunfish, sport-fishing, and charter boats available. Rates on request. Tel. 329–2582 or Neal Watson Underwater Adventures. In the U.S. 800–327–8150 or 305–763–2188.

South Andros–Congo Town Airport Area: *Las Palmas Beach Hotel.* Small-boat rentals available: Sunfish, $4 per hour; Boston Whalers, $6 per hour; 20-foot ski boat, $20 per hour; 20-foot fishing boat, $200 per day, $100 half day. Tel. 325–5441.

Scuba: There's superb diving off Andros's eastern shore, along the Great Andros Barrier Reef. Approximate rates for a half-day reef trip with gear, boat, and guide are $35–$50 per person.

BIMINI

Bimini, known for half a century as the big-game fishing capital of the world, lives up to its reputation. Anglers fishing these waters have rewritten the record books nearly every year since the 1930s when big-name fishermen such as Ernest Hemingway, Zane Grey, and Howard Hughes discovered the big game lurking just off Bimini's shores. Little has changed on the island since those halcyon days. Fishing is still Bimini's biggest draw, but divers are discovering the island, and there are several notable underwater attractions just offshore.

The nearest Bahamian island to the U.S. mainland, Bimini lies 50 miles due east of Miami, across the mighty Gulf Stream that sweeps the island's western shores. Each year Bimini attracts thousands of avid fishermen, divers, cruising yachtsmen, and sporting vacationers from Florida's Gold Coast, the rest of the United States, Canada, Britain, and Europe. Many come to participate in the dozen major international fishing tournaments held on the island each year from March through the first week in August. Reservations for tournament weeks are very difficult to get; they should be booked up to six months in advance.

You won't need a car on Bimini, because most of the "action" sprawls along Queen's Highway (barely wide enough for two cars to pass), which runs through the center of Alice Town for a mile or two, with bars, "nightclubs," grocery stores, souvenir shops, bait-and-tackle emporiums, and brightly painted houses crowded together along both sides of the road. On the Gulf Stream side of the island are long winding beaches, and on the harbor side are a few rustic resorts with busy docks and marinas.

You can bike or walk around most of the island in an hour or two, for there's not a lot to see. Bimini is one big fishing camp, raucous and rowdy at night when anglers crowd the small bars and "nightclubs" to swap tales, merengue to a calypso band, or disco to a rock group. During the day, the island lies sleepy under a golden sun, a perfect place for a picnic on a quiet beach or a leisurely drink in an uncrowded bar. If you choose the beach, drop by Captain Bob's Conch Hall of Fame Restaurant for your picnic lunch; he makes the best ones on the island. Or have a steaming bowl of conch chowder at his sparkling clean counter.

The best beach is opposite the Anchorage, an attractive old Cape Cod–style cottage on a small slope overlooking the sea, now the restaurant for Bimini's Blue Water Resort but once the home of Michael and Helen Lerner and the setting for Ernest Hemingway's novel *Islands in the Stream.* A close friend of the Lerners, Hemingway visited them annually during the big game fishing season. The beach was one of his favorites; it extends for nearly a mile off the Anchorage, with coarse white sand and a surfing sea when the wind is right. A quieter beach with calmer waters can be found north of town, off King's Highway. Take a left when the

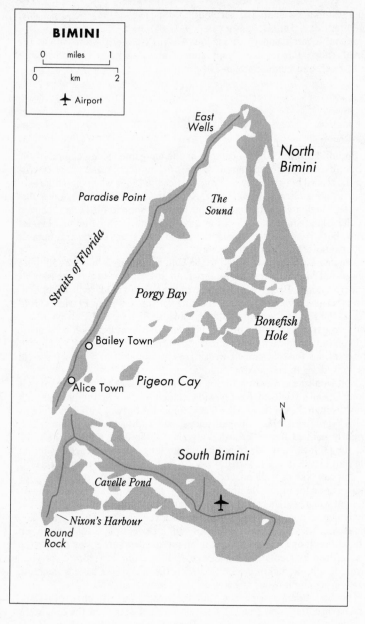

BIMINI

0   miles   1

0   km   2

✈ Airport

East Wells

North Bimini

Paradise Point

The Sound

Straits of Florida

Porgy Bay

Bonefish Hole

Bailey Town

Pigeon Cay

Alice Town

N

South Bimini

Cavelle Pond

Nixon's Harbour

Round Rock

road branches to Bimini Bay. The paved road ends after a few hundred yards, where you'll see a path to your right. Follow it to a lovely casuarina-shaded beach, wonderful for swimming, snorkeling, and a picnic in the shade.

The pathway above the Anchorage beach will take you to Wesley Methodist church, one of the quaintest in the Family Islands. Founded in 1858, its white clapboard, green shutters, and miniature bell tower make it look as though it had been transplanted from New England.

For a real change of pace, wander down King's Highway (the narrow main street) to the End of the World Bar, funkiest spot on funky Bimini, once the hangout for Adam Clayton Powell, the late, always controversial New York congressman who spent more time in Bimini than he did in Washington. Dirt floor, graffiti-covered walls, a lazily turning ceiling fan painted in bright candy stripes, and wide open doors that look out on the harbor. It's a laid-back place, perfect for a tall cold drink on a hot afternoon. Bimini visitors for more than a generation have left their mark on the tables and walls.

Downtown, near Chalk's seaplane ramp (which extends across the road), the Compleat Angler is quiet in the afternoon, the best time for having a look around the old inn with its polished Abaco pine walls, stone fireplace, and a great collection of Hemingway photos and memorabilia. In room #1 he slept (when he wasn't fishing, partying, brawling, or boozing) and worked on the manuscript of *To Have and Have Not.*

Sunset is time to head for the docks and watch the fishing yachts come in; there's always plenty of activity as the giant blue marlin are weighed. For a quick, inexpensive supper, drop into the bright red Red Lion Pub, tiny and somewhat tacky but terrific for fresh seafood, chicken, and ribs. The most elegant dining on the island will be found at the Bimini Big Game Fishing Club, where the "catch of the day" is famous and the grilled lobster memorable.

Cat Cay

Located south of Bimini, Cat Cay (not to be confused with Cat Island) is a posh private island for the rich and famous, founded as a private club in the 1930s. Today it remains strictly private, an enclave with many beautiful homes, a nine-hole golf course, a splendid clubhouse, and fine docking facilities. Cruising yachtsmen are welcome to make Cat Cay a port of call, but they may stay a maximum of only two days, and they have a separate restaurant and bar and may not mingle with club members or guests. The Cat Cay Championship Tournament, a leg of the Bahamas Billfish Championship, held in May, is the only annual fishing tournament open to the public. Cat Cay Club, Box 530950, Miami Shares, FL 33153; tel. 305-757-6439.

PRACTICAL INFORMATION FOR BIMINI

HOW TO GET THERE. By air. Bimini is just a half-hour from downtown Miami via *Chalk's International* seaplanes, and about 40 minutes from Fort Lauderdale or Nassau. The seaplanes operate daily, and land in the harbor at North Bimini, near the resort center. Tel. 800–327–2521, U.S.; 800–432–8807, FL. A paved airstrip on South Bimini, linked to the main island by a short ferry ride, accommodates private planes and *Aero Coach International's* daily service from Miami and Fort Lauderdale.

By mail boat. The *M/V Bimini Mack* sails from Potter's Cay in Nassau every Thurs., calls at Cat Cay and Bimini, returns to Nassau Mon. Contract dock master at Potter's Cay, tel. 323–1064. One-way fare is $25.

TELEPHONES AND EMERGENCY NUMBERS. The area code for Bimini is 809. For police and fire, dial 919; for the medical clinic, dial 327–2210.

HOTELS AND RESTAURANTS. Most hotels in Bimini have restaurants, and hotel restaurants generally accept the same credit cards that the hotel honors. Hotel price categories, based on double occupancy in high season, are: $100 and up, *Expensive;* $75–$99, *Moderate;* under $75, *Inexpensive.*

Bimini Big Game Fishing Club. *Expensive.* Reserve direct: Bimini Big Game Fishing Club, 2857 S.W. 27th Ave., Miami, FL 33133; in Florida tel. 305–444–7480; in the rest of the U.S., 800–327–4149; in Bimini, tel. 347–2391. Owned and professionally managed by the Bacardi Company, the club offers the most luxurious accommodations on Bimini. There are 51 large, attractive rooms and six cottages, all air-conditioned. The dining room offers legendary island fare, specializing in the catch of the day, and there is casual dining and entertainment in the popular bar and on the terrace overlooking the pool and the harbor. Sports include tennis on a hard-surface, night-lit court; big-game fishing, water-skiing, boating, scuba offered at a nearby facility. The club operates a modern 60-slip marina, and there's a broad beach just a few minutes' walk away. For serious anglers, the club sponsors five major fishing tournaments each year, including a leg of the prestigious Bahamas Billfish Championship series in April. AE, MC, V.

Bimini's Blue Water Resort. *Moderate.* Box 627, Bimini, Bahamas; tel. 347–2291. Twelve neat, cozy, air-conditioned rooms and two cottages. One of the cottages is famous as Marlin Cottage, Ernest Hemingway's Bimini hideaway in the 1930s. The resort has a swimming pool, a good 42-slip marina with all water sports, and a beautiful private beach. The resort sponsors four major international fishing tournaments annually, including the Hemingway in April, a leg of the Bahamas Billfish Championship, and the Native Tournament in August—one of the most popular events in the Bahamas. AE, MC, V.

Brown's Hotel. *Inexpensive.* Box 699, Bimini, Bahamas; tel. 334–227. This is another part of Bimini's history, with 37 air-conditioned rooms. Popular bar and restaurant and meeting spot for divers. Scuba equipment available. No credit cards.

The Compleat Angler. *Inexpensive.* Box 601, Bimini; tel. 347–2122. A small historic inn, the oldest on Bimini, and a hangout for Hemingway in the 1930s. The 12 rooms are cozy, comfortable, and air-conditioned, and noisy at night once the action begins downstairs. The popular bar offers entertainment and houses a priceless collection of Hemingway memorabilia and old photographs of early anglers. It was here that Gary Hart entertained Donna Rice and other patrons with a session on the bongos during their infamous Bimini voyage aboard the craft *Monkey Business.*

Boating, fishing, tennis, and diving can be arranged, and rental scooters and bicycles are available. AE, MC, V.

Seacrest. *Inexpensive.* Box 654, Bimini; tel. 347–2071. Neat, cozy 17-room hotel in town; the modestly furnished, air-conditioned rooms have balconies with a splendid harbor view. Two minutes from the beach, restaurants nearby. No credit cards.

SPECIAL EVENTS. A list of **major fishing tournaments** follows. For exact dates, entry fees, and tournament regulations, call the Bahamas Sports Hotline weekdays from 9 A.M. to 5 P.M. toll-free 800–32 SPORT; or contact the sponsoring resort directly.

February: *Bimini Benefit Billfish Tournament,* Bimini Blue Water Resort.

March: *Bacardi Rum Billfish Tournament,* Bimini Big Game Fishing Club. *Hemingway Billfish Tournament,* 1st leg of Bahamas Billfish Championship, Bimini Blue Water Resort.

April: *Championship Billfish Tournament,* 2nd leg of Bahamas Billfish Championship, Bimini Big Game Fishing Club.

May: *Bimini Blue Water Tuna Tournament,* Bimini Blue Water Resort.

June: *Blue Marlin Tournament,* Bimini Big Game Fishing Club.

July: *Jimmy Albury Memorial Blue Marlin Tournament,* Bimini Blue Water Resort.

August: *Native Tournament* (all fish), Bimini Blue Water Resort. *Big Game Rodeo* (all fish), Bimini Big Game Fishing Club.

September: *Small B.O.A.T. Tournament,* boats under 22′, Bimini Big Game Fishing Club.

November: *The Wahoo,* Bimini Big Game Fishing Club. *Adam Clayton Powell Memorial Wahoo Tournament,* Bimini Blue Water Resort.

SPORTS. Fishing and Boating. The following marinas offer fishing boats for charter (rates are approximate, subject to wide swings with the seasons and the tournament schedules, negotiable when business is slow): *Bimini Big Game Fishing Club,* deep-sea fishing charter with tackle and crew, $200 half-day, $400 full day. Tel. 347–2391. *Bimini's Blue Water Resort,* 13-foot Boston Whalers, $70 full day, $40 half-day. Deep-sea fishing charter with tackle and crew, $450 full day, $350 half-day. Tel. 347–2166/2291. *Brown's Marina,* deep-sea fishing, reef and shark fishing with tackle and crew, $350 full day, $225 half-day. Tel. 347–2227. *Weech's Bimini Dock,* deep-sea fishing charters with tackle and crew, $500 full day, $300 half-day. Boston Whalers, $80 full day, $40 half-day. Tel. 347–2391.

Scuba. *Neil Watson's Bimini Underwater Adventures* offers four certified dive masters, equipment rentals, and three dive boats with daily trips to offshore reefs, drop-offs, and blue holes. Two trips visit notorious dive sites: The *Sapona* is the wreck of a concrete barge from rum-running days that was being used for target practice when five Avenger aircraft and a search craft sent to find them all disappeared into the "Bermuda triangle" during World War II; the *Stones of Atlantis* are man-made structures in shallow waters just offshore, the object of investigation by archaeologists and psychics ever since Edgar Cayce said he had a vision of them. Dive packages, including air fare to Bimini and accommodations, available. Air charter service offered daily from Fort Lauderdale. Reserve direct: Bimini Underwater Adventures, Box 21766, Fort Lauderdale, FL 33335; 305–763–2188, or 800–327–8150.

CAT ISLAND

A beautiful, hilly, windswept island lying across the sound from the Exuma cays, Cat Island boasts the highest elevation in the Bahamas: 206-foot Mount Alvernia. Ideal for the sophisticated traveler seeking new islands to conquer, Cat Island is still relatively untouched by the twentieth century, and the small local population fishes and farms much as their ancestors did. Along its hundreds of miles of coastline with untrod beaches, a handful of get-away-from-it-all resorts attracts mostly fishermen and divers. One is located at Fernandez Bay on the western shore, another at Cutlass Bay on the southwestern tip of the island, and a third at New Bight on the western shore. All are served by private airstrips reasonably close by, and all are within close (but rugged) access to the island's prime sightseeing attraction, the Hermitage atop Mount Alvernia. It was the home of Father Jerome, once an Anglican and later a Catholic missionary in the southern Bahamas, builder of the two great churches on Long Island. Father Jerome died in 1956 at the age of 80 and is buried in a cave near the top of the high hill he loved.

Cat Island is a long, narrow island shaped roughly like a lady's stocking; 48 miles long and one to four miles wide throughout most of its length, it splays out to form a foot at the southern end. In the north, Arthur's Town is the commercial center of the island and was the boyhood home of the actor Sidney Poitier, who has written fondly of the island, his parents, and relatives who still live there. The town has changed little over the centuries; the commissioner's office is here, a grocery store, a gas station, and a telephone station. You should be able to negotiate a rental car, with or without a driver, at the airport. Sightseeing is best to the south of Arthur's Town.

The government road winds bumpily the length of the island, fringing the sea and passing through one village after another, many with thatched-roof cottages. Bennett's Harbour is one of the largest and oldest settlements; at the Bluff you'll see whitewashed stone baking ovens, still used for cooking and baking bread, beside many of the homes. At Tea Bay a lovely coconut grove stands along a splendid white beach.

Three miles south, the village of New Bight is set along a stretch of beach that links it with Old Bight. The long curve of beach forms a vast bay, the Bight, one of the most beautiful areas on Cat Island. At the north end of the Bight, the ruin of a 19th-century plantation house, Pigeon Bay Cottage, is set on a gentle rise along the road. At New Bight, the Bridge Inn boasts 12 simple but comfortable bedrooms, each with ceiling fan and private bath, in a low one-story stone building. A second stone building houses a spacious dining room, lounge, and bar. Cars and bicycles are available for rent, and the hire of small boats can be arranged. The inn overlooks a warm, shallow tidal pool, ideal for children, and a stone walkway leads to the Bight's lovely beach. The Atlantic side of the island, just a mile or two away, affords a wild, surfing ocean beach with fine shelling.

Cat Island's most famous attraction, the Hermitage, a miniature abbey and cloister constructed by hand of native stone, sits atop Mount Alvernia. The views, spectacular in every direction, are well worth the hot, dusty climb to the top. To reach the Hermitage, take the dirt road that begins next to the commissioner's office in New Bight and follow it to the foot of the rise. From this point on, you'll need good walking shoes, a stout constitution, and something cold to drink along the way. The steep, tricky trail climbs steadily upward, with Stations of the Cross carved into the hillside along the way. At the top is Father Jerome's retreat, built in his old age with his own hands. Originally an Anglican architect who built the fine Anglican church on Long Island, he converted to Catholicism, built an even more splendid Catholic church on Long Island and the great Augustinian monastery in Nassau, and in his late sixties retired to Cat Island and his mountaintop. (The locals remember him fondly as the Hermit of Cat Island.) The Hermitage is a perfect, child-size abbey with a circular bell tower, a chapel barely big enough to hold three adults, and three closet-size rooms Father Jerome used as living quarters. Pause awhile and enjoy the view across the island from the quiet Exuma Sound to the rocky cliffs and pounding sea on the Atlantic side; the climb down is much easier than the climb up.

On the main road, continue south through the little village of Old Bight, off to the right from the main road. Just beyond, the road forks to circle a large pond, Great Lake. The left branch will take you to Port Howe and the ruins of the Deveaux mansion. Deveaux was the Carolina hero who led a motley band of 100 soldiers, farmers, and fishermen to recapture Nassau from the Spaniards in 1783. As a reward for Deveaux's bravery, the British governor of the Bahamas granted him thousands of acres of land to farm on Cat Island. Today his mansion is just a shell, shrubs growing inside and tree roots winding through the old stone fireplace.

Beyond Port Howe the road curves along the sole of the stocking's foot, hugging the coastline and offering beautiful views of the sea from high rocky cliffs. About midway down the sole you'll come to Cutlass Bay Club, another small island resort, with its own airstrip and a beautiful beach. A rustic bar and a broad veranda are ideal for sitting over a tall drink and gazing out to sea. There's fine swimming in clear, calm waters protected by a coral reef two miles offshore.

The road winds along the southern coast of the island, affording stunning ocean views. The best view is at Devil's Point, a small village by the sea with a cluster of low, thick-walled stone houses, brightly painted in tropical colors with thatched roofs of palm fronds, and children playing in the street. In summer you should be able to buy some of the tiny, delicately flavored pineapples that grow profusely in the area.

From Devil's Point the road curves across the toe of the foot and back to the quiet Exuma Sound side of the island, then turns westward to the tip of the toe at Hawk's Nest. Here the road ends at the Hawk's Nest Club, a small resort and marina that caters to yachtsmen, fishermen, and fliers who land at the club's airstrip. Here are a good dining room, a well-stocked bar, and a small supply store that offers fuel and sundries as well as attractive T-shirts and sweatshirts with the Hawk's Nest Club logo. The sunset views here at the very end of the island may be the most spectacular in the Bahamas.

PRACTICAL INFORMATION FOR CAT ISLAND

HOW TO GET THERE. By air. *Bahamasair* offers twice-weekly service to Arthur's Town Airport at the northern end of the island, and the resorts arrange licensed charter service to private airstrips from south Florida.

By mail boat. The *North Cat Island Special* departs Nassau every Tues., calling at Arthur's Town and Bennett's Harbour on Cat Island and returning to Nassau on Thur. Contact the dock master at Potter's Cay in Nassau, tel. 323–1064.

HOTELS AND RESTAURANTS. All of the hotels on Cat Island have restaurants. None accept credit cards. All Cat Island hotel rates are based on double occupancy in high season. Rates in the low season tend to be 10 to 20 percent lower.

Greenwood Inn/Tabaluga Diving Base. *Expensive.* Reserve direct: Island Services Inc., 750 S.W. 34th St., Fort Lauderdale, FL 33315; tel. 305–462–0300 or 800–635–6366 (after dial tone, 616). Largely a dive operation, but nondivers can enjoy this comfortable inn directly on the beach on the southwest coast of the island as well. There are 20 attractive rooms, a dining room serving notable specialties, a bar with lounge area, and a swimming pool. For divers, there is a 40-foot custom dive boat plus an inland water "blue hole." All-inclusive packages can be arranged. MAP only. No credit cards.

Fernandez Bay Village. *Inexpensive to Moderate.* Reserve direct: Fernandez Bay Village, Box 2126, Fort Lauderdale, FL 33303; tel. 305–764–6945. Eight full housekeeping units, dining room and bar in the main lounge—all well maintained and tastefully decorated in a tropical style. All sports can be arranged, and there are rental vehicles available for exploring. MAP only. No credit cards.

Bridge Inn. *Inexpensive to Moderate.* New Bight, Cat Island; tel. 809–354–5013. Modest 12-room resort of native stone overlooking a tidal pool and linked to a long, lovely beach. Each room has ceiling fan, private bath, and sun porch. Attractive dining room and rustic bar. Baby-sitting, car and bicycle rentals, and boats can be arranged. Nearest resort to Mount Alvernia and the Hermitage. AP only. No credit cards.

Hawk's Nest Club. *Inexpensive to Moderate.* Devil's Point, Cat Island; tel. operator, Devil's Point. 10 comfortable, neatly furnished rooms with tile floors and private patios. Sunny, spacious dining room, good bar, congenial lounge. Marina (10 slips) with a small store for ships' supplies and souvenirs. Private airstrips. AP only. No credit cards.

CHUB CAY

A somewhat luxurious private island at the southern end of the Berry Island chain, across the Great Bahama Bank from Bimini, Chub Cay perches at the edge of a vast deep-water canyon called the Tongue of the Ocean and borders the shallow banks, providing top action for every sort of fisherman—those who troll the deep sea for big blue marlin and those who stalk the feisty bonefish. The island is known for spectacular diving, with easy access to beautiful reefs less than 10 minutes offshore. Owned by members of the Chub Cay Club, it is one of the most exclusive private fishing clubs in the Bahamas. The club has accommodations for visitors.

PRACTICAL INFORMATION FOR CHUB CAY

HOW TO GET THERE. By air. Chub Cay has a private airstrip that is an official port of entry, and the Chub Cay Club offers licensed charter service from Fort Lauderdale or Miami.
By mail boat. The mail boat *M/V Captain Dean* departs Potter's Cay Dock in Nassau each Tues. for Chub Cay, and returns to Nassau on Fri. Contact dock master at Potter's Cay, tel. 323–1064.

HOTEL AND RESTAURANT. The Chub Cay Club. *Moderate.* Reserve direct: Club Cay Club, Box 661067, Miami Springs, FL 33166; tel. 809–325–1490; or call 305–445–7830 in Florida. A beautiful 50-room resort stretched along miles of pristine beach, overlooking a sheltered harbor. There are 15 comfortable, air-conditioned rooms at the Yacht Club on the harbor and villas along the beach, in the gardens, and aboard a moored houseboat. Amenities include a swimming pool, full-service marina with 75 slips, a custom-built 54-foot sportfisherman for charter, two all-weather tennis courts lighted for night play, a 250-yard driving range for golf buffs, and a full scuba program. To reserve, contact *Neil Watson's Underwater Adventures,* Box 21766, Fort Lauderdale, FL 33335; 305–763–2188. For divers, the club provides a PADI instructor, a line of rental equipment, and three dive boats with daily excursions to offshore reefs. For anglers, the club sponsors three major international fishing tournaments annually, including the Chub Cay Blue Marlin Tournament in early July, the last leg of the Bahamas Billfish Championship series. (Major credit cards accepted.)

CROOKED ISLAND

Crooked Island is a remote, friendly, but as yet untamed island in the southern Bahamas that overlooks the famed Windward Passage dividing the Bahamas from the Caribbean Sea, a stopover point for sixteenth- and seventeenth-century galleons and men-of-war sailing the Spanish Main. Today the island hosts just one small "barefoot" resort catering to private plane fliers and offers superb diving off the virtually unexplored virgin reefs. Two beachfront cottages at Colonel Hill, near the airport, are also available for vacation rentals. Among the island's worthwhile sights are Bird Rock Lighthouse, dating from 1872, which guards the Crooked Island Passage; and Castle Island Lighthouse, which marks the southern entrance to the islands.

PRACTICAL INFORMATION FOR
CROOKED ISLAND

HOW TO GET THERE. By air. *Bahamasair* offers twice-weekly service to Colonel Hill Airport on Crooked Island and twice-weekly service to Spring Point on the adjacent island of Acklins. The resort also offers licensed charter flights from Florida to Crooked Island. For private plane fliers, there's a good airstrip just minutes from the clubhouse.

HOTEL AND RESTAURANT. Pittstown Point Landings. *Moderate.* Reserve direct: Pittstown Point Landings, c/o Bahamas Caribbean International, Box 9831, Mobile, AL 36691; tel. 205–666–4482. An attractive, totally self-sufficient little 16-room resort that is gaining a top reputation among divers and private-plane fliers. The resort sprawls along miles of white-sand beach, overlooking a turquoise bay. Informal conviviality marks the nautical bar, and good seafood is served in the comfortable dining room. The resort has its own private airstrip and transportation to and from the Colonel Hill Airport 16 miles away. For divers, there are rental equipment, three dive boats, and certified instruction. The bonefishing nearby is excellent (rental boats available). AE.

Crooked Island Beach Inn. *Inexpensive.* Church Grove, Crooked Island; tel. post office. Several neat and clean guest house-cottages provide a total of 11 rooms with private baths and kitchens. There is a private beach where boating and fishing are available.

T & S Guest House. *Inexpensive.* Cabbage Hill. Reserve direct: 809–326–2096. Five small, pleasant rooms with a dining room. Beach privileges are available nearby where boating and fishing can be organized. No credit cards.

ELEUTHERA

Eleuthera—the Greek word for *freedom*—symbolized hope for dissenters who fled as storms of religious controversy raged over England in the seventeenth century. Most famous of the refugee bands were the Pilgrims, who founded Massachusetts Colony. Others fled to Bermuda, and a small hearty band of adventurers found their way to "Cigatoo" (the Arawak name) in the Bahamas. They renamed the island Eleuthera and set up the first democracy in the New World.

More than a century later, in the 1780s, Eleuthera received a new and even larger band of refugees. They were Loyalists fleeing the American Revolution, with their families and their slaves. Most settled on the offshore islands of Spanish Wells and Harbour Island, where many of their blond, blue-eyed descendants live today. When Bahamian slaves were emancipated, most settled on the main island, where their descendants also live today in small, attractive seaside settlements along the length of Eleuthera.

The island is startlingly beautiful, a long, narrow ribbon of green surrounded by pink-sand beaches and a turquoise sea. Eleuthera is a hundred miles long and barely two miles wide, and a fair road runs the length of the island, making it possible for the adventurous to explore Eleuthera's picturesque villages and beaches by automobile.

The variety of resorts on Eleuthera and its offshore cays is the most extensive on any of the Family Islands. Vacationers may stay in a cluster of cottages along the beach, an elegant old home overlooking the sea, a posh country-club resort, or small family-owned hotels.

Three international airports currently serve the island. North Eleuthera Airport serves the northern third of the island and the offshore cays of Harbour Island and Spanish Wells. The center third of the island is served by Governor's Harbour Airport. The southern third of the island is served by Rock Sound Airport. (Visitors should be certain that they are routed to the proper airport, as transportation between them can be extremely expensive and difficult to arrange.)

North Eleuthera

A driving tour of the northern section of the island, either by rental car or a taxi driver-tour guide (easily arranged at the airport or through your hotel), is an interesting—but slightly bumpy—experience. One of the most famous sites on the island is Preacher's Cave, which lies northeast of the airport, toward the Harbour Island ferry dock. The cave sheltered the early band of Eleutheran Adventures in 1647 after their ship foundered on a nearby reef. They managed to salvage a small boat and sent it to Massachusetts for supplies to start their colony. Later the Eleutherans repaid their benefactors by sending a shipload of Braziletto wood to Boston with instructions that the cargo be sold and the proceeds donated to Harvard College, "to avoid the foul sin of ingratitude." The cave, easy to explore, is near the road north, about ten miles from North Eleuthera. Light filters softly from the holes in the ceiling, illuminating a rough stone altar where the Puritans worshiped.

The main road south from the airport branches; a right turn takes you to the Current, a village separated from the offshore Current Island by a tidal cut, the world-famous Current Cut dive site. The tide roaring through the cut at 5–10 knots sends divers spinning and tumbling through the 65-foot chasm.

Traveling south again on the main road, you'll pass through tiny villages like the Bluff, and vast acres of small farm plots known as the Commonage. These lands were a legacy to the Loyalists from King George III, and are still handed down from generation to generation. Stop for lunch or a snack at Arlie's Place in the village. Continuing south, pass through the villages of Upper and Lower Bogue to reach the Glass Window, where the island narrows to the width of the road and a bridge spans two great limestone cliffs. From the Atlantic side a giant surf pounds through the narrow cut, meeting the tranquil, turquoise waters of the island's western shores. The views are spectacular. The road winds southward through rolling hills and valleys.

Twenty miles from your starting point at the airport, you'll reach the picturesque village of Gregory Town, situated at the head of a narrow, deep cleft in the island's cliffs, with a commanding view. Here you'll find a beach famed among surfers as "the second-best wave in the world." At the least, it's the best surfing beach this side of Hawaii. If the surf does not quite beat Hawaii's, the pineapples do! They grow in profusion in the area, and one bit of the tiny, sweet, and delicately flavored fruit will convince you. A wonderful pineapple rum is made from the local fruit and sold everywhere in the Bahamas. Try a sample from a local liquor store. If the rum samples have sparked your spirit of adventure, ask in the village about a local guide (usually an experienced teenager) to show you the Caves, which lie just a few miles south of Gregory Town. The entrance is marked by a great, gnarled ficus tree that legend claims was planted by pirates in the 1600s to screen the entrance to their favorite hideout and cache of ill-gotten gains. The cave system is formidable, with massive caverns filled with harmless bats, stalactites and stalagmites, and winding, sloping tunnels that end at an 80-foot cliff overlooking a pounding sea. Cambridge Villas near Gregory Town combine hearty Bahamian food and a pretty poolside setting when you're ready for lunch.

Harbour Island

Harbour Island is a centuries-old island village lying just off the windward shore of North Eleuthera, known to generations of visitors as one of the most beautiful towns in the Bahamas. Even if you are vacationing on the main island take a day to explore this gem—ferry boat/water taxis depart regularly from the North Eleuthera docks, and it's just a 20-minute ride.

Just two square miles in area, Harbour Island boasts a three-mile-long strand of perfect pink-sand beach on its oceanside. (Yes, the powdery sands are actually pink—they're made up of eons-worth of crushed conch shells and coral.) At harborside is the delightful colonial village of Dunmore Town, named for Lord Dunmore, who served as governor after being driven from the states by American revolutionaries.

Today, Dunmore Town lies sleepy under a tropical sun, its flowered lanes and pastel-tinted saltbox cottages edged by white picket fences—a reminder of old New England in the Bahamas. Ask anyone to point out Loyalist Cottage, the oldest house on the island, overlooking the harbor. Drop by the two distinguished old churches, St. John's Anglican, built in 1768, and Wesley Methodist, built in 1848. A good, inexpensive Bahamian meal can be had at Angela's Starfish restaurant, a little aqua stucco house where you can eat indoors or out, at a picnic table. (Try the pork chops with peas 'n' rice or cracked conch.) You won't need an auto to explore Harbour Island, although they are available. You'll see and enjoy more by walking or biking from the harborside to the oceanside of "Briland," as generations of "Brilanders" have affectionately called the island. Nestled here and there amid the sea-grape-, palm-, and pine-shaded dunes overlooking the broad ocean beach, are half a dozen resorts, whose styles range from elegant to rustic.

Spanish Wells

This old island village off Eleuthera's northern shores gained its name when sixteenth-century Spanish galleons filled their casks here before heading back across the broad Atlantic to Spain. The blond, blue-eyed people of Spanish Wells trace their heritage back more than three centuries to the original Eleutheran adventurers, and they still earn their living from

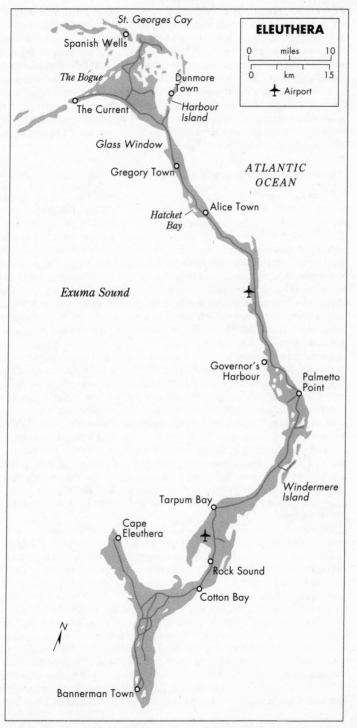

ELEUTHERA

0 miles 10
0 km 15
✈ Airport

St. Georges Cay
Spanish Wells
The Bogue
Dunmore Town
Harbour Island
The Current
Glass Window
Gregory Town
ATLANTIC OCEAN
Alice Town
Hatchet Bay
Exuma Sound
Governor's Harbour
Palmetto Point
Windermere Island
Tarpum Bay
Cape Eleuthera
Rock Sound
Cotton Bay
Bannerman Town

the sea much as their forefathers did. Today the island is the most prosperous in the Bahamas, with a modern commercial fishing fleet specializing in Bahamian lobster, in great demand for export to the Florida mainland as well as Nassau and Freeport. The island is delightfully picturesque, with neat rows of pastel-colored homes, flowered lanes, and tidy farm plots producing fine crops. You can bike around the entire island in an afternoon, with time for browsing in quaint shops, perhaps bargaining for one of the distinctive broad-brimmed fisherman's hats of hand-woven straw or a colorful quilt, a specialty of the island women. There are just two small locally owned resorts on the island, reachable by ferry from the Eleuthera mainland and by taxi from North Eleuthera Airport.

Central and South Eleuthera

From Governor's Harbour Airport, the center of the long narrow island, the government road continues south through tiny settlements, over rolling hills, past harborside beaches and Atlantic side cliffs. To the north of the airport is Hatchet Bay, headquarters of a large American-owned plantation specializing in milk, eggs, chicken, and ice cream. Traveling south, you'll reach the village of Governor's Harbour, nestled in a crescent cove called Cupid's Bay, settled centuries ago by the Adventurers and Loyalists. The town sprawls along the waterfront, the fading Victorian charm of some of its houses partially restored to recapture hints of the town's glory in the nineteenth century, when it was the busiest port in the country. The Club Med village that overlooks a pink-sand beach here is a favorite of young families.

Continuing south for several miles, you'll see a road branching eastward that leads to the small bridge linking Eleuthera to Windermere Island. If you've planned ahead, made reservations, and are dressed properly (designer casuals are the norm), you can stop for a gourmet buffet luncheon at the most elegant resort in the Bahamas, the Windermere Island Club. Here the Prince of Wales and his wife vacationed before the birth of Prince William, and a persistent photographer captured the pregnant Diana in a bikini—a photograph that made the front pages of tabloids around the world. The royal family owns several properties on the island, and the club hosts many titled and distinguished guests. Down the road is one of the most picturesque villages on the island, Tarpum Bay, site of a small artists' colony. Look for local studios where you might find a bargain in watercolors or pastels.

Between Tarpum Bay and Rock Sound, just east of the main road and about a mile down a narrow dirt lane, is a famous Ocean Blue Hole that looks like a little inland lake but is connected by underwater caves and tunnels to the sea. It teems with ocean life; said to be bottomless, its depths have never been sounded.

At the southern end of the island is Rock Sound, the largest settlement on Eleuthera, with a modern airport nearby. In the village there is a small shopping center with shops for food, liquor, gifts, and souvenirs. Neat, quaint homes with flowering shrubs and picket fences line the narrow lanes, and the old church and cemetery are worth a visit. For good, hearty native cooking at modest prices, try Edwina's Place, a favorite of cruising yachtsmen who drop anchor off a nearby beach. Avid golfers may want to continue driving south to Cotton Bay on the Atlantic shore, home of the posh Cotton Bay Club and its world-class 18-hole Robert Trent Jones course. Visitors are welcome, but guests are given preference and greens fees are high.

South of Rock Sound the island splays like the tail of a fish. The west branch of the road leads to Powell Point and the Cape Eleuthera Club, now closed. The east branch passes through the quiet fishing villages of Wemyss, Miller Hill, and Bannerman Town at the tip of the island. Residents say the bonefishing here is the best on the island.

PRACTICAL INFORMATION FOR ELEUTHERA

HOW TO GET THERE. By air. *Bahamasair* offers daily service from Nassau to North Eleuthera, Governor's Harbour, and Rock Sound. Several licensed, scheduled commuter airlines offer nonstop or one-stop daily service to one or more of Eleuthera's airports from south Florida gateways: Miami, Fort Lauderdale, and West Palm Beach. Among these are *Aero Coach, Carribean Express, Eastern Express,* and the *Piedmont Shuttle.* Check with your travel agent for the most convenient carrier and schedule.

To Harbour Island and Spanish Wells. Flights serving Harbour Island and Spanish Wells from Florida or Nassau land at North Eleuthera airport. From the airport, taxis will take you to the Harbour Island ferry dock or the Spanish Wells dock. There small, modern multi-seat power boats take you across to the offshore cays at reasonable rates. Dockside on the island, taxis will be waiting to whisk you to your resort.

By mail boat. The following mail boats sail from Potter's Cay Dock in Nassau to Eleuthera weekly: *M/V Current Pride* departs Nassau Thurs. for Current Island, Lower and Upper Bogue, returning to Nassau on Tues. *M/V Bahamas Daybreak II* departs Nassau Thurs. for North Eleuthera, Spanish Wells, and Harbour Island, returning to Nassau on Mon. *Harley Charley* departs Nassau Mon. for Central Eleuthera, Hatchet Bay and Governor's Harbour, South Palmetto Point, and Tarpum Bay, returning to Nassau on Tues. On Tues. it sails for South Eleuthera, Davis Harbour, Rock Sound, Weymss Bight, Deep Creek, and Bannerman Town, returning to Nassau on Thurs. On Fri. the *Harley Charley* operates a special weekend trip leaving Nassau for Hatchet Bay and Governor's Harbour, returning to Nassau Mon. Contact the dock master at Potter's Cay, Nassau, tel. 323–1064.

TELEPHONES AND EMERGENCY NUMBERS. Area code for Eleuthera, Harbour Island, and Spanish Wells is 809, although not all areas have direct distance dialing yet. Emergency numbers on Eleuthera include: Governor's Harbour police, 332–2111; doctor, 332–2001. Harbour Island police, 333–2111; doctor, 333–2225; clinic, 333–2227. Rock Sound police, 334–2244; clinic, 334–2226.

HOTELS AND RESTAURANTS. Most hotels on Eleuthera have restaurants. Hotels listed here are grouped according to the nearest airport. The telephone numbers given are reservations numbers; in many cases reservations may also be made through the Bahamas Reservation Service (BRS), tel. 800–327–0787. Hotel price categories, based on double occupancy in high season, are $150 and up, *Super Deluxe;* $125–$149, *Deluxe;* $100–$124, *Expensive;* $75–$99, *Moderate;* under $75, *Inexpensive.*

North Eleuthera Airport/Gregory Town

Pineapple Cove Club. *Moderate.* Box 51438, Gregory Town, Eleuthera; tel. 332–2269; or through BRS. A pretty resort on 28 hilly, tropical acres along a sandy beach. 32 attractive, air-conditioned rooms, all newly renovated and refurnished, each with a private porch. Saltwater pool, two lighted tennis courts, excellent dining room, and a well-stocked gift shop. Fishing, sailing, windsurfing available. AE, MC, V.

Bahama House. *Inexpensive.* Box 5206, Gregory Town, Eleuthera; tel. 332–2230. Half a dozen neat, roomy cottages with single, double, and a few three-bedroom units, gift shop on the premises. Nearby beach privileges with boating, snorkeling, fishing, and tennis in the area. Strictly self-catering. Restaurant and grocery stores nearby. Located in Gregory Town, 18 miles from the airport. No credit cards.

Cambridge Villas. *Inexpensive.* Box 1548, Gregory Town, Eleuthera; tel. 332–2269; or through BRS. Twenty-one neat, attractive rooms and apartments (some with air-conditioning and kitchens) owned and operated by a friendly, local Bahamian family. The complex surrounds a shady terrace and saltwater pool. The dining room serves excellent native food, and there's tea every afternoon at 4. The cheerful bar is popular with locals as well as visitors. A bus shuttles guests to a magnificent oceanside beach a mile and a half away, famed for fine surfing and shelling. Boating, fishing, and diving excursions can be arranged. Located 20 miles from the airport. AE, MC. V.

Oleander Gardens Villas. *Inexpensive.* Box 5165, Gregory Town, Eleuthera, tel. 333–2058. Sixteen casual, modern one- and two-bedroom apartments with a central dining room and bar, along a nice private beach. Boating, snorkeling, and fishing trips can be arranged. Located in Gregory Town, 19 miles from the airport. AE, MC, V.

Sea Raider Cottages. *Inexpensive.* Reserve direct: Sea Raider Cottages, 922 N. Broadway, Rochester, MN; tel. 507–288–4009; or 809–333–2290. Nine efficiency and studio apartments by the seaside, all large and airy and equipped with kitchens and patios. No dining room, but there are nearby grocery stores and daily maid service. There's a tennis court nearby and all water sports can be arranged. V.

North Eleuthera Airport/Harbour Island

Dunmore Beach Club. *Super Deluxe.* Box 122, Harbour Island, Eleuthera; tel. 333–2200. An elegant, intimate, beautifully decorated resort with 16 rooms in charming cottages tucked among trees and flowering shrubs. A clubhouse overlooks the sea, and the dining room offers gourmet meals—reputed to be the best on the island. Sports include tennis, deep-sea and bonefishing, and sailing; a beautiful private beach. No credit cards.

Coral Sands Hotel. *Deluxe.* Harbour Island, Eleuthera; tel. 333–2350; or through BRS. On 14 hilly acres overlooking the sea stands this comfortable resort with 33 rooms and cottages along the pink-sand ocean beach. Fine Bahamian and American food in the dining room, and a relaxed lounge, library, and game room. There are three bars—one in the main lounge, one on the beach, and another at the *Nightclub in the Park,* an outdoor pavilion for dancing under the stars, where a local combo entertains on weekends. Sport facilities include a night-lit tennis court, surf riders, snorkeling gear, and small sailboats. Rental golf carts and bicycles. Closed Labor Day–Nov. 14. AE, DC, MC, V.

Romora Bay Club. *Deluxe.* Box 146, Harbour Island, Eleuthera; tel. 333–2325; Box 7026, Boca Raton, FL 33431, tel. 800–327–8286 in FL and Canada or 305–997–9699; or through BRS. A comfortable family-run resort offering 28 air-conditioned rooms and several housekeeping cottages, each with private balconies or terraces overlooking the harbor and tropical gardens, which stretch across the island to the oceanside. The main house on a hillside serves as the clubhouse, with a cheerful dining room, rustic bar with local entertainment weekly, comfortable lounge, and library. Jacuzzi, masseur, tennis court, and hammocks. Four PADI dive instructors give lessons and lead daily dive trips; dive packages are offered. 15 percent service charge. AE, MC, V.

Pink Sands. *Expensive.* Box 87, Harbour Island, Eleuthera; tel. 333–2030; or through BRS. Complete charm with dignified informality is the hallmark of this famous resort, where the third generation of family hoteliers greet the third generation of club guests. First and foremost a private club, the public is invited when accommodations are available. There are 49 cottage suites dotted here and there amid 40 acres of forest glen, paved pathways, and tropical greenery—the site has been designated a bird sanctuary by the Audubon Society. The cottage suites offer huge living rooms and bedrooms, dressing rooms, private baths, kitchens, and spacious patios. Sports include tennis on three fine courts, bird-watching, shelling, sailing or motor-boating. All types of fishing and other water sports are available. The clubhouse offers a lovely dining room (ties or ascots at dinner and long skirts for the ladies), fine Bahamian and American cuisine, a comfortable lounge and well-stocked library. No credit cards.

Runaway Hill Club. *Expensive.* Box 31, Harbour Island, Eleuthera; tel. 333–2150. "Small but elegant" describes this charming old island home with lush tropical gardens, and a broad veranda overlooking a sparkling pool and the sea. Just eight over-size, beautifully decorated rooms upstairs or in an adjacent wing, most with patios or balconies. The ground floor of the main house is a superb dining room where "houseguests" dine free (most room rates include MAP), and visitors from all over the island reserve days in advance to enjoy the gourmet cuisine and impeccable service (expensive, full-course, fixed-price menu). All island sports and activities can easily be arranged, and the ocean is just a stroll away. AE, MC, V.

Valentine's Yacht Club. *Expensive.* Box 1, Harbour Island, Eleuthera; tel. 333–2142; or through BRS. Twenty-one comfortable rooms in a friendly, homelike atmosphere. There's a tranquil harborside beach, a refreshing freshwater pool, and the resort's private *Dunes Club* on the ocean side of the island. All water sports are available, from jet-skiing to windsurfing, but the resort is best known for an excellent dive program featuring free scuba lessons for beginners, advanced instruction, and full certification, with a range of dive packages and daily trips to offshore reefs. Dining room and nautical bar—a gathering spot for cruising yachtsmen who dock at the resort's harborside marina. AE, MC, V.

North Eleuthera Airport/Spanish Wells

Spanish Wells Beach Resort. *Moderate.* Box 31, Spanish Wells, Eleuthera; tel. 333–4371; in the United States 800–262–0621; in Florida 800–451–8891; or through BRS. Twenty-one attractive, simply furnished oceanfront rooms and six beach cottages with kitchenettes, comfortable for up to four people. All overlook a broad, beautiful, unspoiled beach. There's a cozy dining room with good Bahamian cooking, and a relaxing bar and lounge with entertainment on weekends. Sports include free bicycles, windsurfing, water-skiing, Sunfish sailing, boat trips to nearby cays for picnics, and half-day trips to Harbour Island for sightseeing. But the resort's prime attraction is an excellent dive program for beginners through experts, including certification. Two dive masters conduct daily dive trips to the legendary reefs that fringe Eleuthera's northern shores, and the sister resort on the harbor has a complete dive shop. AE, MC, V.

Spanish Wells Harbour Club. *Inexpensive.* Reservations information same as above for Spanish Wells Beach Resort. Twenty crisply clean, simply furnished, airy rooms in the village overlooking the harbor and marina. The club has its own dining room, bar, and entertainment and shares other amenities with the beach resort. Boating and fishing expeditions are easily arranged at the marina, and the dive boats leave from here. AE, MC, V.

Spanish Wells Yacht Haven. *Inexpensive.* Box 27, Spanish Wells, Eleuthera. Tel. 333–3428. Five air-conditioned one-bedroom efficiencies and a two-bedroom apartment. Beach privileges nearby and boating available. Swimming pool, restaurant, and bar. MC,V.

Governor's Harbour Airport

Wykee's World Resort. *Expensive.* Box 176, Governor's Harbour, Eleuthera; tel. 332–2701. Seven rustic stone cottages on hilly acres with terraced lawns from oceanside to harborside. Cottages have one to four bedrooms, fireplaces, and unrestricted views of the sea. Private beach, pool, tennis court, boating available. No credit cards.

Club Med Eleuthera. *Moderate.* Box 80, Governor's Harbour, Eleuthera; tel. 332–2270; or 800–258–2633. Continental Club Med ambience with a distinctive Bahamian flair, set along a pink-sand ocean beach. Three hundred air-conditioned rooms, large free-form pool, dining room, disco, boutique, library, and café/bar with dance floor and stage for nightly entertainment. The club offers a scuba program for beginners, underwater photography, deep-sea fishing, water-skiing, and sailing. There are eight tennis courts and areas for basketball and volleyball. The Mini-Club for youngsters operates 9 A.M.–9 P.M. daily; children under eight stay at the resort free in May, June, Sept., and Oct. Accommodations are neat, modestly furnished rooms with twin beds and showers. Rates are all-inclusive, and may be booked through travel agents or any Club Med office in the U.S., Canada, U.K., and Europe. No service charge. Eight miles from the airport. AE, DC, MC, V.

Laughing Bird Apartments. *Moderate.* Box 76, Governor's Harbour, Eleuthera. Tel. 809–332–2012 or 809–332–2342. Four efficiency apartments and a two-bedroom home. The apartments front on the beach and the house is just a two-minute walk away. The complex, in delightfully landscaped grounds, is operated by Jean and Dan Davies. No credit cards.

Cigatoo Inn. *Inexpensive.* Box 86, Governor's Harbour, Eleuthera; tel. 332–2343; or through BRS. The inn sits on a hilltop amid flowering shrubs and gardens and overlooks an attractive pool. There are 24 nicely decorated, air-conditioned rooms and a popular dining room and bar featuring native specialties. Cigatoo offers beach privileges and a tennis court, and all water sports—from deep-sea fishing to scuba trips—are easily arranged. Weekly entertainment by an island combo makes the inn one of the liveliest spots in town. Located eight miles from the airport. AE, MC.

Palmetto Beach Inn. *Inexpensive.* Box 102. Governor's Harbour, Eleuthera; tel. 332–2533. Eight attractive, air-conditioned rooms, apartments, and villas, each with private bath, TV, and telephone, set along a lovely private beach. There's a nearby marina and dock, with boating, fishing, and dive trips readily accessible. Located 13 miles from the airport at South Palmetto Point. No credit cards.

Palmetto Shores Vacation Villas. *Inexpensive.* Box 131, Governor's Harbour, Eleuthera; tel. 332–2305; or through BRS. Fourteen air-conditioned villas. Private beach with marina and dock. Snorkel gear and windsurfers available. Casual and friendly atmosphere. Located 12 miles from the airport at South Palmetto Point. MC.

Rock Sound Airport

Cotton Bay Club. *Super Deluxe.* Box 28, Rock Sound, Eleuthera; tel. 334–2101; in the U.S. 800–433–5079; in Texas 800–433–2171; or through BRS. The Cotton Bay is where Who's Who in America goes barefoot in the Bahamas. The 77 refurnished rooms are in the main lodge or scattered in cottages and villas set amid acres of gardens and manicured lawns, overlooking a pool and miles of beautiful beach. The resort offers four fine tennis courts and one of the top 18-hole championship golf courses in the Bahamas. Deep-sea fishing and bonefishing trips with local guides, sailboats, and power runabouts are available at the resort's Davis Harbour Marina. At Powell Point, 12 miles from the airport. Packages available, MAP only. AE, MC, V.

Windermere Island Club. *Super Deluxe.* Direct reservations (preference given to members): Box 25, Rock Sound, Eleuthera; tel. 332–2538; in the U.S. 800–237–1236; in New York 212–839–0222; 800–451–2253 in Canada; 800–451–2253; in the U.K. 01–261–1744. Ultra-elegant private club where royalty mingles with business tycoons, heads of state, and international stars. Offers pricey visitor accommodations with temporary membership fees added. A rustically beautiful clubhouse; six tennis courts with a resident pro; stunning pool, bar, library, game rooms, and gourmet dining on the terrace or formal dining room—all this overlooking five miles of magnificent pink-sand beaches. Accommodations include 22 air-conditioned, elegant tropical rooms, apartments, and villas. 18 miles from the airport. Packages available, AP only. AE.

Edwina's Place. *Inexpensive.* Box 30, Rock Sound, Eleuthera; tel. 334–2094; or through BRS. A tidy, relaxed colony of small cottages and ten air-conditioned motel-type rooms set amid flowering hibiscus and overlooking a swimming pool. There's a central dining room and a nearby private beach. Fishing, boating, and diving are easily arranged. Atmosphere is friendly and informal, with owner-operated care and attention. One mile from the airport. No credit cards.

Hilton's Haven. *Inexpensive.* Hilton's Haven, Tarpum Bay, Eleuthera; tel. 334–2216; or through BRS. Neat, comfortable, folksy ten-room inn operated for a decade by nurse Mary Hilton, formerly Public Health Officer for the island. Located across from a lovely ocean beach in the village of Tarpum Bay, the genteel resort offers rest and relaxation and is a favorite hideaway for convalescent visitors. The cozy dining room has down-home cooking and a small, friendly bar. Six miles from the airport. No credit cards.

HOW TO GET AROUND. Auto rentals and motor scooter rentals are available through most resorts. The following car-rental agents are located in settlements near resorts. At **Palmetto Point:** *Bethel Maitland,* tel. 332–2504. At **Harbour Island:** *Johnson's Rental,* tel. 333–2376. *Ross Garage,* tel. 333–2122. At **Governor's Harbour:** *ASA Rent-A-Car,* tel. 332–2305. *Highway Service Station,* tel. 332–2077. At **Rock Sound:** *Dingle Motor Service,* tel. 334–2031.

SPORTS. North Eleuthera: *Fishing and Boating.* Harbour Island and Spanish Wells are noted for fine bonefishing in the shallows on the leeward side of the islands and excellent reef and drift fishing along the miles of reef that line the windward shores. Charter boats with guides and gear are available on Harbour Island at the following minimum rates: deep-sea fishing, $250 per day; bottom fishing and bonefishing, $60 per half-day. Tel. 333–2350. On Spanish Wells at *Spanish Wells Beach Resort* at the following minimum rates: deep-sea fishing at $400 per full day, $250 half-day; reef fishing and bonefishing at $120 full day, $70 half-day. Tel. 332–2645.

Scuba. Some of the finest diving in the Bahamas is located off North Eleuthera. Noted dive sites are Devil's Backbone, a treacherous barrier reef that has claimed a number of wrecks, and Current Cut, a narrow tidal channel separating Eleuthera Sound and the open sea—divers experience the thrill of a lifetime as they soar through the cut on an incoming tide. Scuba-dive operators in the area are on Harbour Island at *Romora Bay Club,* tel. 333–2324. *Valentine's Yacht Club,* tel. 333–2080 or 333–2142, and on Spanish Wells at the *Spanish Wells Beach Resort,* tel. 333–4371.

Central and South Eleuthera: *Fishing and Boating.* Boats may be chartered and fishing excursions arranged at the following locations (rates listed are approximate): *Cotton Bay Club.* Located at Davis Harbour. Reef-fishing excursions, $15 per person per half-day; deep-sea fishing for a party of four, $175 per half-day including gear and guide. Tel. 334–2156.

Golf. The *Cotton Bay Club* course, designed by Robert Trent Jones, par 72. Lessons and all equipment available for rental. Greens fees year-round are $20 for the day; caddy, $8 for 18 holes, $4 for 9 holes; electric cart, $20 for 18 holes, $10 for 9 holes. At Davis Harbour. Tel. 334–2101.

THE EXUMAS

Little has changed in the two centuries since fleeing Loyalists sought these islands in the sun. The long, languid chain of islets and cays, which stretches 140 miles from Nassau in the north to Little Exuma in the south, still offers miles of beautiful crescent-shaped beaches, turquoise waters, and swaying palms. They are still unspoiled, unsophisticated, and mostly untrod.

No one has counted the Exuma cays. Some say there are 365 of them, one for every day of the year. Fliers, yachtsmen, anglers, and divers especially love these islands. A flight over the Exuma chain offers one breathtaking view after another. For sailors they are the ultimate cruising grounds, with hidden coves, quiet harbors, and sheltered anchorages throughout the length of the chain. For divers, the emerald, turquoise, and aquamarine waters are as clear as liquid sunshine and the islands and cays are fringed by living reefs, sea gardens, colorful coral, and schools of brilliant tropical fish. For anglers, there's everything from deep-sea big-game fishing and reef trolling to light-tackle angling from a skiff or hand-casting from shore.

Fewer than 4,000 Bahamians live in the Exumas, most in tiny, widely scattered island settlements where they earn their living in small-scale farming or from the sea. Over half of them are named Rolle—a legacy from the Loyalists who settled the islands two centuries ago. Lord John Rolle, Baron of Steventon, was the largest of the landholders in the Exumas, with hundreds of slaves. When Britain passed the emanicipation laws abolishing slavery in her colonies, Lord Rolle deeded his name and his land to his slaves. The land may never be sold; it is passed from generation to generation of Rolles.

There are just two resort centers in the Exuma cays. About midway down the island chain is Staniel Cay, 80 miles southeast of Nassau, and at the southern end of the chain is George Town on Great Exuma Island, about 130 miles southeast of Nassau.

Staniel Cay

Staniel Cay, about a square mile in size, is surrounded by white beaches and crystalline seas. Here is a Bahamian village with fewer than 100 inhabitants, and several vacation homes owned by wealthy Americans and Europeans dot the island and surrounding cays. A favorite port of call for cruising yachtsmen and island-hopping private-plane fliers and the center of social activity on the island is the Staniel Cay Yacht Club and the nearby Happy People Marina.

The village of Staniel Cay has just one paved road, which runs through town from the yacht club to the airstrip. Drop into the rustic, red-roofed church, exchange pleasantries with the postmaster, and bargain with the straw ladies who weave their magic on hats and bags and souvenirs under a shady tree. The village boasts two stores for groceries and supplies and the only telephone station on the island. A visitor might go down to the docks and swap tales with the guides and fishermen or the cruising yachtsmen around the marinas, wander the beach on the ocean side of the cay, search for shells, or just lie in the sun. The waters are sheltered and calm for swimming, and the good snorkeling is just offshore. The only "nightclub" on the island is the Royal Entertainer Lounge, where Bahamians and visitors mix and mingle with typical out-island music and style. The restaurant serves three meals a day, and the lounge really jumps twice weekly when local musical talent takes over. Check with the folks at Happy People Marina to find out which nights the "action" takes place.

To explore the half-dozen isles and cays within a few miles to the north or south, rent a Boston Whaler or a small sailboat for the day and bring along a picnic lunch. Or join a dive group heading for one of the spectacular underwater sites just a few miles offshore.

Exuma Cays Land and Sea Park, accessible only by boat, offers miles of protected cays, islands, reefs, and sheltered waters set aside for bird-watching, beachcombing, skin diving, and the preservation of natural beauty for future generations. Founded by the Bahamas National Trust, the park begins just north of Staniel Cay at Conch Cut and extends 22 miles north to Wax Cay Cut. Visitors may not remove any plant life or coral specimens from the park, but fishermen and divers are permitted a limited "day's catch" by hand, Hawaiian sling, or hook and line. A resident warden offers assistance and information to park visitors and enforces regulations and wildlife laws.

Thunderball Grotto, a massive cliff, an underwater cave, and grotto formations a few miles off Staniel Cay, is said to rival the famed Blue Grotto of Capri. The site was made famous in the James Bond movies *Thunderball* and *Never Say Never Again*. There is no souvenir hunting in this area, which is protected by the Bahamas National Trust.

George Town

A timeless village by the sea, George Town is the undisputed "capital" of the Exuma chain. The picturesque community overlooks beautiful Elizabeth Harbour, one of the largest and finest in the Bahamas. Running through the middle of the village is the Tropic of Cancer, that imaginary dividing line that marks the beginning of the tropics.

George Town is steeped in history. During the pirate days of the seventeenth century, its deep-water harbor sheltered buccaneers from the seven seas. In the eighteenth century it was populated by a plantation aristocracy from the Carolinas who sought refuge under the British flag. In the nineteenth century the island served as a refitting base for British man-of-war ships, and in this century it became an important U.S. naval base during World War II. Today, George Town boasts the largest population in the Exumas, with some 800 Bahamians living on Great Exuma Island and the surrounding cays. There are accommodations for around 400 tourists on the island, with a broad choice of lifestyles from crisply clean apartments above a general store in the village to elegant villas on a private beach.

A dozen small shops provide groceries, supplies, and souvenirs in George Town. An absolutely charming strawmarket in the center of town sprawls under an ancient ficus tree. By the harbor there's a miniature town square with a white picket fence, surrounded by a quaint little library on stilts and the imposing pink government building that houses the commissioner's office, police, courts, and jail. Atop a hill is St. Andrew's Anglican Church, dating from 1802, and an interesting old graveyard. There are beautiful views of sparkling Elizabeth Harbour everywhere, and of tiny Lake Victoria, which fringes the other side of the village. Stroll down to Government Wharf, where the mail boat calls and out-island farmers and fishermen gather to load their wares for the Nassau market. You can buy nearly every variety of fresh tropical fruits and vegetables and bargain with the fishermen for a fresh catch.

To explore the settlements and cays to the north and south of George Town, you'll need a motor scooter, taxi/tour guide, or rental car. The Queen's Highway runs the full length of Great Exuma Island and is in reasonable repair. To the north, you'll travel through "generation land" estates—Ramsey, Mount Thompson, Steventon, and Rolleville with such interesting villages and sights as Moss Town, the Forest, and Roker's Point. All along the route you'll see the ruins of old plantation houses and meet the "descendants" of Lord Rolle. The road has been extended north and a causeway built so that you can now drive to the settlement of Berreterre (pronounced Barry-Tarry). From here the views of the nearby cays are breathtaking. And the names are fascinating—Children's Bay Cay, Rat Cay, Pigeon Cay, and, heading south, Pudding Cut. At Rolleville, stop for lunch or a snack at Kermit's Hilltop Restaurant and Tavern, where

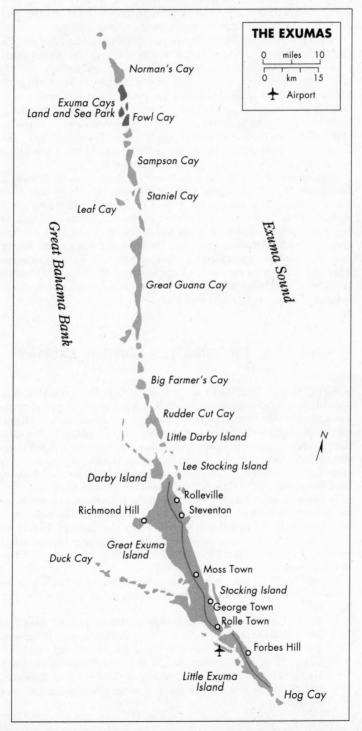

THE EXUMAS

0   miles   10

0   km   15

✈ Airport

Norman's Cay

Exuma Cays
Land and Sea Park

Fowl Cay

Sampson Cay

Staniel Cay

Leaf Cay

Great Bahama Bank

Exuma Sound

Great Guana Cay

Big Farmer's Cay

Rudder Cut Cay

Little Darby Island

Lee Stocking Island

Darby Island

N

Rolleville

Richmond Hill

Steventon

Great Exuma
Island

Duck Cay

Moss Town

Stocking Island

George Town

Rolle Town

Forbes Hill

Little Exuma
Island

Hog Cay

there's always fresh seafood on the menu, friendly villagers to meet, and a superb view seaward. On weekends there's a local combo.

Heading south from George Town, you'll reach Flamingo Bay and Pirate's Point. Nearby is Kidd Cove, a favorite anchorage for the notorious pirate Captain Kidd in the early years of the 1700s, and Rolle Town, another large "generation land" estate with plantation ruins and friendly Rolles. At a small settlement called the Ferry, a concrete bridge links Great Exuma Island to Little Exuma. There you'll find rolling farmland, stunning views, and Pretty Molly Bay. Traveling south almost to the tip of the island, you'll find the Hermitage in William's Town. Built by Loyalists and their slaves, it is the Exumas' only remaining intact plantation house from the era, now a privately owned dwelling.

Stocking Island may be the most beautiful island in all the Bahamas. Just a mile offshore of George Town, it is accessible only by boat from several hotels and the government dock. The hilly, seven-mile-long island shelters Elizabeth Harbour, and almost its entire coastline is fringed by exquisite beaches and swaying coconut palms. Atop a rocky cliff a 200-foot beacon offers breathtaking views over the turquoise water of the harbor and the intricate line of tropical cays that form the reef. There's fine swimming and sunning on the sheltered harborside, with Peace and Plenty's rustic beach club offering drinks and snacks. On the ocean side, a superb mile-long beach has excellent shelling.

PRACTICAL INFORMATION FOR THE EXUMAS

HOW TO GET THERE: By air. *To Staniel Cay:* There is a 3,000-foot paved airstrip serving the island, although it is not an official port of entry. *Tropical Airways* in Fort Lauderdale offers U.S. carrier-licensed and Bahamas-certified charter flights on a regular basis to Staniel Cay with a stopover at a port of entry for customs clearance. The firm also handles reservations for resorts, scuba programs, and yacht cruises, offering a variety of moderate to expensive all-inclusive packages. 4250 S.W. 11th Terrace, Fort Lauderdale, FL 33315; 305–522–3814 or 800–635–6366.

To George Town, Great Exuma: Daily flights from Nassau on *Bahamasair;* daily flights from Miami on *Caribbean Express;* and daily flights from Fort Lauderdale on *Aero Coach.* George Town International Airport, an official port of entry, offers a paved 5,000-foot landing strip approximately five miles from the village. Expansion and upgrading of the airport facilities is scheduled for completion in 1989.

By mail boat. To make arrangements for all mail boats sailing to the Exumas out of Nassau, contact the dock master at Potter's Cay (tel. 323–1064).

To Staniel Cay: The *M/V Lady Blanche* departs every Wed. from Potter's Cay in Nassau, calling at Staniel Cay, Rolleville, and Barreterre, Exuma, returning to Nassau Fri. One-way fares are $20–$25.

To George Town, Great Exuma: The *M/V Grand Master* departs every Tues. from Potter's Cay in Nassau, calling at George Town, Rolleville, Forest, Farmers Cay, and Black Point, returning to Nassau Fri. One-way fares are $25–$30.

THE EXUMAS

157

TELEPHONES AND EMERGENCY NUMBERS. Staniel Cay: The only telephone on the island is located at the telephone station in the village of Staniel Cay, with an operator on duty a few hours each day, seven days a week. Hours may vary, but are generally 9–10:30 in the morning and 12–1:30 and 4–5:30 in the afternoon. Service is unreliable, but worth a try if you must reach someone in an emergency. The telephone number is 334–2217.

George Town, Great Exuma: Area code for George Town is 809, and may be reached by direct distance dialing. Emergency numbers on the island include: police, 336–2152; Ministry of Health Clinic, 336–2088; the resident doctor, 336–2606.

HOTELS AND RESTAURANTS. Most hotels in the Exumas have restaurants. The telephone numbers given are reservations numbers; in many cases reservations may also be made through the Bahamas Reservation Service (BRS), tel. 800–327–0787. Generally speaking, hotel restaurants accept the same credit cards that the hotel honors. Hotel price categories, based on double occupancy in high season, are: $100 and up, *Expensive;* $75–$99, *Moderate;* under $75, *Inexpensive.*

Staniel Cay

Staniel Cay Yacht Club. *Expensive.* Tel. 809–355–2024. Reserve through BRS or Tropical Airways, tel. 305–522–3814 or 800–635–6366. The clubhouse with its nautical decor is the gathering spot for vacationers, cruising yachtsmen, and private pilots. It offers hearty dining, a genial bar, and a barefoot, relaxed ambience. Just steps away, tucked amid pines at the water's edge, are four guest cottages (each ideal for two), a permanently moored houseboat (accommodating up to four), and a two-bedroom guest house with full kitchen (comfortable for up to six). All have private baths and hot-water showers. A well-equipped marina accommodates 15 yachts and offers fuel, metered electricity, water, ice, and shower facilities. Boston Whalers, small sailboats, windsurfers, and scuba gear available for rent. Rates include all meals, and guests staying three nights or longer have complimentary use of sailing skiffs and runabouts. AE, MC, V.

Sampson Cay Club. *Moderate.* Reserve through RSVP Air, tel. 305–467–6850; in the U.S. 800–822–7787; in Florida 800–235–7787. A small cottage colony on Sampson Cay just a few miles north of Staniel Cay. The club has accommodations for only ten guests in private villas overlooking the sea and a sheltered harbor, each with housekeeping facilities and bath. The clubhouse has a bar, lounge, dining room, and video movies for entertainment. For yachtsmen, there is protected dockage, a commissary, fuel, ice, and water. Boat rentals and guided dive trips to nearby reefs are available. No credit cards.

Happy People Marina. *Inexpensive.* Tel. 809–355–2008. A friendly, informal Bahamian-owned resort, offering 11 comfortable motel-style rooms along a sandy beach near the village of Staniel Cay. The small hotel has a popular restaurant for visitors and natives alike, a congenial bar and "nightclub," the *Royal Entertainer Lounge,* where a local band plays a few nights a week. The dock and marina will accommodate nine yachts and offers fresh water and electricity. No charge for children under 12 sharing a room with parents. No credit cards.

George Town, Great Exuma

Out Island Inn Village. *Expensive.* Box 49, George Town, Exuma. Tel. 336–2171; or through BRS. The largest resort center in the Exumas, the village has 80 rooms spread through low, one- and two-story native stone buildings. Rooms are air-conditioned, neat, and comfortably furnished. The inn sprawls along a lovely palm-shaded white-sand beach, with thatched-roof sun shelters. The dining room, located oceanside, offers hearty Bahamian and American fare. The Reef Bar overlooks the sea and is a popular gathering spot for guests, locals, and private pilots harbor-hopping the island chain. Amenities include a freshwater pool, two tennis courts, volleyball and shuffleboard courts, and a game room with darts, checkers, and backgammon boards. Rental cars, boats, scooters, bicycles, windsurfers, and water skis are available. From the 30-slip marina, there's a twice-daily service to nearby Stocking Island beaches. Cost includes three meals, all drinks including wine with lunch and dinner, all sports, tax and gratuities. Five miles from airport, AP only. AE, MC, V.

Hotel Peace and Plenty. *Moderate.* Box 55, George Town, Exuma; tel. 336–2551; Box 21584, Fort Lauderdale, FL 33335; or through BRS. A historic inn overlooking Elizabeth Harbour. Thirty-two charming, air-conditioned rooms, each with a balcony; the choice rooms are those over-looking the sea and a freshwater pool on the terrace. The nautical bar is a favorite hangout for cruising yachtsmen, divers, and the angling set, both local and international. There's entertainment on weekends, and the casu-al dining room serves good Bahamian and American dishes. The inn offers a private beach club on exquisite Stocking Island, just a mile across the harbor, with regular ferry service back and forth. Car rentals, scuba trips and equipment, fishing boats and guides, and island tours can be arranged at the front desk. A small boutique offers nautical souvenirs and a large selection of Androsia fashions. No children under six. Located 3½ miles from the airport. AE, MC, V.

Pieces of Eight. *Moderate.* Box 49, George Town, Exuma; tel. 336–2600; or through BRS. A sister resort of the Out Island Inn, the two-story stone hilltop lodge lies just across Queen's Highway from the larger hotel and shares its beach and all amenities. There are 32 nicely furnished, air-conditioned rooms with balconies overlooking the sea and a patio with freshwater pool. There are superb views from the dining room, which serves good, down-home dishes, and from the Pirate's Den Bar, which fea-tures occasional evening music. Exchange dining privileges with the Out Island Inn. Excellent dive program, offering lessons and daily reef trips. Five miles from the airport. AE, MC, V.

Marshall's Guest House. *Inexpensive.* Box 27, George Town, Exuma; tel. 336–2571 or 336–2081. Adjoining Marshall's Grocery Store, 12 tidy, air-conditioned rooms and an inexpensive restaurant. Nearby beach privi-leges. In town, three miles from the airport. No credit cards.

Two Turtles Inn. *Inexpensive.* Box 51, George Town, Exuma; tel. 336–2545; or through BRS. Attractive wood-and-stone resort with just 12 cozy, comfortable rooms (some air-conditioned). Good local food served in a small dining room or in the cool green surroundings of the courtyard. There's a very nice gift shop, and guests have beach privileges nearby. Four miles from the airport. AE, MC. V.

APARTMENT AND VILLA RENTAL. Flamingo Bay Club. *Moderate.* Box 23, George Town, Exuma; or Box N-8727, Nassau; tel. 327–8471.

Four elegant two-bedroom villas, amid palm trees and tropical flowers, beautifully furnished and fully equipped for self-catering holidays. Amenities include a lively private beach, marina, and a tennis court. Rental vehicles and sports excursions arranged. An additional 33 villas are under construction for vacation rental, time-sharing, or purchase. The Flamingo Bay Club is part of a major land development half a mile from the airport, with 1,300 acres stretching from oceanside to harborside, 17 miles of paved roads, and more than 30 private vacation homes. No credit cards.

Regatta Point. *Inexpensive.* Box 6, George Town, Exuma; tel. 336–2206. Just five roomy, attractive, one- and two-bedroom apartments with full kitchens and ceiling fans. On Kidd Cay in Elizabeth Harbour, linked to George Town by a causeway. No restaurant; daily maid service provided. A private beach, lawns, and gardens. Three miles from the airport. No credit cards.

HOW TO GET AROUND. George Town, Great Exuma: Local taxis are available at the airport for transportation to all hotels in the area. Taxi drivers also serve as tour guides for the island. You may negotiate rates directly with them or book through your hotel. Motor scooters and bicycles are available through most resorts, and cars may be rented from the following agencies: *Exuma Transport,* Box 19, George Town, tel. 336–2101; *Peace and Plenty Hotel,* Box 55, George Town, tel. 336–2551; *R & M Tours,* Box 68, George Town, tel. 336–2112.

SPECIAL EVENTS. Staniel Cay: *New Year's Cup Race.* International yachts compete in a fun-filled racing series over the New Year holiday each year, with hundreds of boats making up the spectator fleet and their crews joining the revelry ashore. Headquarters for the race and center of the partying ashore is the Staniel Cay Yacht Club, with the Happy People Marina helping to absorbe the overflow crowds.

Emancipation Day Regatta. Native workboats and their crews compete in a series of races off the settlement of Black Point, a few miles from Staniel Cay by boat. The annual regatta celebrates the freeing of slaves on August 1, 1834, and is accompanied by barbecue picnics, singing, dancing, and merriment ashore. Emancipation Day is a legal holiday, celebrated on the first Monday of August.

George Town, Great Exuma: *Bonefish Bonanza.* Held annually in early November, sponsored by Hotel Peace and Plenty. Teams of international anglers stalk the feisty, elusive Bahamas bonefish in the reefy shallows off George Town. Good-natured fun and parties; prizes awarded. A similar *Bonefish Bash* tournament is held in January. For information, tel. 800–327–7678; or write Hotel Peace and Plenty, Box 55, George Town, Exuma.

Family Island Regatta. The most important annual event in the Bahamian sporting calendar. Each year in mid-April, the usually tranquil village of George Town comes alive with rivalry and revelry during out-island race week. The native workboat regatta, held for more than 30 years, pits handcrafted wooden sailing sloops against each other in a series of hotly contested races for trophies and cash prizes. Ashore, there are Junkanoo masquerades, goombay music, and the Royal Bahamas Police Force Band in concert and on parade; arts and crafts for sale; and thatched-roof stands serving an endless variety of down-home dishes. The small hotels and inns of George Town overflow with celebrating locals and visiting revelers, and the harbor is crowded. Book very early if you plan to join in the fun.

SPORTS. Staniel Cay: *Scuba.* Scuba gear is available for rent by qualified divers, and guided dive trips are available at Sampson Cay. One of the most famous dive sites in the area is Thunderball Grotto. Another popular dive trip goes to the Exuma Cays Land and Sea Park. The firm offers a variety of packages that include airfare and accommodations at moderate rates. They may be booked through *RSVP Air,* tel. 305–467–6850; in the U.S. 800–822–7787; in Florida 800–235–7787.

Fishing. There is fine bonefishing in the turquoise shallows of the Great Bahama Banks to the west of the island and good game fishing in the dark blue depths of Exuma Sound, which borders the eastern shore. Skilled local guides are available, and rates are "negotiable" for fishing excursions complete with boat, bait, tackle, and crew. Arrangements can be made at the *Staniel Cay Yacht Club, Happy People Marina,* and the *Sampson Cay Club.*

Other Sports. Windsurfers, Boston Whalers, small sailboats, and snorkeling gear may be rented at each of the resorts at moderate rates.

George Town, Great Exuma: *Scuba and Snorkeling.* Shallow- to medium-depth coral reefs and sea gardens off George Town draw snorkelers and divers, and a unique attraction is a series of ocean blue holes. Popular dive spots are Stingray Reef and Angelfish Blue Hole. The most famous dive site is Mystery Cave on Stocking Island, which tunnels for more than 400 feet beneath the island. Dive trips may be arranged through most George Town hotels or directly with *Exuma Divers,* Box 110, George Town, Exuma; tel. 336–2710 or 336–2030. The firm offers an experienced PADI instructor and a 38-foot houseboat that carries up to 18 divers, and operates two dive shops in the George Town area with all equipment for rental. Or *Exuma Aquatics,* Pieces of Eight Hotel, Box 49, George Town, Exuma; tel. 336–2600. Take advantage of an Underwater Photo Center, certified instruction, a range of programs from basic diving to dive master and instructor training, plus daily dive trips to offshore reefs.

Fishing. Fine game fishing may be found in the cobalt depths of Exuma Sound and in the Tongue of the Ocean beyond the shallow banks to the west of the cays. But the George Town area is best known for bonefishing along the banks and reefy shallows just offshore. Fishing boats may be rented at *Minn's Watersports,* Box 20, George Town, Exuma; tel. 336–2604; or may be arranged for at your hotel. Guided bonefishing and bottom-fishing trips may also be arranged for at your hotel or through *Exuma Docking Services,* Box 19, George Town, Exuma; tel. 336–2578. Rates may be negotiated with individual guides.

GREAT INAGUA

One of the farthest "out" of the Family Islands, 325 miles southeast of Nassau, Great Inagua is little developed for tourists but highly regarded by nature lovers, wildlife enthusiasts, and serious bird watchers. The island shelters a 287-square-mile wilderness preserve for the once nearly-extinct West Indian Flamingo, national bird of the Bahamas. These magnificent, long-legged, long-necked, brilliantly pink birds are year-round dwellers and constitute one of the largest remaining flocks in the Western Hemisphere—an estimated 50,000. Dozens of other species of birds, both migratory and resident, enjoy the protected acreage that sprawls along the shores of Lake Windsor near the center of the island. Tours of the park are arranged by the Bahamas National Trust.

The island is also known for the Morton Salt Company complex, the world's second largest solar evaporation center for salt production; and a green turtle hatchery where the endangered species is bred and released to the wild, a joint project of the Bahamas Ministry of Agriculture and Fisheries and the Caribbean Conservation Corporation. Most Inaguans work in the salt fields or earn their living by small-scale farming or fishing.

Matthew Town is the only village on Great Inagua Island. It has friendly people, a few houses, churches, bars, a telephone station, post office, government offices, and a medical clinic. A picturesque 1870 lighthouse at Southwest Point guides ships to the Windward Passage between Inagua and Hispaniola and the entrance to the Caribbean Sea.

PRACTICAL INFORMATION FOR GREAT INAGUA

HOW TO GET THERE. By air. *Bahamasair* offers twice-weekly flights from Nassau to Great Inagua's Matthew Town airport, which is also used by charters and private craft and has a nearby ramp for seaplanes.

EMERGENCY NUMBERS. The number for police is 255; for the clinic, 249; for the doctor's residence, 226.

HOTELS AND RESTAURANTS. The hotels in Inagua have restaurants. Inagua hotels fall into the *Inexpensive* category (under $50), based on double occupancy in high season.

Ford's Inagua Inn. Matthew Town, Inagua; tel. Inagua 277. Five neat, airy rooms, some with shared bath facilities. Dining room and bar. A beach nearby and sports can be arranged. One mile from the airport. No credit cards.

Main House. Matthew Town, Inagua; tel. 267. Eight comfortable air-conditioned rooms and a neat, modern dining room. A beach nearby and sports can be arranged. 1½ miles from the airport. No credit cards.

HOW TO GET AROUND. There are no rental cars, but you can negotiate a tour of the island with taxi drivers at the airport or through the hotel desks.

LONG ISLAND

Long Island is a long, narrow ribbon of land in the southern Bahamas, about four miles wide at its broadest and just over a mile at its narrowest point. It was one of Christopher Columbus's stops during his voyage of discovery in 1492. He anchored near the northern tip and called it Cape

Santa Maria, naming the rest of the island Fernandina after his patron, King Ferdinand of Spain. On the island's Atlantic shore towering cliffs plunge to a surging sea, but on the sheltered leeward side of the island there are long, quiet beaches, a gentle surf, and hidden coves. The only major resort center on Long Island, Stella Maris Inn and Estates, is located on the northeastern shore near the village of Burnt Ground, very near the spot where Columbus landed.

There's a fair-to-good government highway running the 57-mile length of the island, which Long Islanders call Rhythm Road. It passes through a dozen delightful settlements with such names as Deadman's Cay and Hard Bargain. Deadman's Cay is a pleasant village near the island's main airport. Look for sponges strung on lines to dry before being packed and shipped to Nassau markets. Note the "pothole" farming which flourishes in the area: natural or manmade holes in the coral rock containing fertile soil, sprouting crops of bananas and corn. Nearby are fascinating caves with stalactites and stalagmites, some with ancient Indian drawings on the walls, and the ruins of Lord Dunmore's plantation overlooking the sea.

Clarence Town, one of the prettiest settlements in the Family Islands, boasts the two huge twin-spired churches of Father Jerome. As a devout Anglican architect named Hawes, he built St. Paul's Church. Following his conversion to Catholicism, he determined to top his previous achievement by building St. Peter's Church, whose near-Gothic architecture is startling in a tiny out-island village.

As you drive along the island, be sure to watch for the "hex" signs drawn on houses along the road. You can picnic on a remote beach and hunt for shells or drop by a village tavern for a snack, a cool drink, and a chat with the locals. Don't miss the strawmarkets—nearly every village has one. Long Island is famed throughout the Bahamas for its fine straw work. In Nassau they say "you can tote water in a Long Island hat." Look for strawwork by Ivy Simms; it is exquisite and is sold in exclusive Nassau shops. Fisherman, farmers, salt rakers, or straw weavers, you'll find the 3,300 Long Islanders friendly, courteous, and helpful. They'll point out interesting sights, guide you to old caves and plantation ruins, or share island tales and folklore.

In May the Long Island Regatta matches George Town's races for rivalry and revelry. The annual workboat series attracts up to 50 entrants from all over the Bahamas. The best place for viewing the races is at Salt Pond, between Stella Maris and Deadman's Cay.

PRACTICAL INFORMATION FOR LONG ISLAND

HOW TO GET THERE. By air. *Bahamasair* provides four flights each week from Nassau to Stella Maris airport in the north and Deadman's Cay in the center of Long Island. The Stella Maris Inn also operates frequent licensed charter flights from Fort Lauderdale; tel. 305–467–0466 or 809–336–2106; in the U.S. 800–426–0466; or through BRS.

By mail boat. The *M/V Nay Dean* sails weekly from Potter's Cay in Nassau to Clarence Town, Simms, Salt Pond, and Stella Maris on Mon. and returns to Nassau on Fri. Contact the dock master at Potter's Cay,

Nassau; tel. 323–1064. The *Windward Express* departs every Wed., calling at Clarence Town, Saline Point, and Acklins.

EMERGENCY NUMBERS. Area code for Stella Maris is 809, available through direct distance dialing. For on-island emergencies, call the operator.

HOTELS AND RESTAURANTS. K.B. Resort Company Limited. *Moderate.* Tel. operator, Stella Maris. This 10-room guest house has a private beach, restaurant, and bar. It is located in the settlement of McKanns.

Stella Maris Inn and Estates. *Moderate.* Box 105, Long Island; tel. 305–467–0466; in the U.S. 800–426–0466; or through BRS. A truly international resort and land-development center, popular with Europeans, Canadians, and Americans. The attractive lodge is set amid broad lawns and flowering shrubs, overlooking the sea. Charming dining room with excellent Bahamian, Continental, and American fare, rustic bar for relaxing, and attractive patio for dancing. Accommodations are air-conditioned and scattered over the vast acreage, with hotel rooms adjacent to the lodge; villas, apartments, townhouses, or cottages in the landscaped grounds—a total of 50 rooms. The Inn offers three miles of protected beach, two tennis courts, three swimming pools, a 12-slip marina, and a delightful yacht club where there is frequent entertainment such as Sunday afternoon guitar concerts and an occasional goombay "rake 'n' scrape" band. The resort offers a full dive program. Rental cars, jeeps, bikes, small sail and power boats, water skis, jet skis, and even small private aircraft are available through the Inn. Deep-sea fishing and cruising boats may be chartered at the yacht club, and overnight excursions can be arranged for diving, fishing, or exploring nearby Rum Cay and Conception. The resort operates the Stella Maris Charter Service, with frequent licensed air charter service and a good range of inclusive packages available. AE, MC, V.

K.B. Resort Company Limited. *Moderate.* Tel. operator, Stella Maris. This 10-room guest house has a private beach, restaurant, and bar. It is located in the settlement of McKanns.

Carroll's Guest House. *Inexpensive.* Tel. operator, Deadman's Cay. Neat two-story wood and stone guest house, four bedrooms downstairs (two share baths) and two one-bedroom apartments upstairs, each with living room, dining room, kitchen, and bath. Beaches nearby; boating can be arranged. A well-stocked grocery and general store on the property. Meals on request. AE, V.

Thompson Bay Inn. *Inexpensive.* Tel. operator, Salt Pond. A two-story stone building with a popular bar and lounge, restaurant, dance hall, and game room. Nine neat, comfortable bedrooms with four shared baths. Beaches nearby. Boating, fishing, and sightseeing excursions arranged. No credit cards.

HOW TO GET AROUND. Cars may be rented at the Stella Maris Inn, tel. 336–2106. Sidney Burrows and Joseph B. Carroll at Deadman's Cay offer vehicles for hire; telephone the operator at Deadman's Cay to make arrangements. Bicycles and motor scooters may be rented at Stella Maris Inn for nearby exploration and day excursions.

RUM CAY

Rum Cay is one of the most remote of the Family Islands, primitive and appealing, with just one small resort, the Rum Cay Club. The island was discovered by Columbus in 1492. He named it Santa María de la Concepción, after the Virgin Mary. It received its modern name in the 1700s when a West Indian man-of-war laden with rum was wrecked on the reef off its shores. Once a major salt-raking center, it was devastated by a hurricane in 1908. The sleepy little island today has a population of fewer than a hundred people, almost all of whom live at Port Nelson, a picturesque village in a coconut grove hugging the seashore on the island's southeast coast. There are historic ruins to explore, miles of deserted beaches, lovely scenery with rolling hills, and a necklace of coral reef encircling the island's shores. Offshore is one of the Bahamas' most unusual dive sites, the wreck of the *H.M.S. Conqueror,* Britain's 101-gun man-of-war, which sank in 1861. The wreck is the property of the government, and no contents of the ship may be removed, but snorkelers and divers may easily see and visit it, as it lies in just 25 feet of water.

PRACTICAL INFORMATION FOR RUM CAY

HOW TO GET THERE. By air. The Rum Cay Club offers licensed air charter service from Fort Lauderdale.

By mail boat. The *Maxine* departs Tues. from Potter's Cay Dock in Nassau, calling at San Salvador and Rum Cay and returning to Nassau on Sat. Dock master, Potter's Cay, tel. 323–1064. One-way fare is $30.

HOTEL AND RESTAURANT. The Rum Cay Club. *Moderate to Expensive.* A variety of packages available. Reserve direct: Rum Cay Diving Club, Box 22396, Fort Lauderdale, FL 33335; tel. 305–467–8355; 800–334–6869; or through BRS, 800–327–0787. A very attractive, surprisingly luxurious, casual get-away-from-it-all resort. 19 rooms ranging from standard to deluxe, including a dormitory for dive groups. The comfortable dining room serves excellent Bahamian and American cuisine and tall, cool drinks on the terrace; there's a video lounge with an extensive library of underwater films. The club offers a complete dive center with certified instructors; rental equipment; three 34-foot Flattop dive boats that carry 18 divers each; a photo-processing center; plus catamarans, windsurfers, and fishing boats for rent; a hot tub overlooks miles of beach. The Rum Cay Club has its own airstrip, and offers all-inclusive eight-day/seven-night packages with private, licensed air charter service from Fort Lauderdale. AE, DC, MC, V.

SAN SALVADOR

It seems appropriate to end this book with San Salvador, where the story of the Bahamas and the New World began. Little has changed in the nearly 500 years since Columbus landed. The handful of native Arawak Indians he found have been replaced by a handful of native Bahamians, descendants of freed slaves. They live in much the same simple fashion as the Arawaks lived, cultivating small farm plots and fishing in the bountiful waters that fringe the island's shores. The primitive beauty of the island is virtually unchanged, with lush tropical greenery, forest-covered hills, pristine beaches, and unexplored reefs.

When Columbus arrived, the natives called their island Guanahani. He renamed it San Salvador, and in the seventeenth century it became known as Watling's Island, after a resident buccaneer. It wasn't until this century that university expeditions and intensive research by archaeologists and historians determined that the island was the actual site of Columbus's landfall in the New World. In 1926 the Bahamas Parliament officially renamed the island San Salvador. Although the exact spot where Columbus first stepped ashore is unknown, three different monuments claim the honor.

Today the largest settlement on the island is Cockburn Town (pronounced Coburn Town) on the western shore. Tiny wooden pink and yellow houses cluster around a giant flowering almond tree—which the locals call the "lazy tree"—overlooking the harbor. An Anglican church and a Catholic church, the commissioner's office, police station, courthouse, library, telephone station, and health clinic surround the "lazy tree," and a pair of old cemeteries are nearby. The most exciting day of the week is when the mail boat calls from Nassau and the whole town goes down to the dock to welcome it.

From the village the rugged but paved Queen's Highway circles the island. To the north is Palmetto Grove, where Columbus described an Indian village. Archaeologists have discovered Arawak artifacts here, and you can see them in the New World Museum in the North Victoria Hill settlement. At the northern end of the island is Graham's Harbour, which Columbus described as a harbor that would "hold all the ships of Christendom." The long narrow spit of land to the east, North Point, would be excellent for a fort, Columbus wrote, because it could easily be separated from the island by a moat. The Spanish or the English may have built a fort here in later years; a cannon and shot have been discovered underwater near the spit of land. Walk out to the end and you'll see the calm waters of the harbor meet the crashing waves of the Atlantic. The building located off the beach at Graham's Harbour belongs to the College Center of the Finger Lakes, a field station for a group of U.S. colleges that bring students here to study the archaeology and ecology of the island.

On the opposite side of the island, on the northeast shore, stands the Dixon Hill lighthouse, built in 1856. It stands 163 feet above the sea, and its beacon is the last of the original hand-operated, kerosene-burning lights in the Bahamas. A climb to the top for a look at the intricate machinery that operates the light is a must. The lighthouse keeper is usually happy to show visitors around. The view from the top is breathtaking. To the east is East Beach, excellent for shelling and beachcombing for the old bottles and glass floats that frequently wash ashore.

Not far south of the lighthouse is the rocky promontory called Crab Cay, where the *Chicago Herald* Columbus Memorial is the oldest monument to Columbus on the island. Built by the Chicago newspaper in 1892 to commemorate the 400th anniversary of Columbus's landing, it can be reached by a hard, rocky hike from the lighthouse.

Traveling south from Cockburn Town, a narrow road cuts off to the east from the Riding Rock Inn and leads to a lookout tower that affords extraordinary views of the island and the myriad inland lakes that sparkle under the tropical sun. South on the main road are two later monuments to Columbus. A simple but starkly beautiful white cross marks the spot where historians believe Columbus first came ashore; it was erected in 1956 by the historian Ruth Wolper, who operates the New World Museum. Nearby is the eternal flame that lit the 1968 Olympic Games in Mexico City. In the vicinity of these monuments archaeologists have discovered fifteenth-century European artifacts, an indication that this area was indeed the site of Columbus's landing in the New World.

At the southern end of the island is French Bay and a government dock. The high rocky promontory that marks the tip of the island is Sandy Point, with superb snorkeling and diving offshore. The broad white-sand beach offers fine beachcombing and swimming and snorkeling in calm, protected waters. The old ruin atop the hills, outlined against the sky, is Watling's Castle, named for the seventeenth-century pirate. However romantic the legend, the ruins are much more likely to be the remains of an eighteenth-century plantation house than a castle from buccaneering days.

Of late there has been considerable interest in San Salvador and the uninhabited, remote, reef-fringed island of Samana Cay some 65 miles away. In November 1986 *National Geographic* published findings, based on computer studies, that determined that Columbus landed not on San Salvador but on Samana Cay. The argument still rages, but the experts agree at least that the Bahamas were the site of Columbus's first landfall in the New World.

Meanwhile, the Bahama Islands prepare for the 500th anniversary of Columbus's arrival, hoping to have a world-famous attraction in San Salvador in 1992.

PRACTICAL INFORMATION FOR

SAN SALVADOR

HOW TO GET THERE. By air. *Bahamasair* offers two weekly flights from Nassau to the island. The Riding Rock Inn offers weekly licensed air charter service from Fort Lauderdale every Sat.

By mail boat. The *Maxine* departs Tues. from Potter's Cay Dock in Nassau, calling at San Salvador and Rum Cay and returning to Nassau on Sat. Dock master, Potter's Cay, tel. 323–1064. One-way fare is $30.

HOTELS AND RESTAURANTS. Riding Rock Inn. *Inexpensive to Moderate.* Out Island Service Co., 701 S.W. 48th Street, Fort Lauderdale,

FL 33315; tel. 305–761–1492 or 809–322–2631; in the U.S. 800–272–1492. San Salvador's only resort, located just north of Cockburn Town, attracts diving enthusiasts from around the world to the island's magnificent reefs just offshore. The moderately priced inn offers 24 comfortable, newly reno-vated, air-conditioned rooms, tennis court, freshwater pool, restaurant and lounge, conference center and classroom for divers, and a darkroom with film processing for underwater photography. Three well-equipped dive boats make two daily reef trips. The full-service marina has eight slips for visiting yachtsmen. MC, V.

Ocean View Villas. *Inexpensive.* Tel. operator, Cockburn Town. Small, friendly, attractive guest house, nicely landscaped with a private beach. Two single-story stone buildings with four bedrooms and two sharing baths. Kitchenette and sitting room. No credit cards.

INDEX

Index

Abacos, the, 116–127
  hotels and restaurants on, 122–125
  map of, 115
Adelaide Village, 56
Air travel, xii, 10–11, 58, 98, 121, 130, 135–136, 140, 141, 142, 143, 147, 156, 161, 162, 164, 166
  from Britain, 4
  interisland, 12–13, 104, 114, 130, 136, 140, 141, 142, 147, 156, 161, 162–163, 164, 166
  seaplane, 51
Alvernia, Mount, 138
American Civil War, 31, 43–44
American Embassy, 46
American Revolution, 29–30, 53, 116, 126, 142
Andros, 129–133
  freshwater for Nassau from, 47
  map of, 128
Androsia, 129
Apartment rentals
  Family Islands, 116, 118, 124–125, 158–159
  Freeport/Lucaya, 101
  New Providence Island, 63–65
Aquarium, Seafloor, 48, 71
Ardastra Gardens, 48, 70

Area of the Bahamas, 1
Arthur's Town, 138
Artworks, 49, 54–55, 121, 166
Auto rental services, 14, 66, 102, 125, 132, 138, 143, 151–152, 163

Bacardi Rum Distillery, 57, 68
Bacardi Tournament, 8
Backgammon championships, 8
Bahamas Financial Center, xi
Bahamas, origin of name of, 28
Bains Town, 57
Banking, x
Barrier Reef, Andros, 129
Batik fabric, 129
Beaches, xi, 1, 48, 51, 55, 56, 71, 93, 96, 119, 120, 129, 133, 135, 138, 143–144, 153, 156, 164, 166
Beverages, 37–38
Bevin Town, 96
Bimini, 8, 133–137
  map of, 134
Bird-watching, 118, 160–161
Blackbeard's Tower, 53, 68
Blue Holes, 34
  Andros Island, 129
  Grand Bahama Island, 96
Boat cruises, 73–74, 104, 125

Boating, 71, 105, 117, 126–127, 132–133, 137, 152, 159–160, 162. *See also* Yachting

Boat races, 7–10, 66–67, 126, 159–160, 162

Boatyard, Albury, 120

Bonefish Bonanza, 9, 159

Book Shop, United, 54

Botanic Gardens, 70

British visitors' information, 4–5

BRS, Bahamas Reservation Service, 6

Buena Vista Estate, 70

Buses, 65–66

Cable Beach, x, 55
  casino on, xi, 55, 86, 87
  hotels on, xi, 59–60, 63–64
  nightlife in, 86–87
  restaurants on, 80–81, 87–88

Calendars of events, 7–10, 66–68, 102–104, 126, 137, 159–160

Camperdown, 54

Canada
  import duty for residents of, 16
  tourist information in, 3–4

Candy factories and stores, 44, 120

Casinos, xi, 20, 33, 51, 55, 87–88, 113

Casino Theaters, 86

Cat Cay, 135

Cat Island, 138–140

Caves. *See also* Grotto, Thunderball
  Eleuthera, 143, 144
  Grand Bahama Island, 96
  Long Island, 162
  New Providence Island, 55

Cenotaph, 43

Changing of the Guard, 45, 69

Children, traveling with, 21–22

Choral groups, 74

Christ Church Cathedral, 46, 69

Chub Cay, 140–141

Churches, 45, 46, 49, 69

Clarence Town, 162

Clifford Park, 48

Clothing. *See* Packing

Cockburn Town, 165, 167

Columbus, Christopher, xii, 9, 27–28, 161–162, 165, 166

Conch, in Bahamian cuisine, 36–37

Conch-Cracking Contest, 103

Conference Corner, 55

Coral Harbour, 57

Coral World Hotel and Marine Park, 48, 70

Cost of your trip, 17–18

Credit cards, 17

Crooked Island, 141–142

Cruise lines, xi–xii, 11–12, 58, 98. *See also* Boat cruises
  British, 5

Crystal Palace Hotel and Casino, xi

Cuisine, Bahamian, 36–37

Currency, 17

Customs and duty, 15–17

Dance, 74

Deadman's Cay, 162

Departure Taxes, 16–17

Devil's Point, 139

"Dine-Around" plans, 85–86

Discos, 86

Discovery Season, xii, 67, 103–104

Diving, xi, 33–34, 72, 106, 127, 133, 137, 141, 152, 160, 164

Dog show, 9

Dolphin Experience, xi, 93–94

Drama, 74–75, 106–107

Dundas Town, 118

Dunmore House, 53, 57, 70

Dunmore Town, 144

Duty-free allowances, 16

Elbow Cay. *See* Hope Town

Electric current, 21

Eleuthera, 142–152
  map of, 145

Emergencies. *See* Telephones

EP (European Plan), 19
Exumas, the, 152–160
  map of, 155

Family Islands, x, 33, 114–167
  beaches of, 120, 129, 133, 135,
    138, 143–144, 153, 156, 164,
    166
  hotels and restaurants on,
    122–125, 130–132, 136–137,
    140, 141, 142, 147–151,
    157–158, 161, 163, 164,
    166–167
  shopping on, 117, 119, 120, 146
FAP (Full American Plan), 19
Financial Center, xi
Fishing, 8–10, 34–35, 71, 105,
    118, 126–127, 132–133, 135,
    137, 140–141, 152, 159, 160
Flamingos, 48, 70, 160–161
Forts
  Charlotte, 30, 47, 69
  Fincastle, 30, 44, 69
  Mantagu, 53, 69
  Nassau, 46
Fox Hill Day, 9, 54, 67
Fox Hill Village, 54
Freeport/Lucaya, x, xi, 33, 89–94
  hotels in, 99–100
  map of, 90
  restaurants in, 109–111
  shopping in, 91–92
French Cloister, 50, 70–71

Gambier Beach, 55
Gaol Alley, 43
Garden of the Groves, 93, 104
Gardens. *See* Parks and gardens
George Town, 153, 154, 156,
  158
Glass-bottom boat tours, 70, 104
Golf, xi, 8–10, 33, 72, 103, 105,
    127, 146–147, 152
Goombay, 6–7, 38–39, 45, 67, 86,
  103
Goombay Punch, 37

Goombay Summer Festival, 6–7,
  9, 45, 67, 103
Government House, xi, 41, 45, 69
Governor's Harbour, 146, 150–151
Grand Bahama Island, x, 33,
  89–113. *See also* Freeport/
  Lucaya
  casinos, 113
  hotels on, 98–101
  map of, 95
  nightlife on, 112–113
  parks and gardens on, 92–93,
    96, 104–105
  restaurants on, 108–112
  shopping on, 91–92, 107–108
Grant's Town, 45, 57
Graycliff, 46, 70
Great Britain
  Bahamas and, x
  import duty for residents of, 15
  rule of the Bahamas by, 28–32
  tips for visitors from, 4–5
  tourist information in, 4
Great Guana Cay, 119, 123
Great Inagua, 160–161
Green Turtle Cay, 118, 120–121,
  124–125
Gregory Arch, 45, 69
Gregory Town, 143–144, 148
Grotto, Thunderball, 154

Hammocks, 27
Handicapped travelers, 22
Harbour Island, 142, 144, 148–149
Hawk's Nest, 139
Health, 22–23
Hemingway, Ernest, 135, 136
Hermitage, the (Mount Alvernia),
  138–139
Historic sites and buildings, 68–70
History of the Bahamas, 27–32
Hope Town, 119, 122–123
Horseback riding, 51, 72, 106
Horse shows, 9, 54
Hotels, xi, 18–19, 33
  Abacos, 122–125

Hotels (*continued*)
  Andros, 130–132
  Bimini, 136–137
  Cable Beach, xi, 59–60, 64
  Cat Island, 140
  Chub Cay, 141
  Crooked Island, 142
  Eleuthera, 147–151
  Exumas, the, 157–158
  Grand Bahama Island, 98–101
  Great Inagua, 161
  Long Island, 163
  New Providence Island, 58–65
  Paradise Island, 61–63, 64
  Rum Cay, 164
  San Salvador, 166–167
House of Assembly, 43

Inagua. *See* Great Inagua
Independence Day, 9, 32, 47
Interisland travel, 12–13, 104, 114,
    130, 136, 140, 141, 142, 147,
    156, 161, 162–163, 164, 166
International Bazaar, x, 89, 91–92,
    107–108, 111

Jerome, Father (Fra), 54, 138–139,
    162
Jewish cemetery, 49
Johnston family, 119–120
Junkanoo celebrations, 6, 7, 9, 38,
    67, 103, 159
  museum of, 55

Kidd Cove, 156

Legal drinking age, 19
Library, Nassau Public, 43, 68
Lighthouses, 31
  of Crooked Island, 141
  Hope Town, 119
  on Inagua, 161
  on San Salvador, 165–166
Little Harbour, 119–120
Long Island, 161–163
Lowe, Alton Roland, 121
Lucaya. *See* Freeport/Lucaya

Lucayan National Park and
    Caverns, xi, 96
Lyford Cay, 56

Mailboat travel, 13, 121, 130, 136,
    140, 141, 147, 156, 162–163,
    164, 166
Malone, Brent, 49
Man-O-War Cay, 120
MAP (Modified American Plan),
    19
Marsh Harbour, 117–118, 122
Matthew Town, 161
Monastery, St. Augustine's, 54, 69
Morgan's Bluff, 130
Murphy's Town, 118
Museums
  art, 54–55, 121, 166
  history, 44, 105, 119
  Junkanoo, 55
Music, xi, 45, 74, 106. *See also*
    Goombay; Nightlife

Nassau, x, 33, 40–50
  calendar of events in, 7–10
  drinking water of, 56
  guided walking tour, 68
  history of, 28–31, 40–41
  horse-drawn surreys of, 68
  hotels in, xi, 60–61
  map of, 42
  nightlife in, 86–88
  restaurants in, 81–85
  shopping in, 35–36, 49–50,
    75–79
Nassau Botanic Gardens, 47, 70
Nassau Conference (1962), 55
Native Nightclubs, 87
New Plymouth, 120–121, 125
New Providence Island, x, 40–50,
    51–88. *See also* Cable Beach;
    Nassau; Paradise Island
  beaches on, 48, 51, 55, 56, 71
  historic sites and buildings on,
    68–70
  hotels on, 58–65
  map of, 52

outside of Nassau, 47–57
parks and gardens on, 47–48, 50, 70–71
restaurants on, 79–86
shopping on, 35–36, 75–79
Nightlife, 86–88, 112–113, 153

Old/New Free Town, 94, 96
"Out Islands," x, 114
"Over the Hill," 45, 57, 69

Package programs (air and hotel), 2
Packing, 14–15
Paradise Beach, 51
Paradise Island, x, 33, 50–51
    casino on, x, 51, 86
    hotels on, 61–63, 64
    map of, 42
    nightlife on, 86–88
    restaurants on, 84–85, 87–88
    shopping on, 50
Paradise Lagoon, 51
Parasailing, 72, 106
Parks and gardens, 47–48, 50, 70–71, 92–93, 96, 104–105
    Exuma Cays Land and Sea Park, 153–154
    Garden of the Groves, 93, 104
    Inagua wilderness preserve, 160–161
Parliament Square, 43, 69–70
Passports and visas, 15
People to People Program, 10, 66, 91
Pets, 21
Photographing, 50
Pindling, Sir Lynden O., x, 32
Pine barrens, 56
Pirates, 28–29, 53, 130, 154, 156.
    See also Wreckers
Planning your trip, 2
Population of the Bahamas, ix
Port Lucaya, xi, 89, 94
Postage, 21
Potter's Cay, 49–50
Preacher's Cave, 143
Private houses in Nassau, 45–47, 70

Private-plane flying, 13–14
Prohibition, 31, 98

Queen's Staircase, 44, 70

Rand Memorial Nature Center, 92, 104
Rawson Square, 43
Red Bays Village, 130
Remembrance Day. See Supreme Court Assizes
Restaurants, 19, 36–38
    Abacos, 117–118, 122–125
    Andros, 130–132
    Bimini, 133, 136–137
    Cat Island, 140
    Chub Cay, 141
    Crooked Island, 142
    Eleuthera, 147–151
    Exumas, 157–158
    Grand Bahama Island, 108–112
    Great Inagua, 161
    Long Island, 163
    New Providence Island, 79–86
    Paradise Island, 84–85, 87–88
    Rum Cay, 164
    San Salvador, 166–167
Retreat, The, 71
Rock Sound, 146, 151
Roker, Angelo, 55
Rolle Town, 156
Royal Bahamas Police Force Band, xi, 45
Royal Victoria Hotel and Gardens, 43–44, 70
Rum Cay, 164

Safety and security, 23
St. Augustine's Monastery, 54, 69
St. Francis Xavier Cathedral, 57, 69
St. Matthew's Anglican Church, 49, 69
Salt-production center, 161
Samana Cay, 166
Sandy Point, 118
San Salvador, 27, 165–167
Scooter and bike rental, 66, 132, 151, 159, 163

Scuba. *See* Diving
Sea Gardens, 70
Seasonal events, 7–10, 66–68,
    102–104, 126, 137, 159–160
Security precautions, 23
Seminole Indians, 130
Shipwreck at Rum Cay, 164
Shopping, 35–36. *See also specific*
    places
Silkscreened fabrics, 49
Slavery and emancipation, 9, 28,
    30, 31, 47, 54, 56, 67, 153,
    159
Spanish Wells, 142, 144, 146,
    149–150
Sports, xi, 7–10, 33–35, 71–74,
    105–106. *See also specific*
    sports and islands
Staniel Cay, 153–154, 156–157,
    159, 160
Stocking Island, 156, 160
Strawmarkets, 35–36, 41, 75, 77,
    92, 108, 154, 162
Student and youth travel, 22
Student Getaway programs, 8,
    67–68, 103
Supreme Court Assizes, 7–8, 9, 67

Taxes, 16–17
Taxis, 65, 102, 125, 159, 161
Taylor, Peanuts, 87
Telephones, telegrams, telex, 20,
    58, 98, 121–122, 130, 136,
    147, 157, 161, 163
Tennis, xi, 10, 73, 105, 106
Theatre, 74–75, 106–107
The Retreat, 71
Time sharing

Freeport/Lucaya, 101–102
    New Providence Island, 65
Time Zone, 21
Tipping, 20
Tongue of the Ocean, 1, 129, 140
Tourist information services, 5–6,
    43, 46, 66, 91, 102, 116
Tourists, number of, x
Tour operators, 2–4
Tours, 68, 91, 104, 125
Travel agents, 2–4
Traveler's checks, 17
Treasure Cay, 117, 118, 123–124
Treasure Island, xii

UNEXSO, x, 93–94, 96, 105, 106
United States Navy, 129

Versailles Gardens, 50, 70
Vintage Car Speed Week, 10, 103

Water Tower, 44, 68
Weather, year-round, 6–7
West End, 97, 100–101
Windermere Island, 146
Windsor, Duke and Duchess of,
    32, 38, 45
Windsurfing, 8, 67, 73, 106, 127,
    160
Windward Passage, 141, 161
Wreckers, 117

Yachting, 13–14, 53, 94, 117, 126,
    159
    British charter agencies for, 5
Yellow Elder development, 54

Fodor's Travel Guides

U.S. Guides

Alaska
Arizona
Atlantic City & the
  New Jersey Shore
Boston
California
Cape Cod
Carolinas & the
  Georgia Coast
The Chesapeake Region
Chicago
Colorado
Dallas & Fort
  Worth

Disney World & the
  Orlando Area
Florida
Hawaii
Houston &
  Galveston
Las Vegas
Los Angeles, Orange
  County, Palm Springs
Maui
Miami, Fort Lauderdale,
  Palm Beach
Michigan, Wisconsin,
  Minnesota

New England
New Mexico
New Orleans
New Orleans *(Pocket
  Guide)*
New York City
New York City *(Pocket
  Guide)*
New York State
Pacific North Coast
Philadelphia
The Rockies
San Diego
San Francisco

San Francisco *(Pocket
  Guide)*
The South
Texas
USA
Virgin Islands
Virginia
Waikiki
Washington, DC
Williamsburg

Foreign Guides

Acapulco
Amsterdam
Australia, New Zealand,
  The South Pacific
Austria
Bahamas
Bahamas *(Pocket
  Guide)*
Baja & the Pacific
  Coast Resorts
Barbados
Belgium & Luxembourg
Bermuda
Brazil
Britain *(Great Travel
  Values)*
Budget Europe
Canada
Canada *(Great Travel
  Values)*
Canada's Atlantic
  Provinces
Cancún, Cozumel,
  Mérida, the
  Yucatán
Caribbean

Caribbean *(Great
  Travel Values)*
Central America
China
China's Great Cities
Eastern Europe
Egypt
Europe
Europe's Great Cities
Florence & Venice
France
France *(Great Travel
  Values)*
Germany
Germany *(Great Travel
  Values)*
Great Britain
Greece
The Himalayan
  Countries
Holland
Hong Kong
Hungary
India, including Nepal
Ireland
Israel

Italy
Italy *(Great Travel
  Values)*
Jamaica
Japan
Japan *(Great Travel
  Values)*
Jordan & the Holy Land
Kenya, Tanzania,
  the Seychelles
Korea
Lisbon
Loire Valley
London
London *(Great Travel
  Values)*
London *(Pocket Guide)*
Madrid & Barcelona
Mexico
Mexico City
Montreal &
  Quebec City
Munich
New Zealand
North Africa
Paris

Paris *(Pocket Guide)*
Portugal
Rio de Janeiro
The Riviera *(Fun on)*
Rome
Saint Martin &
  Sint Maarten
Scandinavia
Scandinavian Cities
Scotland
Singapore
South America
South Pacific
Southeast Asia
Soviet Union
Spain
Spain *(Great Travel
  Values)*
Sweden
Switzerland
Sydney
Tokyo
Toronto
Turkey
Vienna
Yugoslavia

Special Interest Guides

Bed & Breakfast
  Guide: North America
Health & Fitness
  Vacations

Royalty Watching
Selected Hotels of
  Europe

Selected Resorts
  and Hotels of the U.S.
Shopping in Europe

Skiing in North
  America
Sunday in New York